Sustainability and Firms

ADVANCES IN ECOLOGICAL ECONOMICS

General Editor: Robert Costanza, *Director, University of Maryland Institute for Ecological Economics and Professor, Center for Environmental and Estuarine Studies and Zoology Department, USA*

This important series makes a significant contribution to the development of the principles and practices of ecological economics, a field which has expanded dramatically in recent years. The series provides an invaluable forum for the publication of high quality work and shows how ecological economic analysis can make a contribution to understanding and resolving important problems.

The main emphasis of the series is on the development and application of new original ideas in ecological economics. International in its approach, it includes some of the best theoretical and empirical work in the field with contributions to fundamental principles, rigorous evaluations of existing concepts, historical surveys and future visions. It seeks to address some of the most important theoretical questions and gives policy solutions for the ecological problems confronting the global village as we move into the twenty-first century.

Titles in the series include:

Transition to a Sustainable Society
A Backcasting Approach to Modelling Energy and Ecology
Henk A.J. Mulder and Wouter Biesiot

Modelling Global Change
The Art of Integrated Assessment Modelling
Marco Janssen

Valuation for Sustainable Development
Methods and Policy Indicators
Edited by Sylvie Faucheux and Martin O'Connor

Sustainability and Firms
Technological Change and the Changing Regulatory Environment
Sylvie Faucheux, John Gowdy and Isabelle Nicolaï

Valuation and the Environment
Theory, Method and Practice
Edited by Martin O'Connor and Clive Spash

Sustainability in Question
The Search for a Conceptual Framework
Jörg Köhn, John Gowdy, Fritz Hinterbergr and Jan van der Straaten

Sustainability and Firms

Technological Change and the Changing
Regulatory Environment

Edited by

Sylvie Faucheux

C3ED, Université de Versailles-Saint Quentin en Yvelines, France

John Gowdy

Rensselaer Polytechnic Institute, USA

Isabelle Nicolaï

C3ED, Université de Versailles-Saint Quentin en Yvelines, France

ADVANCES IN ECOLOGICAL ECONOMICS

Edward Elgar
Cheltenham, UK • Northampton, MA, USA

Published by
Edward Elgar Publishing Limited
Glensanda House
Montpellier Parade
Cheltenham
Glos, GL50 1UA
UK

Edward Elgar Publishing, Inc.
6 Market Street
Northampton
Massachusetts 01060
USA

A catalogue record for this book
is available from the British Library

Library of Congress Cataloguing in Publication Data
Sustainability and firms : technological change and the changing
  regulatory environment / edited by Sylvie Faucheux, John Gowdy, and
  Isabelle Nicolaï.
    (Advances in ecological economics series)
    1. Sustainable development. 2. Technological innovations—
  Environmental aspects. 3. Competition, International.
  4. Environmental policy—Economic aspects. I. Faucheux, Sylvie,
  1960– . II. Gowdy, John M. III. Nicolaï, Isabelle, 1965– .
  IV. Series: Advances in ecological economics.
  HD75.6.S859   1998
    338'.064—dc21   98-22536
                                                                      CIP

ISBN 1 85898 809 8

Printed and bound in Great Britain by Bookcraft (Bath) Ltd.

Contents

Figures

Figures

Tables

1. Introduction

Sylvie Faucheux, John Gowdy and Isabelle Nicolaï

1.1 THE CONTEXT

Since the 1970s the view has been widely expressed that industrial production and consumption patterns need to be guided and circumscribed so as to respect ecological 'limits to growth'. The task of regulation has, traditionally, been confined to the public sector, although accompanied sometimes by doubts about the efficacy of the state apparatus. The promotion of the policy goal of sustainable development represents an attempt to reduce the apparent conflict between economic growth and environmental protection. Indeed, sustainable development aims at reconciling the pursuit of goals traditionally associated with economic growth (such as material wealth and consumer satisfaction) with ecological constraints on economic activity. A related evolution has taken place in the private sector and in regulatory theory and practice. On the one hand, firms have come increasingly to consider the necessity of 'taking the environment into account' not just as an exogenously imposed cost or constraint, but as a strategic opportunity. Necessity is thus converted into virtue. Furthermore, public authorities and theorists concerned with environmental regulation have given increased attention to the extent to which environmental goals might be 'internalized' in norms of good commercial practice. Today, sustainable development is often presented as a reconciliation between free-market economics, with its perceived benefits (productivity incentives, technological innovations, representing the basis for increasing material wealth and consumer satisfaction), and the protection of environmental quality as a prerequisite for sustainable economic activity and direct source of general welfare. This view has implications for, and reflects changes of attitude by, all the economic partners, particularly firms.

These interrelated developments give some *prima facie* support to Porter's suggestion, that the growth of environmental controls (laws, policies, standards and public expectations) is not incompatible with continued economic competitiveness. However, it cannot simply be assumed that these simultaneous changes in public attitudes, business policies and government regulations are going to guarantee the conditions for long-term ecologically and economically sustainable development. The risk remains that changes are made merely in response to certain environmental problems, while other and perhaps more serious environmental impacts are being overlooked. So we must look with an open mind at the prospects for reconciling economic competitiveness with the priority of environmental protection.

During the past ten years, competitiveness has become the catchword in a great number of debates, even though it is difficult to define the term accurately. The dangers of this overuse have been pointed out by certain economists, who see too much being claimed in the name of competitiveness and its derivatives. The idea remains none the less at the forefront of debates on economic policy. For example, in Europe, the Commission's 1994 *Livre Blanc* (*White Book*) refers to competitiveness as a key issue in a chapter entitled 'Towards global competitiveness'. Likewise, in the United States, the Competitiveness Policy Council reports annually to the President and to Congress. In this book we consider competitiveness and competition as two aspects of a dynamic process which requires proactive and reactive adjustments by business and governance institutions.

In this regard, we emphasize that competitiveness takes on a significantly different meaning depending on whether one places oneself at the level of a firm, an industry, or of government. From a business point of view, major competitiveness factors are still those described by the traditional variables of competition, that is profitability, keeping costs down, and the setting of prices, even though these variables are strongly influenced by how a company adapts to and positions itself in the market. Firms will focus particularly on their own input and output markets, and this competitivity can be illustrated by the adoption of interfirm relations (as cooperative forms). On the other hand, states are strongly concerned with international competitiveness for sectors as a whole, such as measured by aggregate trade flows and so on. This can be complicated by interplays between firm and state. In its home country a firm or an industry may consider an environmental pressure as a constraint and thus oppose the application of controls. Yet, after regulations have been adopted, industry may cooperate with the government to ensure that other countries enact rules that are at least as strict. Hence the same regulation can represent a constraint for an industrial company at the domestic level, while it constitutes an opportunity in the international marketplace if the country manages to impose it internationally in such a way that it works to that country's advantage.

This leads to the triple focus of the book:

- *Evolutionary dynamics,* meaning the ways that individual strategies that are employed by firms to remain competitive in the short and medium run can, over time and because of their compound impact, lead to new difficulties that require quite new strategies.
- *Technological change,* and the fundamental role which technological innovation can play in procuring greater freedom for firms to opt for strategies at all levels. The focus is on the decision to engage the firm in an innovation process oriented to a sustainable development strategy. The technological innovation is a strategic decision that is thought of as a sequence of successive constraints of building a path in which there are no initial states of reference. The productive capacity is built step by step over time in a sequence in which each step is dependent on inherited past steps and on anticipations formation.
- *Public policy,* that is, the capacity of governments to bring about changes in market conditions, in part through the creation or expansion of regulatory institutions.

The book illustrates the diversity and the plurality of perspectives that were presented during the International Conference organized by the Centre d'Economie et d'Ethique pour l'Environnement et le Développement (C3ED), which was held in Saint-Quentin on 23–25 May 1996. This idea of complementarity is, perhaps, the distinctive feature but also the point of difficulty of the book. It is difficult because our approach forces us to present a wide spectrum of perspectives and schools of thought differentiated in terms of theoretical, disciplinary and national logics. These do not necessarily sit comfortably together, but this also constitutes a stimulating challenge. We then refer in this book to various theoretical fields such as ecological economics, evolutionary dynamics and the neo-classical tradition.

What is needed is a coherent, theoretically based and empirically defensible typology of perspectives that involves the essence of different views of the firms and governance actions in respect of pursuit of sustainable development. The following sections outline the contents of the three parts of the book.

1.2   CORPORATE ENVIRONMENTAL STRATEGIES

Part I presents the emergent practice of environmental assessment and strategy development, with its own specificity, within the private sector. This practice, which is most evident at the levels of corporate enterprise and of sectoral associations, has emerged *de facto* as a response by firms to the necessity and desirability of 'taking the environment into account'. Elements of corporate environmental strategy may, *inter alia*, include identifying new market opportunities, responding to (and, in some cases, moulding) the regulatory framework, or establishing a positive public image through positioning in relation to environmental concerns. These emerging corporate practices warrant study for several reasons. First, they have been developed in situations of high-stake commercial decision making. Second, they must reconcile commercial imperatives with requirements for social legitimacy, for example with regard to industrial risks and pollution control. So a documentation of current corporate environmental strategies and practices can be a valuable source of lessons about effective integration of scientific, economic and wider social considerations for decisionmaking. Third, an understanding of corporate practice furnishes a vital knowledge base for effective public policy design and communication aimed at implementation of sustainable development norms. Three analyses of such practices are proposed in the three chapters which make up the first part of the book.

In Chapter 2, *Globalization, competitiveness, governance and environment: what prospects for a sustainable development?* by Sylvie Faucheux, Isabelle Nicolaï and Martin O'Connor, the purpose is to develop a clear view of the problems related to competitiveness and environmental controls. For that the authors use examples provided by small, medium-sized and large firms in European countries and elsewhere and provide a conceptual framework for assessing risks and prospects for environmental quality associated with firms' actions within the ongoing economic globalization process. Citing examples, the authors identify various forms of competitive activity (resulting in the deregulation of national and international markets), which have an adverse impact on the environment. The assessment of risks and aspirations from the process of economic globalization leads to identification of the crucial roles of governance (at the local, national and international level) required by the search for a win–win strategy combining business competitiveness and environmental quality.

In Chapter 3, *Environmental regulations and foreign direct investment flows within the European Union*, António Castro Guerra and Vitor Santos develop an econometric model that analyses the impact of the strictness of environmental regulations on the location of polluting industries within the European Union (EU). Their analysis focuses on the interdependences between economic integration and national environmental regulations in the concrete case of the European Union. Their estimates suggest a significant effect of the strictness of environmental regulations on foreign direct investment, FDI. Moreover, empirical evidence indicates that lax regulations tend to attract foreign capital, thereby validating the pollution haven hypothesis (free trade will contribute to increasing industrial pollution in developing countries).

In Chapter 4, *Environmental regulations, firms' strategies and market behaviour: modelling to learn*, Rui Santos, Luís Jordão, Paula Antunes and Nuno Videira propose a simulation approach, based on the use of systems dynamics models, to help study the effects of environmental regulations on firms' strategies and market behaviour. They show how environmental efficacy of the different instruments and their corresponding impact on firms' competitiveness and market behaviour, are matters of debate in theoretical and practical arenas. They show to the managers that, in some situations, the adoption of environmental regulations can increase their profits, instead of being an extra burden to the firm. The development of learning tools which allow managers to understand these interactions can give them an incentive to adopt innovative and more efficient approaches to pollution control. This improved knowledge also shows the importance of adopting a system approach and to illustrate the types of variables and issues that should be taken into account by managers and regulators in the design and implementation of environmental strategies.

1.3   TECHNOLOGICAL CHANGE AND SUSTAINABILITY

The second part of this volume considers the fundamental role played by technological innovations in providing all types of firms (small businesses, multinationals, government-owned companies) with a certain amount of freedom to implement their own strategies. Environmental technology refers to all techniques, processes and products playing an important role in reducing pressures on scarce natural resources, in reducing pollution flows, and in the prevention and reduction of environmental hazards.

Many debates about prospects for sustainable development hinge on views about the potential of technological change to reduce pollutant emissions and improve efficiency of natural resource, land and water use. If products, manufacturing processes and services are to be made significantly less intensive from an environmental viewpoint over the coming ten years, it is obvious that technological progress must play a fundamental role, even though changes in consumption patterns should also be taken into account. Recently in several parts of the world there have been initiatives to use information on technology as a frame of reference for the implementation of environmental regulatory policies.

Firms' process and product innovations that simultaneously enhance environmental performance and maintain competitivity can contribute to wider objectives of ecological and economic sustainable development. Major business corporations and alliances are, indeed, in a position to influence the direction taken by environmental technological innovations and also to change various aspects of public policies. However, environmental technological innovations are not isolated processes having to do exclusively with the strategy of firms. Changed business practices and regulations may bring solutions to certain environmental protection problems while ignoring serious and potentially irreversible processes of resource depletion and the deterioration of ecosystems. This is why, in the pursuit of sustainable development, a social partnership is necessary. For example, it has become commonplace to speak of the Precautionary Principle as a guideline for public policy and commercial behaviour, meaning the obligation to refrain from actions that would impose serious risks on future generations. The growing popularity of concepts such as the extended responsibility of producers has helped solidify relationships between business and the environment while at the same time making them more complex. There are examples of new social obligations that are being placed on firms to reflect environmental quality concerns. It is to developments of this sort that the three chapters of Part II are dedicated.

In Chapter 5, *After the age of abatement technologies? Technological change for sustainable development*, Roberto Malaman treats the question of cleaner technologies, thanks to a survey of 192 innovations developed by 168 companies in Italy and analysed by means of 28 variables. He explains how these technologies are extremely widespread within industry and why we should call attention to a special effort by medium- and large-sized companies, by sensitive industries that have strong specific technological opportunities, and by companies with an international base and market. The integration of environmental and economic objectives at the company level appears to be a pursuable goal in most cases through the targeted use of available technologies, without changing the dominant technological paradigms. Italian firms move with agility within these bounds.

In Chapter 6, *Socio-technological innovation and sustainability*, Frank Beckenbach introduces an evolutionary market model to explain economic evolution in terms of technical change. The author analyses the relation between a decentralized evolutionary process of technical change and the sustainability objective. The model and its interpretation indicate that the process of technological innovation cannot be regulated directly. Innovation and imitation activities are bound into a complex system of economic, social and political conditions. Specific constellations of these conditions may induce a self-organizing process towards a more sustainable path of technological change. Making the signalling of ecological scarcities more effective and stabilizing the use of ecological stocks in a sustainable corridor are the main tasks for an evolutionary environmental policy in such a framework.

In Chapter 7, *All Production is joint production – a thermodynamic analysis,* Malte Faber, John L.R. Proops and Stefan Baumgärtner outline the danger in following the optimistic vision of technical change for the environment. They describe real production processes in terms of joint production. Joint production means that the production of a good is necessarily accompanied by the production of one or more by-products. It is often argued that joint production of wastes is only an inefficiency of production which could, in principle, be overcome by inventing and innovating new techniques or by operating existing techniques efficiently. This is the idea behind process- and product- integrated environmental protection. In contrast, by employing thermodynamic relations the authors argue that joint production is a necessary characteristic of all production. This is why it is also important to promote changes in consumption patterns, in addition to technical change, to attain sustainability paths.

1.4 SUSTAINABLE DEVELOPMENT AS A SOCIAL PARTNERSHIP BETWEEN FIRMS, CITIZENS AND GOVERNMENT

The third part of the book is devoted to the important roles of governance (at the local, national and international levels) required in the search for firms' win–win strategies combining business competitiveness and improved environmental performance, and also for promoting the larger social goal of sustainable development. The achievement of the social cohesiveness and environmental quality objectives normally associated with the objective of sustainable development hinges on developing new systems in the regulatory environment.

Allowing competition among manufacturers to become the only factor determining strategies in response to environmental considerations could lead to 'locked' technological and social options being chosen which do not contribute to overall goals of ecological and economic sustainability. This is why it is important to introduce, as complements to competitiveness, other notions such as the public interest and collective responsibility for the future which must be taken into account in adopting new environmental regulatory systems.

There is no general consensus on the collective approach to be used in order to resolve the problem of imbalances in the relationship between the economy and the environment. Many agree that sustainable development is an ethically attractive social goal, and from this point of view it is tempting to point to prospects for firms grasping win–win opportunities. This does not necessarily mean undermining competitivity. Rather, it means that changes are taking place in the background against which competitiveness is pursued. These are changes in social values and preoccupations that show up in the aspirations and expectations of market participants. In a way, it is the collective dynamics of those aspirations which, through their translation into measures taken by organizations and institutions, determine future economic activity.

Chapter 8, *The company environmental scheme,* by Valérie Martin and Françoise Garcia, is about new policy approaches such as voluntary agreements, eco-auditing schemes, informal approaches and so on. This chapter highlights the role of the Business Environmental Plan in the French context, contributing to the promotion of a global approach and facilitating integration of environmental awareness with business strategy. After studying the reasons behind companies' commitments, and the different actors involved in thinking about environmental management, comes a look at the regulatory framework and emerging tools. The authors outline how the Business Environmental Plan scheme can be a suitable response in the French context for industrial needs and how the integration of environmental concerns in businesses now involves all the stakeholders.

In Chapter 9, *The use of regulatory mechanism design in environmental policy: a theoretical critique*, Matthieu Glachant treats the strategic problem of informational asymmetry between the regulator and regulated firms. He discusses the extension of the normative theory of incentives in environmental economics (it clearly leads to a renewal of the theoretical debate on the efficiency of environmental policy making). According to the author this approach proposes truth-revealing mechanisms which may solve information asymmetry problems between the regulator and the regulated firms. Such mechanisms appear as new and sophisticated policy options which allow the solution of an important problem: information collection by the regulator about pollution abatement costs.

In Chapter 10, *Environmental privatization and technological norms*, Martin E. Diedrich shows that the privatization of natural resources is normally accompanied by various forms of supporting government regulation. Such regulatory support can be justified by imperfect competition or environmental externalities. According to the author, the unregulated privatization of natural resources would create an inflationary process that would gradually erode the long-term viability of the economy. By imposing technological norms on the use of natural resources, government regulation stabilizes resource rents and makes private ownership of natural resources compatible with a viable income distribution. Rather than being a response to market failure, technological norms act as a fundamental precondition for the normal operation of markets under private ownership of natural resources.

Chapter 11, *Financial transfers to ensure cooperative international optimality in stock pollutant abatement,* by Marc Germain, Philippe Toint and Henry Tulkens, is about the transnational character of many environmental problems which require cooperation amongst the countries involved, if a social optimum is to be achieved. Using the theory of non-cooperative games in the framework of a model of intertemporal transboundary pollution, they construct a sharing scheme for the abatement costs between the countries involved which makes their cooperation coalitionally rational. This sharing scheme is strategically stable in the sense that no coalition of countries can guarantee to its members a total cost lower than that obtained at the international optimum with financial transfers. This cost-sharing approach can be useful for regulations of the global environmental issues at the international level.

In Chapter 12, *The implementation of the international climate regime: how to finance the reduction of CO_2 emissions*, Michel Trommetter and Laurent Viguier propose a model of cooperation involving international, national and local actors for global environmental problems. After describing the climate regime as a 'negotiated international regime', they construct a finer typology of regimes that leads to a 'collaboration regime' based on a hierarchical relationship. Institutional bargaining is not limited to situations where actors' interests are convergent, and situations where interests are divergent can lead to regimes other that imposed regimes. The effectiveness of a given measure concerning global environment will depend on legal, political, economic and physical conditions of concerned countries. The system of negotiated norms, integrating economic, biological and social imperatives, leads to the governance question in environmental regulation.

PART I

Corporate Environmental Strategies

2. Globalization, Competitiveness, Governance and Environment: What Prospects for a Sustainable Development?

Sylvie Faucheux, Isabelle Nicolaï and Martin O'Connor

It is easy to identify instances of competitive activity that have adverse impacts on the environment. We can also, however, identify ways that competitive economic activity can evolve so as to be respectful of environmental quality, and in some instances to provide a positive solution to environmental quality and sustainability issues. In this paper we explore the following general questions. First, what are the social and technological preconditions necessary for the identification of *win–win strategies for firms*, that is (as defined by Porter and van der Linde 1995a, 1995b), business strategies that secure a healthy competitivity while also achieving a desired level of environmental protection? Second, under what circumstances might competitive free-market business activity work in the direction of a *sustainable development*, that is, a form of economic activity that respects long-run concerns for the maintenance of ecological life-support systems and economic welfare prospects for future generations?

Today, sustainable development is often presented as a reconciliation between free-market economics, with its perceived benefits (productivity incentives, technological innovations, representing the basis for increased material wealth and consumer satisfaction), and the protection of environmental quality as a prerequisite for sustainable economic activity and direct source of general welfare. This view has implications for, and is reflected in, changes of attitude by all the economic partners:

- In the private sector, firms have shifted (to varying extents) from a position of simple hostility towards environmental regulations – perceived as obstacles and as the source of additional expenses – to a more positive consideration of the environment as a strategic opportunity.

- Government agencies and scientists involved in environmental regulations have recently started giving more attention to the manner in which environmental objectives can be incorporated into standard business practices.
- Increasing numbers of 'green consumers' or individuals concerned about the environment express their support for environmental quality goals and for the principles of cross-generation equity, and for commercial practices and policies respectful of these ideals.

However, it cannot simply be assumed that these simultaneous changes in public attitudes, business policies and government regulations will guarantee the conditions for long-term ecologically and economically sustainable development (Palmer et al. 1995). The risk remains that changes are made merely in response to certain environmental problems, while other and perhaps more serious environmental impacts are being overlooked. So in this paper we look with an open mind at the prospects for reconciling economic competitiveness with the priority of environmental protection.

- In section 2.1, we suggest a typology of business approaches to the environment – what we can call firms' *environmental strategies* – emerging from our review of empirical studies covering various economic sectors.
- In section 2.2, we explain, using examples, the crucial role that environmental technological innovation can at times play in the search for a competitive edge and for an improvement in environmental performance.
- In section 2.3, we raise the question of how to modify the organizational structure of firms in order to operationalize the implementation of technological innovations aimed at linking competitiveness with sustainability.
- In section 2.4, we consider overall global trends in business–environment performance, and conclude that the current situation is a long way from translating 'win–win' firm opportunities into a genuinely sustainable development at global and national scales.
- In section 2.5, we conclude by hinting at some of the attitude changes and governance measures that would be required in order to bring about a society-wide win–win relationship between healthy competition and the protection of the environment, that is to say an authentic ecological–economic sustainable development.

2.1   A SIMPLE TYPOLOGY OF BUSINESS STRATEGIES ON THE ENVIRONMENT

Firms producing all kinds of goods and services are required to respond to controls that reflect increased concerns over health, safety, the quality of the environment and the preservation of natural resources. Environmental policies can be looked upon as simply causing additional expenses, as barriers to flexibility and, hence, as going against the grain of competitiveness. Nevertheless, the need for local, national and international environmental policies is an accepted fact. Moreover, and to an increasing extent, the private sector is actively involved in the negotiation and implementation of environmental policies. Existing analyses suggest that strategies implemented by firms with respect to the environment fall along a line between two extremes:

(1) Firms pursuing a defensive strategy with respect to environmental issues. These are firms which view environmental restrictions as extra costs that must be kept to a minimum, or even reduced to zero whenever possible.
(2) Firms opting for proactive or integrated environmental strategies. These firms anticipate new regulatory requirements and turn to their own advantage business opportunities provided by new research required to solve environmental problems.

Between these two extremes there is a wide spectrum of positions, such as that of the 'follower' firms which adjust to new environmental regulations without participating in their drafting.

2.1.1   Defensive Environmental Strategies

Traditionally, up to the 1980s, firms have regarded environmental performance requirements defensively, that is, as an additional constraint to be side-stepped if possible. According to a study by the European Commission's DG III (1995), firms most likely to engage in defensive strategies in Europe are major companies that are leaders in their field at home, but not multinationals, and, to a lesser extent, small and medium-sized firms. The sectors where this typically occurs are the machine, textile, food-processing, wood and paper, automobile and metallurgical industries. Within the EU, the tendency was particularly pronounced in some of the Mediterranean countries.

To see how environmental performance can be a factor in competitivity, it is useful to give some examples of different kinds of defensive strategies. First of all, firms may refrain from reporting their pollution-causing activities or from cutting back on the pollution they cause, simply in order to avoid the costs of such measures. Or they may make reluctant adjustments to environmental regulations after the fact.

For example, in the case of concern with sulphur and nitrogen oxide emissions causing acid rain, German manufacturers anticipated the arrival of controls requiring the use of catalytic converters, and indeed in some cases were pushing for such regulations (BMW announced that all of its cars would have catalytic converters starting with the 1989 models). By contrast, the French automobile industry was hostile to those measures. The German manufacturers had gained expertise in the technology. Not only were their cars ready to add converters (at low costs to owners), but also Bosch had a monopoly on some of the components of catalytic converters. The French automobile industry (in particular PSA) then declared that the proposed catalyser solution was a bad one, and offered instead to develop a clean engine. But rapid progress in regulations and the estimated 5 billion francs cost of the suggested research programme dissuaded the French from fighting for their point of view. They subsequently had to accept European regulations imposing catalysers and to meet the extra costs of adjustments in their car design and manufacturing processes (Faucheux and Noël 1990).

A more aggressive strategy is either to bypass or to block regulations. Firms may engage in transfers of production or in dumping practices to export markets where the safety or environmental regulations are non-existent or not enforced. An example involves some Western cement corporations, which have started operating subsidiaries in countries where regulations were virtually non-existent (Latin America) or where controls existed but were lightly enforced (Turkey, Poland, Hungary) (Gramond and Setbon 1996).

Historically, the adoption of environmental controls in industrialized countries is correlated with the phenomenon of hazardous waste being exported to developing countries and in the expansion of operations of highly polluting industries, such as leather, metallurgy or asbestos in these countries. However, according to several studies (Jacobs 1994; Sprenger 1995), if environmental considerations are sometimes a factor in decisions to relocate a firm, they are seldom the only one and seem to have, at least until now, always played a secondary role as compared to other factors such as labour costs, the availability of raw materials, barriers to trade, access to markets, and so on. It should also be noted that defensive strategies, while sometimes profitable in the short run, can expose firms to high adjustment costs if changes in standards or market conditions should catch up with them. They can also be the cause of serious disruptions in the event of an accident. In 1984, prior to the Bhopal accident, which caused the death of several thousand persons, Union Carbide was the world's tenth largest chemical firm. By 1994, it had fallen to 44th place (Cairncross 1995).

2.1.2 Proactive and Integrating Strategies of Firms towards the Environment

Some highly publicized accidents, such as the Seveso toxic cloud release in Italy (De Marchi 1997) and the Bhopal disaster in India, have changed public and regulatory opinion so that firms are now obliged to take a more proactive position. A growing number of polluting firms have begun to consider environmental protection not just as a constraint but as providing a potential competitive edge, owing to their competitive situation and falling margins as well as to the increase in consumer awareness of ecology.

Since the 1980s, the world has witnessed the development of what Porter (1990) refers to as the new competitiveness paradigm, based on a dynamic vision. According to this view, competitiveness at the industry level may well be achieved through higher productivity or lower prices, but also by the ability to provide different and better-quality products priced higher than others. Armed with this new concept of competitiveness, many firms take the view that, rather than maximizing profits within a fixed set of environmental constraints, it is better to modify those constraints in order to gain a competitive advantage. In that perspective, environmental considerations may cause a firm to cease distributing an old product or to bring out a new one. They may also lead to the discovery and use of outlets for certain goods resulting from the manufacturing process. Under this technical arrangement, materials which used to be considered waste become by-products that can be sold. The environment hence introduces a new criterion for differentiating among products, including on the basis of the development of environmental standards or labels (ISO 14000 at the international level), or else causes changes in the properties of products, such as their useful life or their price-to-weight ratio. Leading European automobile manufacturers, for example, have been looking for a way to compute a recyclability index that could be used for business purposes. Concerns about the disposal of old vehicles have also given rise to discussions concerning the useful life of cars.

Commercial success, then, depends on a combination of technical expertise (innovative processes and products, life cycle analysis), the attitude of consumers (demand for 'green' products) and public relations. The firm, by developing a proactive strategy, does not limit its business exclusively to already existing market segments but also seeks to influence changes in consumer perceptions and demand (product differentiation, acceptance, changes in behaviour, and so on). Lastly, a proactive environmental strategy contributes to the firm gaining a more positive image. Firms today often refer to their responsibilities with regard to energy efficiency, the scarcity of resources, chemical waste, the disposal of polluting substances, waste management, recycling and nature conservation.

This kind of proactive strategy is evident among many large multinational corporations in some industries, especially those that see themselves threatened by environmental controls – namely electrical utilities, chemical firms, oil refineries and water-treatment plants (survey by the European Commission, DG III 1995). The strategy requires a considerable expenditure of time and financial resources by firms, including the hiring and employing of experts in various fields (political analysts, legal advisers, consultants on technical feasibility, market researchers, lobbyists, and so on). This high cost means that the practice is principally limited to large companies as well as to industry associations in which firms have a shared interest, in particular with respect to control measures.

The famous example of DuPont can be cited. Anticipating that regulations on CFCs were unavoidable, the company, one of the world's leading chemical firms and the largest manufacturer of CFC, had been conducting research into CFC substitutes since 1975 in order to obtain a decisive advantage in the distribution and manufacturing of those substitutes when the moment was right.

Another example is that of Arco, the world's eighth-ranking oil company. Having developed a major research and development programme starting in 1988, it put out a clean automobile fuel at the end of 1990. Arco had sales in 1990 of 19.9 billion dollars, or four times its total for 1986. Similar results were reported for 1992 and 1993. The company owes its success to a proactive environmental strategy which led it to bring out a new product that ended up influencing and anticipating environmental regulations (including some 1990 amendments to the Clean Air Act) in order to obtain a competitive edge in the highly competitive oil industry (Piasecki 1995).

2.1.3　The Follower Strategy regarding the Environment

A follower is a firm that does not introduce new innovations or lobby for regulatory change, but adjusts purposefully to the new ground rules. Such behaviour can be motivated by a variety reasons, such as on grounds of legitimacy, in order to avoid future accusations, or to secure future markets, or else simply to avoid being a loser in tomorrow's competitive race. For example, in the field of waste disposal, European automobile manufacturers are now preparing for new guidelines being progressively introduced at the European Union level (1991 Amendment to the 1975 General Directive, and 1991 Directive on Hazardous Waste), without seeking to change those directives. They are also making ready to respond to provisions concerning packaging and priority waste as defined by the

European Commission, which includes automobile carcasses (Serret 1996). The case of European cement manufacturers can also be cited. Despite a generally defensive approach to regulations concerning their main business, they have grasped at one significant advantage which could be gained from environmental controls. This is to develop their very minor side-business of waste disposal for industrial liquids and solids with a high and low energy content, such as hydrocarbon sludge, tar, pitch, solvents, varnishes, distillation residues, spent oils, tyres, residue from automobile-body crushing (Setbon 1997).

If European evidence is generalizable, then the 'follower' strategy seems to have been adopted by a majority of firms. A survey of a large number of firms, made in 1995 by the European Commission's DG III, revealed that more than half of the firms surveyed implemented measures in response to environmental regulations, from simple registration to the installation of capital-intensive pollution-fighting equipment. But most of these (55 per cent of the firms in the study), regardless of their industry, deal with environmental problems only to the extent required by regulations, and no more. The main reason for this seems to be that environmental performance is usually perceived by small companies as a problem of compliance associated with non-productive expenditures.

These conclusions are corroborated by a 1994 survey, done in the south of England, of 175 firms (medium-sized and large) in the chemical and pharmaceutical industries and in the financial and information services sectors (Garrod and Chadwick 1996). This situation seems comparable to what has been observed in the United States (Frosh 1995). For France in particular, it has been noted there that (1) only a minority of firms have become aware of the opportunities that are afforded by the consideration of environmental issues in management areas; (2) most measures, when implemented, are taken by large corporations; (3) the majority of small and medium-sized firms do not take any action with respect to the environment unless forced to do so, on the grounds of cost, personnel or diversification considerations (Chailloux 1996).

2.2   ENVIRONMENTAL TECHNOLOGY INNOVATION

A close connection exists, in theoretical terms, between technological change, industrial competitiveness and sustainable development (Skea 1994; Faucheux 1997). This section reviews those links, focusing mainly on long-term changes in environmental technology. *Environmental technology,* as we use the term, refers to all techniques, processes and products playing an important role in reducing pressures on scarce natural resources, in reducing pollution flows, and in the prevention and reduction of environmental hazards.

2.2.1   Technological Innovation: a Key Variable in Win–Win Strategies

A dynamic competitiveness process is characterized by changes in technological as well as marketing opportunities. Inherent in this are elements of unpredictability, incomplete information and organizational inertia. But, while specific innovations and decisions may be unpredictable, maintaining competitivity may depend on organizational features that enhance creativity and responsiveness to newly perceived opportunities.

According to studies made by the Japanese government (MITI), some 40 per cent of the world's production of goods and services over the first half of the twenty-first century may be from environment or energy-linked products and technologies. This forecast explains why, for almost 20 years, Japan has been making the development of these technologies a priority, followed at some distance by Germany, The Netherlands, Sweden and Denmark (see MITI 1988; Miller and Moore 1994; Erkman 1996). In this context, innovation potential is seen as closely related to political choices, social conditions and economic institutions. Sustainable development depends on trajectories of sustained innovation and associated institutional changes that yield continually improved environmental performance as well as new market opportunities.

The links between environmental technology innovation and competitivity prospects can be explored by identifying the different sorts of objectives or improvements that the innovations may attain (Coenen et al. 1996). For example, performance improvements may be achieved in regard to pollution control, or problems associated with the end of the life cycle of products, or repairing ecological damage and rehabilitating ecosystems, or monitoring and controlling the quality of the environment, reducing technological and ecological hazards, improved efficiency in use of natural resources, and so on (Valenduc and Vendramin 1996). The significance of innovation for competitiveness depends also on the way that the innovation is incorporated within the production or service provision system.

2.2.2   Add-on Technologies versus Integrated Technologies

Much of the new environmental technology can be considered to be of the 'natural capital augmenting' type. That is, it either seeks to improve the productivity of natural resources or else make it possible to reduce the adverse effects of pollution and waste corresponding to a given level of production of goods and services. In this connection, it is useful to distinguish between the following:

(1) *Add-on, or end-of-process technology,* is any modification made *ex post* to a production or machine use process that alters its environmental performance. It frequently consists of incremental changes to existing technology, including processes and products for waste separation, storage and disposal, such as incinerating techniques for industrial waste or systems for cleaning up contaminated soil. The techniques do not prevent the creation of polluting substances; rather they are employed to reduce the impact of the toxic substances through controlling the final destination and form of the emissions. One problem is that such measures frequently shift the environmental problem from one place to another (for example, toxic solid wastes rather than toxic smoke) instead of eliminating it. During the past 20 years, many firms have incorporated this sort of end-of-pipe technology, either to help their own business comply with regulations (if they cause pollution), or in order to provide a service (acting as a part of the cleanup sector) ensuring that others may comply *ex post* with regulations.

(2) *Integrated technologies, also referred to as clean technologies* (see Duchin et al. 1995; Frosh 1995), are new production or service methods whose whole conception is to reduce environmental harm. Rather than, for example, capturing polluting substances after they have been produced (as with the end-of-process technologies), the ideal is not to produce the harmful substance at all, or to produce less of it, or a less harmful one.

Here, the consideration of environmental issues has the potential to act as a factor of technical change for the entire productive chain associated with a product. This allows the prioritizing, if desired, of specific environmental performance criteria such as the availability of inputs over time or environmental impacts at the various stages of a product's life cycle. Research and development can aim at progressive improvements in any designated direction.

European car manufacturers, for example, already incorporate, from the design stage onwards, various criteria having to do with the end of the useful life of vehicles. These include:

(1) Substitution mechanisms among new raw materials, tending to limit the varieties of materials used (in particular in the case of polymers); increased use of certain plastics (polyolefins); preference given to parts made out of a single material rather than composites.

(2) Substitution mechanisms between new and regenerated raw materials.

(3) Reduced toxicity of products. Certain substances have been given special attention, including asbestos, CFC gases, PVC or heavy metals.

(4) The generalized labelling of plastic parts, for easier disassembly and
sorting (Serret 1996).

The technical aspects of the manufacturing process can also be affected,
leading to an alteration of existing techniques (addition of technology,
equipment alterations) or to the development of new processes. This can
give rise, for example, to a reexamination of technical aspects having to do
with the assembly stage, in light of the new notion of 'disassembly'. Xerox,
for example, has become a leader in component products which can be
disassembled. Canon has innovated by inventing recyclable and reusable
cartridges.

Investment in integrated environmental technology is part of a proactive
environmental strategy which can, in the long run, be a win–win approach.
The competitive advantage of the innovation gives access to, or creates, a
specific market segment.

2.2.3　Incremental Innovations/Radical Innovations

The question may be asked whether integrated technologies can generate a
new impulse to innovation in favour of genuinely sustainable growth,
which goes beyond mere environmental protection imperatives. We will
conclude later that very substantial technological change will probably be
necessary for long-run ecological–economic sustainability, but is not
sufficient on its own; attitudinal changes would also be necessary. At this
stage, the distinction may usefully be introduced between 'incremental'
and 'radical' innovations (Freeman 1982). This distinction does not apply
exclusively to environmental technology, but rather comes from the
evolutionary theory of technology change.

(1) *Incremental innovations* are improvements to products or
manufacturing techniques occurring continuously throughout the
history of the class of technology. They do not result in major
transformations but are essential to secure productivity improvements,
gain market share, or deal with fashion trends. For example, the
successive versions of existing software programs represent
incremental innovations.

(2) *Radical innovations* cause breaks in the continuity of evolving
processes or products, leading to the transformation of methods of
production or distribution. They serve as a starting point for the
development of new technical systems or new technological
trajectories. The convergence of several new technical systems, at a
time of economic recession, causes a turnaround and makes it possible
for a new business cycle to start. The personal computer and the CD-
ROM are examples of radical innovations.

Most environmental technology innovations in recent years, whether add-on or integrated, belong to the category of incremental innovations. Nevertheless, radical innovations also can occur in response to environmental objectives. Chlorine-free chemical processes, organic fuels, photovoltaic energy and hydrogen-based fuels would fall into that category, because their introduction can have far-reaching consequences for economy-wide production and consumption and lifestyles. This raises the important point that environmental technology innovations often result from radical innovations made in other technical fields, such as synthetic chemicals, new materials, biotechnology, electronic data processing, and so on. In part this may be because of relatively low investment in environmental research (Valenduc and Vendramin 1996), but it also shows the transversal character of discovery and innovation. For these reasons, improvements in environmental performance can be expected as one product of a strong research/innovation culture, not just through the specification of environmental goals. This may be an important lesson for regulatory policy.

2.2.4   Advantages and Shortcomings of Environmental Innovation

Environmental technology innovation provides many competitive advantages but is also held back by many obstacles. The advantages include:

(1) *Opportunities for reducing costs.* Environmental technology provides opportunities for lowering production and distribution costs by making use of potential increases in ecological efficiency. Integrated technology can help reduce production costs and increase productivity, a great deal more so than add-on technology.

(2) *Quality improvements.* Environmental technology innovation is easily made part of the 'total quality management' approach (the ISO 9000 series). There are even references today to 'total quality environmental management' (the ISO 14000 series). The US-based multinational corporation 3M provides a perfect illustration of this trend, with its Pollution Prevention Pays (3P) programme, whereby every project must fulfil four criteria: eliminate or reduce a polluting substance, contribute to the environment through energy savings or a more efficient use of manufacturing materials and resources, demonstrate an ability for technological innovation and save money by reducing cleanup costs (Shrivastava 1995a).

(3) *Competitive advantages.* As indicated earlier, environmental technology innovation may provide firms with an opportunity to pursue unique and exclusive strategies. A small or medium-sized business can gain a competitive edge and become a leader within a strategic market

segment. Examples of this were cited earlier. The Body Shop is another. The company has created a genuinely 'green' business within a cosmetics industry that used to be dominated by major multinational chemical corporations.

(4) *Social responsibility.* Environmental technology innovation makes savings possible in public health-care budgets and helps firms gain social acceptance and legitimacy in the marketplace.

(5) *The possibility of influencing legislation.* Firms developing or implementing environmental technology innovation have the possibility of influencing legislation to their benefit. This can in turn give them a competitive edge over others in the industry. For example, Germany's head start in regulations applicable to the cement industry and their implementation has enabled German cement manufacturers to develop and make use of the latest end-of-process technology, while at the same time conducting research into integrated technology for recycling and reusing gaseous emissions, as well as for improving energy efficiency (OECD 1993). At the same time, the German cement industry, by pushing for European regulations, has secured a medium- and long-term competitive advantage in certain segments of the market.

Japan is one country where the importance of competitive advantage has been well appreciated. The general policy there has been to encourage industry through fiscal and research incentives to develop a wide environmental technology 'portfolio', so as to ensure that there is flexibility of response in the face of unpredictable economic and environmental changes. It is further presumed that such a portfolio will enhance Japanese international competitivity in the medium and long run (5 to 50 years ahead), during which period environmental technology innovation is expected to play a crucial role. Outside of Japan, many large corporations, including chemical companies such as Du Pont and Dow, have also seen the advantages of this flexibility and acquired considerable expertise in various fields of environmental technology (recycling, waste and water treatment, disposal of toxic waste, risk management, and so on).

With so many potential benefits at stake, why do not more firms invest sooner in environmental technology innovation? In fact, many obstacles stand in their way (Shrivastava 1995a, 1995b). Among those obstacles are the fact that environmental performance is only one axis of possible competitive advantage and an ambiguous one at that. Environmental policy is marked by complicated, vague and contradictory regulations (in particular for different jurisdictions, that is, local, regional, European, and so on). Added to this is the inertia displayed by many firms. All this said, two particular hindrances are the following:

(1) *Lack of environmental expertise and information.* Technological solutions have not yet been found for certain environmental problems, and there is uncertainty about regulatory obligations. Under such circumstances, many firms have chosen to wait because they are not in a position to finance basic research nor to take too many investment risks if policy changes leave them in a cul-de-sac. In the European Commission DG III report (1995) referred to above, more than 75 per cent of those polled (the percentage was significantly lower in Germany and The Netherlands) stated the desire for additional and clearer information about environmental regulations and available technological solutions.

(2) *Development costs.* Although technical solutions may be available, the cost of implementing them may still be high. When this happens, some firms – especially small and medium-sized ones – prefer to adopt a wait-and-see attitude. Capital investment for environmental technology takes longer to pay for itself than most investment outlays. This can act as a disincentive for firms that are ruled by requirements of short-term performance. Furthermore, given a firm's limited financial resources, different types of capital expenditures compete for funds.

An example is the European pesticide industry. Data supplied by the agrochemical sector reveal that research and development expenditures have increased considerably over the past ten years and environmental testing accounts for a significant share of the costs. Environmental and toxicological tests reportedly combine to account for between 25 and 40 per cent of R&D expenditures, estimated at some 150 million dollars per molecule (Nadaï 1996). Yet, in the case of agricultural chemicals, market conditions make it impossible to earn an adequate return on investment in environmental technology. The European Crop Protection Association reports that profit margins at agrochemical firms operating in the European Union over the past 20 years fell to 6.8 per cent of sales in 1990, from 10.5 per cent in 1981, and it is claimed that environmental regulations were the primary cause of the drop. The situation has led a growing number of firms to put pressure on governments to improve patenting and to extend the life of patents. This would, however, result in a trade-off between the profitability of innovations and their availability.

2.3 ORGANIZATIONAL STRUCTURES FOR WIN–WIN STRATEGIES

In a firm, the process of environmental technology innovation can require changes in working relationships and result in the need for new research and monitoring. Consideration of environmental issues can occur at several levels. It can involve the creation of a specialized field with its own structures, the addition of an extra variable to an organizational chart or the implementation of environment-specific concepts throughout management. In-house discussions can result in the creation of new departments (environment division, recycling division, and so on) and cause the inclusion of an additional parameter at existing ones. The environment can also cause the business of the firm to evolve or be a catalyst for new activities. Major innovations can also result in external organizational changes, such as in the case of the establishment of new connections for obtaining raw materials and semi-finished inputs, as well as new marketing strategies (in particular in the case of product innovations) and measures aimed at recycling and processing waste. Many changes can then be introduced by means of vertical and/or horizontal integration, through the setting up of new cooperation alliances among firms and within sectors, and even, as will be discussed in Section 2.4, through new types of agreements between firms and governments.

2.3.1 Changing the Internal Organization of Firms

A simple way to discuss organizational change of firms is in terms of the structure of the market (S), the behaviour of firms (B) and performance (P), as proposed by Bain (1956). These three elements can be seen as interactive over time. For example, a firm's profitability, market share or environmental performance has an impact on its subsequent strategies (or behaviour), which can contribute to modifying market structures. The Du Pont Corporation, for example, adopted early on a particular research strategy (behaviour) when it elected to emphasize research into CFC substitutes. Subsequently, a strong negotiating activity (in support of regulations on the reduction of CFC emissions) enabled Du Pont to improve its performance by securing a competitive edge in the new market conditions and structures that changed to its advantage.

Changes in the market structure generally go hand in hand with changes in a firm's internal organization. The trend is particularly visible in the chemical industry. Rhône–Poulenc, ICI, Bayer, Union Carbide and Ciba, for instance, have added special 'environment' horizontal divisions and, at the same time, created incentives (for example, the Proforis employee-motivation programme, or PRISE) to ensure that activities are horizontally coordinated (Chailloux 1996).

The trend is also in evidence in the automobile industry. For example, Renault has focused on the disposal of used vehicles and created new structures as a result (recycling programmes). Also, while Renault's policies were until recently based on four considerations, that is, quality, cost, time and weight, recycling has now been added. In addition, the French automotive manufacturer, which used to operate according to a matrix-like business structure, has now included recycling as part of its projects as well as operations.

Consideration of environmental issues can cause a firm's business to change dramatically, and/or result in its expanding into new fields. For example Ricoh, an electronics company, single-handedly developed a substitute for a polystyrene that is easier to recycle, to be used in packaging. The company has developed a cardboard-based packaging with the same properties as packaging made of polystyrene. Ricoh has improved its cardboard packaging so that its electronic components will cause less environmental pollution (Persson et al. 1995).

2.3.2 Changing the External Organization in Response to the Environment

The environment can become a factor in the evolution of relationships between firms and others they do business with, either vertically (as in the case of industries and business contacts upstream or downstream from production), or else horizontally (companies in the same sector), or even with respect to links with other entities (government, consumers, and so on).

For example, influenced in part by questions of liability in relation to environmental impacts and accidental damages, insurance companies and other financial institutions are revising their relations with business firms. For insurance companies, environmental hazards belong to a special category of risks (Schmidheiny 1992), not just because accidental damages can be very severe but also because of the uncertainties associated with gradual pollution, occurring over a long period of time. Likewise, banks have been expanding the scope of their management audits to include environmental aspects, in particular in the case of mergers and acquisitions or in connection with the creation of environmental funds.

Changes in relations with 'upstream' participants in the system (subcontractors and suppliers) may also occur, bringing about stronger links and demands for evidence of the environmental quality of goods. Many factors are contributing to this, including the certification procedures required of suppliers in certain instances. In the automobile industry, for example, the fact that manufacturers are taking into consideration the disposal of scrapped vehicles has had repercussions for all firms operating upstream, whether they are parts suppliers or processors and chemical companies supplying raw materials. Giving consideration to the environment and in particular to the disposal of used products has also resulted in the development of a new set of interconnections between firms operating downstream from manufacturers. It can lead to the joint creation of business entities. For example, a joint project by PSA, Compagnie Française des Ferrailles (CFF) and the Vicat cement company resulted in the creation of a facility for pre-industrial applications at Saint-Pierre de Chandieu. In addition, the organization of the sector has tended to put more emphasis on quality (merger of two trade associations of scrapyard companies in 1995) (Chailloux 1996; Serret 1996). Finally, the growth of certain environmental policy instruments such as voluntary agreements also illustrates this trend. The French master agreement of March 1993 on the processing of scrapped cars was signed jointly by representatives of the automobile industry and the government.

In the case of horizontal relations among firms in the same line of business, mergers can be encouraged in order to achieve greater concentration and economies of scale. Given the unpredictability of environmental developments and the importance of capital outlays for environmental protection, cooperation is particularly attractive for firms pursuing a proactive environmental strategy. Many categories of agreements call for sharing environmental risks and costs. Alliance strategies range from simple cooperation agreements to mergers and acquisitions. Their typology can be derived from examples taken from various industries and countries.

(1) *Cooperation agreements for the development of new processes.* France's Rhône–Poulenc and Sweden's Kenura set up a jointly owned subsidiary in 1990 to look for more efficient and cheaper ways of fighting water pollution. In September 1992, SITA (a subsidiary of Lyonnaise des Eaux) and Rhône–Poulenc jointly created TERIS to develop their know-how in the treatment of industrial waste. The principal manufacturers of CFC have formed a strategic alliance known as ICOLP (Industry Cooperative for Ozone Layer Protection) to develop substitutes. There are also cooperation agreements between European cement makers and parts manufacturers, for the development of new processes and to conduct basic research into combustion and flame control. One of the objectives of the research is to measure the influence of the type of burner and fuel used on the production of NO_x, in order to develop burners with lower emissions of NO_x (Gramond and Setbon 1996).

(2) *Cooperation agreements for the development of new products.* Siemens and Bayer have developed catalytic converters for the denitrification of flue gases in order to lower nitrogen oxide emissions. Elbo, the public authority operating the Athens bus system, and Rhône–Poulenc have designed a catalytic converter for diesel engines which cuts back on exhaust fumes.

(3) *Cooperation agreements for the recycling of packaging and products.* Eco-emballages is a company founded in 1992 in France by a group of packaging firms and manufacturers and distributors of packaging materials. In the automobile industry, the issue of scrapping vehicles

has been the subject of several agreements involving either just manufacturers or other industry firms as well. Agreements on the development of a recycling network have been signed, such as the 1994 pact between Renault, BMW and Fiat, which Rover later joined. Research agreements have in addition been signed by French manufacturers and some of their competitors (the 1995 agreement between Renault and Mercedes–Benz).

(4) *Mergers and acquisitions.* This type of strategy can be justified by a desire on the part of firms to focus on their core business and to reduce risk exposure and the cost of implementing environmental technology innovation. Rhône–Poulenc and Sita have acquired, through their jointly owned subsidiary TERIS, the business of SCORI, a company specializing in the disposal of waste with cement makers. Elf Atochem has taken over several small CFC manufacturers in Greece and the United States in order to increase its capacity to conduct research into substitutes.

This sort of cooperation may be a significant factor in commercial globalization. The process of strategic alliances leads, typically, either to more concentration or to the creation of network entities or networks of firms. These alliances and mergers by firms alter the balance of power, and in the process of organizational changes it is easy to foresee the disappearance of certain market participants. In certain instances, this leads to a loss of local control (or of national economic sovereignty), and can lead to more concentration within a sector or domain of activity.

2.4   SOCIAL AND ENVIRONMENTAL TENSIONS WITHIN THE NEW COMPETITION

There exists a complex and significant interplay between environmental technological innovations and political, social and economic developments (Smeets and Weterings 1996). Firms pursuing a win–win environmental strategy ought to reconcile business considerations with the requirements of social responsibility. That is,

(1) On the one hand, business practices based on the need to earn a profit reflect that need in costs, product prices and competitiveness considerations, as well as in market shares and positioning.
(2) On the other hand, a problem of social legitimacy exists which has to do with a notion of public interest that ought to encompass current environmental problems along with the interest of future generations.

The European Commission, for example, frames this in its document *Towards Sustainable Development* (1993) as a three-way cooperation between the private sector, governance, and citizens. National and international political institutions, as well as the public at large, play roles complementary to that of business in choosing technological trajectories. But it cannot simply be assumed that the simultaneous adjustment of business practices and of regulations is going to provide adequately for long-term sustainable development (see for example, the discussion by Duchin et al. 1995). Business strategies that may seem win–win from a firm's point of view in relation to specific environmental targets may in the longer term be judged, from wider social points of view, as wrong–wrong.

Successful innovations may improve environmental performance in certain ways, yet cause the economy to develop along locked-in technological trajectories that turn out to be suboptimal environmentally. Worth citing here is the example of the development of catalytic converters as the exclusive technological solution to the problem of acid rain attributable to pollution caused by automobile exhaust fumes. The case of phosphate-free detergents is also interesting. In this case, the technological lock-in did not originate with an institution or regulation, but was linked to increasing returns from the products' popularity. Henkel based its strategy on a hypothesis of increased return from the popularity of phosphate-free laundry detergents, which caused the market penetration theory to be confirmed by their growing acceptance (with all brands gradually bringing out their own phosphate-free detergents). All manufacturers came out with phosphate-free laundry detergents not because it had been ascertained that they were safer than traditional products, but because every time one company brought out a phosphate-free detergent, the probability rose that another company would do likewise. The manufacturer Rhône–Poulenc, which found itself on the wrong technological track (as the world's leading producer of phosphates), tried to postpone the manufacturing of phosphate-free detergents for as long as possible by financing research into alternatives and by denouncing the unreliability of substitutes. The argument was that more time needed to be given for the 'alternative' technology (in this case the traditional technology) to demonstrate its advantages (Moreau 1994; Benhaïm and Schembri 1995); this debate is still going on.

From these examples we can see the danger that successful innovations can cause the economy to take off in new directions which, while viable from a business point of view and satisfying for consumers in the short run, are in the longer run suboptimal or even directly in conflict with objectives of a sustainable environment. There is also the problem of 'green window-dressing'. There was a revealing case of Mobil Chemical Company. After the firm started marketing its biodegradable garbage bags, a company spokesman declared to the *Tallahassee Democrat* in 1991 (cited by Worldwatch and by *The New York Times*) that

> degradability is just a marketing tool (...) We're talking out of both sides of our mouth because we want to sell bags. I don't think the average consumer knows what 'degradability' means. Customers don't care if it solves the solid waste problem. It makes them feel good.... (cited in Piasecki 1995).

Mention here might also be made of the well-publicized replacement by McDonald's of a white polyethylene packaging sheet with polystyrene foam, which makes no significant difference from an environmental point of view – it is a matter of air pollution versus water pollution (Duchin et al. 1995).

Further, there are concerns that commercially driven environmental innovation can, in some cases, worsen social inequalities on an international level. The environmental protection sector, which generated estimated revenues of 200 billion dollars in 1990 and is expected to grow by 50 per cent during the coming ten years (OECD 1993), operates primarily in OECD countries (90 per cent of world production); the main exporting countries are Germany, the United States and Japan. Demand for products and services is expected to increase during the coming ten years in some developing countries, including the newly industrialized countries of Southeast Asia, as well as in Eastern Europe. However, both the manufacturing and consumption of products and services will continue to take place chiefly in OECD countries.

More generally, the fear is sometimes expressed that the movement in favour of deregulation, within states and internationally, could mean that governments are playing a less clear part in environmental protection and handing the reins over to business. Indeed, a process by which industry seeks to self-regulate is emerging through an increase in so-called voluntary collective agreements (Aggieri and Hatchuel 1996). In some instances, the trend is supported by developments within the governments themselves. An example is the adoption, at the European level, of an 'eco-audit' regulation designed to incite industry to implement environmental policies on a voluntary basis.

It is interesting, in this respect, to note that far from slowing down the setting of standards, deregulation has actually coincided with more and more technical standards being adopted by trade and industry bodies. At the international level, a new generation of ISO standards on environmental management is being drafted. These ISO 14000 standards (especially 14020, 21, 22, 23 and 24; some are still being developed), which contain provisions relating to environmental labelling, in some respects resemble the ISO 9000 standards on quality. Furthermore, national standards are being adopted, as illustrated by the French X 30–200 and the British BS 77–50 standards. Environmental standards are also being developed for specific sectors at the initiative of industries. This was the case, for example, with the standard on the environmental properties of electrotechnical products created by the International Electrotechnical Commission (IEC).

So the question returns: what are the discernible trends of current processes of business practices and globalization? The evolutionary systems view of economic and ecological change that underpins our analysis of competitiveness is exemplified in the work of Krupp (1992), who writes:

> Technologically, this century is characterized by an unprecedented rate of innovation triggered by and triggering a fast competitive race of economic and political entities (...) All production and feedback has become polarized towards profit generation (...). Today's numerous incremental decisions by politicians and businessmen on energy, made wittingly and willingly or not, will accumulate to form fundamental constraints and contingencies shaping the lives of future generations. They determine whether, with all their growing wealth, they might have to cope with unfavourable climate changes, billions of tons of radioactive materials, millions of square kilometers of genetically-manipulated monoculture, including biomass for energy conversion, to name but a few examples, or, alternately, whether early resourceful self-restraint has avoided the related risks without impairment of the quality of future life on earth.

This economic dynamism is manifest, says Krupp, through technological innovation and the incessant release of new and 'improved' products. The commodity economy and circuits of capital now become the main engines and beneficiaries of this dynamic of innovation, a positive feedback loop driven by the quest for profits, and characterized by incessant liquidation and renewal. Yet, the intensification and extensification (through the growth of output and mass consumption levels) of this innovation process now threatens global resources and ecological conditions of life for hundreds of millions of people.

However, there are continuous improvements in environmental performance and natural resource use efficiency; improved efficiency can permit continued output growth; and the sheer scale of many sectors of industrial activity is now of serious worldwide concern. Moreover, the social and environmental costs of this innovation process are unevenly distributed (see Altvater 1993; O'Connor 1994a, 1994b; and Beckenbach 1994, who in turn draws on the cost-shifting notion of William Kapp). Under pressures of commercial survival, firms seek to off-load environmental and social performance burdens on to other social partners – for example, on to the state and taxpayers, on to workers (in terms of bad working conditions, commuting costs, and so on) on to future generations and non-human nature. According to the polluter pays principle, business and consumers ought to take full account of the burdens they impose upon communities and ecosystems. But this is a responsibility which, considered an additional cost, is clearly in conflict with the profit motive.

In the context of observations about globalization, increased attention has been given to instances of international externalities, cases of alleged cost-shifting by economic players separated by very large distances. Many of these involve multinational firms, such as the mining companies RTZ-CRA and Freeport-McMoRan, under attack in the courts and in the boardrooms for the adverse social and ecological impact of their gold and copper mining operations in Irian Jaya ('The Fun of Being a Multinational' in *The Economist*, 20 July 1996). These and other sorts of experiences are giving rise to a growing literature on 'unequal ecological exchange' between the North and South countries. For example, conflicts over the control of the commercial exploitation and profits generated by agriculture and 'wild' biodiversity have led to accusations of 'biopiracy' against multinational firms.

Analyses are increasingly being conducted of the 'ecological footprints' left by production and consumption in rich countries, in terms of land area, water and photosynthesis requirements, compared with the availability of these resources in the producing and consuming countries (Rees and Wackernagel 1994; Rees 1996; Wackernagel and Rees 1995). The opportunity costs of forests and fisheries depletion are being discussed in terms of intersociety and intertemporal injustice (McEvoy 1986; McGrath 1993; O'Connor 1993). Many commentators have raised concern about uneven social distribution of the benefits of economic globalization (Gedicks 1993; Anderson et al. 1991). For example, the destruction of the communal fabric of economic infrastructures by large-scale dam and irrigation projects in India and China is well documented (Goldman 1993). Relatively more aluminium is imported into Japan today from countries such as Canada where hydroelectricity is very cheap than in the 1970s. Similarly, Japan is 'developing hydroelectric power in countries such as Brazil and Indonesia' (Mukaibo, cited in Krupp 1992). For reasons such as these, as well as for reasons of technological innovation, within Japan itself 'pollution will not seriously worsen' (ibid. p.17). A large part of the pollution and ecological damage associated with Japan's economic dynamism is currently being shifted offshore. Again, the fairness of distribution of the benefits of economic globalization is being questioned. A proposal for the North's response to environmental stresses is provided by a recent study on the future of Japan, entitled 'MITI's Centennial Vision of Global Environment and Technology and the Response to Global Warming: Concerning New Earth 21' (Okamatsu, in Krupp 1992). The report envisages, *inter alia*, the greening of deserts and space-based energy sources as solutions to global greenhouse problems. For the South, a parallel image might well be that of the urban or rural poor being obliged to walk long distances in order to obtain minimally drinkable water piped at considerable expense from distant sources, because of the contamination or exhaustion of local water supplies.

This sort of vision emphasizes the fact that 'improved environmental performance', as measured for an individual firm or production process, has to be set against the backdrop of non-sustainable high levels of fish and forest harvesting, and intensive agricultural and animal husbandry practices that are degrading the soil and water quality, in some cases irreversibly (for example, aquifer and soil salinization and soil structure breakdown).

Environmental innovation may, in some cases, be like taking steps up an escalator (improved environmental performance) while the escalator itself (overall environmental quality) is sliding rapidly down. Worsening resource exhaustion and environmental problems can indeed provide stimulus for innovation, and hence renewed competitivity for some firms and sectors, while the overall situation worsens.

2.5 FROM WIN–WIN FIRM STRATEGIES TO SUSTAINABLE DEVELOPMENT?

In order to ensure that a win–win type of environmental strategy for whole nations and for the community of nations – a vision of ecologically and economic sustainable development – it seems indispensable to take into consideration other factors besides innovation and competitiveness alone. These additional factors include the notion of 'public interest' extended to future generations (and, more arguably, to ecosystems and other species as non-human living communities). It is, or would be, the task of governance to put out clear signals to orient all participants (including those in governance itself) towards the desired trajectory. To what extent will this be something that firms, government leaders and consumers really want to make an investment in?

The outlook for a social partnership on win–win environmental strategies, and, more generally, on sustainable development strategies is at best highly uncertain. Prospects can be examined in various ways, with social legitimacy being considered and challenged by various categories of participants from the environmental field. Many firms fear loss of competitivity if they are forced to make major improvements to their environmental performance. This may often be true if end-of-pipe measures are employed. In such situations, the marginal and total costs of abatement for any given pollutant can rise quite sharply as the abatement target is made more severe. Firms are also concerned about getting locked in to expensive environmental protection measures that become obsolete if regulations or market conditions change. This is a problem of uncertainty. However, for several reasons, business outlooks may not be as bad.

- First, there are often significant gains in (for example) energy and raw materials use by improved efficiency practices within the production and transportation processes, at relatively low (or even negative) costs.
- Second, if a dynamic view of competitivity is taken, then investments may be targeted on new generations of products and process technologies, through which substantial improvements in environmental performance may be obtained in the longer run without prohibitive extra costs (Stephan 1998; Faucheux and O'Connor (eds) 1997, Chapters 10 and 11).
- Third, if clear signals are provided through public policy, including international conventions, that improved environmental performance is a basic 'rule of the game', then firms can be reassured that all players are obliged to respond to the same standards.

We do not say that 'sustainability' is around the corner. Yet these last two points represent possible starting points for building alliances between the public, private and communal sectors, so that at least the contradictions between economic growth and ecological resilience can be addressed. Firms are under vertical pressure (from outside the business) from public opinion and regulations imposed by governments and their agencies; they are also subject to lateral pressure (from within the business) linked to the demands of principals, banks, insurance companies and shareholders; that pressure takes longer to bring about but it is also more productive as it is directly reflected in the order books of companies.

It is not necessary to convince small and medium-sized enterprise (SME) managers and business executives of the scientific need to treat the environment in a strategic manner in order for them to agree to do so. It may suffice if they find it likely that their competitors, government institutions and consumers grant the environment such a status. At times when there is hesitation about future trends, a key factor for economic coordination becomes the development of collective alliances of government (national and international institutions), the private sector (trade and industry associations) and the people (consumer associations, non-governmental organizations – NGOs – of all types) to promote a common understanding and vision of the world along with new standards of conduct giving legitimacy to a given orientation. It is interesting to note, for example, that almost 20 per cent of all adults in the United States and Canada belong to consumer groups supporting the environment, such as True Blue or Greenback (Gallup International 1992; Stisser 1994). The commercial demand for environment-friendly products is estimated to be worth 120 million dollars and expected to reach 200 million dollars by the end of the century.

Under those circumstances, the negotiation of voluntary agreements can be given a new dimension in the crystallization of common concepts. Here, as the chairman of AKZO, a chemical corporation, recently commented (Schot 1996):

> History shows that no firm has ever outlived a permanent conflict with society. Dialogue, adjustments and cooperation are therefore not luxuries but rather necessities.

REFERENCES

Aggieri, F. and A. Hatchuel (1996), 'A Dynamic Model of Environmental Policies. The Case of Innovation Oriented Voluntary Agreements', paper presented at a conference on The Economics and Law of Voluntary Approaches in Environmental Policies, Venice, 18–19 November.

Altvater, E. (1993), *The future of the market*, London: Verso.

Anderson, A.B., P.H. May and M.J. Balick (1991), *The Subsidy from Nature. Palm Forests, Peasantry, and Development on an Amazon Frontier*, New York: Columbia University Press.

Bain, J. (1956), *Barriers to New Competition*, Cambridge, MA: Harvard University Press.

Beckenbach, F. (1994), 'Social Costs in Modern Capitalism', in M. O'Connor (ed.), *Is Capitalism Sustainable?*, New York: Guilford Publications, pp. 91–105.

Benhaïm, J. and P. Schembri (1995), 'Technical Change: an Essential Variable in the Choice of a Sustainable Development Trajectory', in S. Faucheux, D.W. Pearce and J.L.R. Proops (eds), *Models of Sustainable Development*, Cheltenham, UK and Brookfield, US: Edward Elgar.

Cairncross, F. (1995), *Green Inc., A Guide to Business and the Environment*, Covelo, CA: Island Press.

Chailloux, N. (1996), 'Implications de la Mondialisation de l'Economie sur la Relation Environnement–Entreprise', *Rapport C3ED* sous la direction de S. Faucheux, Ministère de l'Environnement, janvier.

Coenen R., S. Klein-Vielhauer and R. Meyer (1996), *Umwelt, Technik und Wirtschaftliche Entwicklung*, Büro für Technikfolgen-Abschätzung (TAB), Bonn G: Bundestag.

De Marchi, B. (1997), 'Seveso: from Pollution to Regulation', *International Journal of Environment and Pollution*, 7 (4), 526–38.

DG III (1995), *Attitude and Strategy of Business Regarding Protection of the Environment*, Common Environmental Framework, November, European Commission DG III.

Duchin F., G.M. Lange and G. Kell (1995), 'Technological Change, Trade, and the Environment', *Ecological Economics*, 14, 185–93.

Erkman, S. (1996), 'Industrial Ecology: A Historical View', *Industrial Ecology: Special Issue*, (1/2) 1–10.

Faucheux, S. (1997), 'Technological Change, Ecological Sustainability and Industrial Competitiveness', in A.K. Dragun and K.M. Jacobsson (eds),

Sustainability and Global Environmental Policy: New Perspectives, Cheltenham, UK and Lyme, US: Edward Elgar, pp. 131–48.

Faucheux, S. and J.F. Noël (1990), *Les Menaces Globales sur l'Environnement*, Paris: Collection Repères, La Découverte.

Faucheux, S. and M. O'Connor (eds) (1997), *Valuation for Sustainable Developmement: Methods and Policy Indicators*, Cheltenham, UK and Lyme, US: Edward Elgar.

Freeman, C. (1982), *The Economics of Industrial Innovation*, London: Pinter.

Frosh, R.A. (1995), 'Industrial Ecology, Adaptating Technology for a Sustainable World', *Environment*, December, 16–24 and 34–37.

Gallup International (1992), *Survey of Environmental Opinions*, Princeton.

Garrod, B. and P. Chadwick (1996), 'Environmental Management and Business Strategy: Towards a New Strategic Paradigm', *Futures*, 28 (1), 37–50.

Gedicks, A. (1993), *The New Resource Wars. Native and Environmental Struggles against Multinational Corporations*, Boston, MA: South End Press.

Goldman, M. (1993), 'Tragedy of the Commons or the Commoners' Tragedy', *Capitalism, Nature, Socialism*, 4 (16), December, 49–68.

Gramond, V. and V. Setbon (1996), 'Analyse des Implications Stratégiques des Contraintes et Opportunités Environnementales: une Comparaison France–Allemagne à partir d'une Etude du Secteur Ciment', rapport sous la direction de S. Faucheux, Programme Environnement, Société, Entreprise: la Nouvelle Donne, octobre.

Jacobs, M. (1994), 'Green Jobs? The Employment Implications of the Environmental Policies', Report for WWF, Brussels.

Krupp, H. (1992), *Energy Politics and Schumpeter Dynamics: Japan's Policy Between Short-Term Wealth and Long-Term Global Welfare*, Tokyo: Springer-Verlag.

McEvoy, A.F. (1986), *The Fisherman's Problem: Ecology and Law in the California Fisheries, 1850–1980*, Cambridge: Cambridge University Press.

McGrath, D. et al. (1993), 'Fisheries and the Evolution of Resource Management in the Lower Amazon Floodplain', *Human Ecology*, 21 (2).

Miller, A. and C. Moore (1994), 'Strengths and Limitation of Governmental Support for Environmental Technology in Japan', *Industrial and Environmental Crisis Quarterly*, 8 (2), 155–70.

Ministry of International Trade and Industry (MITI) (1988), White Paper on Industrial Technology: Trends and Future Tasks in Japanese Industrial Technology, MITI, Tokyo.

Moreau, F. (1994), 'L'Entreprise face aux Diverses Formes du Risque Environnemental', *Revue d'Economie Régionale et Urbaine*, 4, 668–80.

Nadaï, A. (1996), 'From Environment to Competition – The EU Regulatory Process in Pesticide Registration', in F. Lévêque (ed.), *Environmental Policy in Europe: Industry, Competition and the Policy Process*, Cheltenham, UK and Brookfield, US: Edward Elgar.

O'Connor, M. (1993), 'Valuing Fish in Aotearoa: The Treaty, the Market, and the Intrinsic Value of the Trout', *Environmental Values*, 3.

O'Connor, M. (ed.) (1994a), *Is Capitalism Sustainable?*, New York: Guilford Publications.

O'Connor, M. (1994b), 'The Material/Communal Conditions of Production', *Capitalism, Nature, Socialism*, 5 (3), 95–104.

OECD (1993), *Environmental Policies and Industrial Competitiveness*, Paris: OECD.

Palmer, K., W.E. Oates and P.R. Portney (1995), 'Tightening Environmental Standards: The Benefit-Cost or the No-Cost Paradigm', *Journal of Economic Perspectives*, 9 (4), Fall, 119–32.

Persson, J.G., C. Luttropp, S. Ritzen and A.M. Akermark (1995), 'Design for Recycling – A Survey on Activities in Industry and at Universities', Royal Institute of Technology, Stockholm, June.

Piasecki, B.W. (1995), *Corporate Environmental Strategy – The Avalanche of Change since Bhopal*, New York: J. Wiley and Sons.

Porter, M.E. (1990), *The Competitive Advantage of Nations*, New York: Free Press.

Porter, M.E. and C. van der Linde (1995a), 'Green and Competitive', *Harvard Business Review*, September–November, 120–34.

Porter, M.E. and C. van der Linde (1995b), 'Toward a New Conception of the Environment–Competitiveness Relationship', *Journal of Economic Perpectives*, 9 (4), Fall, 97–118.

Rees, W.E. (1996), 'Revisiting Carrying Capacity: Area-based Indicators of Sustainability', *Population and Environment: A Journal of Interdisciplinary Studies*, 17 (39), January.

Rees, W. and M. Wackernagel (1994), 'Ecological Footprints and Appropriated Carrying Capacity', in A.M. Jansson et al. (eds), *Investing in Natural Capital: The Ecological Economics Approach to Sustainability*, ISEE, Covelo, CA: Island Press.

Schmidheiny, S. (1992), *Changer de cap*, Paris: Dunod.

Schot, J. (1996), 'Facing the Sustainable Challenge; Strategic Choices for Industrial Firms', Public lecture in Paris Conference, 25 March.

Serret, Y. (1996), 'Effets dans la Représentation de Compétitivité par les Firmes sur le Traitement de la Dimension Environnementale', Environment, Long-term Governance and Democracy, Conference held in Abbaye de Fontevraud, France, 8–11 September.

Setbon, V. (1997), 'Waste Incineration in Cement Plants: Constraints and Development Opportunities (a French–German Comparison)', *International Journal of Environment and Pollution*, 7 (4), 547–60.

Shrivastava, P. (1995a), 'Environmental Technologies and Competitive Advantage', *Strategic Management Journal*, 16, 183–200.

Shrivastava, P. (1995b), 'Democratic Control of Technological Risks in Developing Countries', *Ecological Economics*, 14, 195–208.

Skea, J. (1994), 'Environmental Issues and Innovation', in M. Dodgson and R. Rothwell (eds), *Handbook of Industrial Innovation*, Aldershot, UK and Brookfield, US: Edward Elgar, pp. 421–31.

Smeets, E.R.W. and R.A.P.M. Weterings (1996), 'Implementing Long Term Considerations in Industrial Innovation Strategies', Environment, Long-term Governance and Democracy, Conference held in Abbaye de Fontevraud, France, 8–11 September.

Sprenger, R.U. (1995), 'Croissance Economique et Protection de l'Environnement: les Thèses en Présence', *Problèmes Economiques*, 2407, Paris: La Documentation Française, janvier.

Stephan, G. (1998), 'Short Run and Long Run Adjustment to Environmental Policy: a Neo Austrian Approach', in S. Faucheux, M. O'Connor and J. Van der Straaten (eds), *Sustainable Development: Concepts, Rationalities and Strategies*, Dordrecht: Kluwer.

Stisser, P. (1994), 'A Deeper Shade of Green', *American Demographics*, 16 (3), 24–9.

Valenduc, G. and P. Vendramin (1996), *Le travail au vert; Environnement, Innovation et Emploi*, FTU Emerit, EVO société.

Wackernagel, M. and W.E. Rees (1995), *Our Ecological Footprint: Reducing Human Impact on the Earth*, Gabriola Island, BC and Philadelphia, PA: New Society Publishers.

3. Environmental Regulations and Foreign Direct Investment Flows within the European Union

António Castro Guerra and Vitor Santos

3.1 INTRODUCTION

One common concern among environmentalists is the so-called pollution haven hypothesis which states that free trade will contribute to increased industrial pollution in developing countries through two different mechanisms: on the one hand, stricter environmental regulations stimulate the displacement of pollution-intensive industries from developed to developing countries; on the other hand, the competitive discipline imposed on domestic industries is a common argument used by business lobbies in order to persuade governments to reduce further their environmental standards. Both phenomena could lead to excessive pollution in developing countries, thus inducing negative impacts on welfare. Any judgement about free trade should take into consideration the trade-off between economic growth and environmental quality and their net impacts in terms of welfare.

This is the background and the main motivation of our paper. However, our discussion is mostly devoted to the analysis of the interdependences between economic integration and national environmental regulations in the concrete case of the European Union. Theoretical results proposed by Rauscher (1992) suggest that the process of European economic integration might induce a relocation of capital from the northern to the southern countries. Furthermore, the same author concludes that this process tends to be amplified by environmental regulations. The relative scarcity of environmental goods in northern European countries associated with more restrictive environmental regulations leads to industrial flight of pollution-intensive industries to southern countries.

These adjustment processes lead to an increase in emission levels in southern countries – the pollution haven hypothesis – and most likely to a reduction of welfare in those countries.

As far as we know, there is no empirical evidence on the pollution haven hypothesis applied to the European Union. However, existing empirical studies covering other geographical areas,[1] with the exception of Kolstad and Xing (1992), conclude that environmental regulations do not significantly determine the location of polluting industries. The basic argument suggested in those studies to explain the non-relevance of pollution abatement and control costs on industrial location is the small share of these costs within most industries of the total production costs. In order to avoid this shortcoming, we have decided to focus our empirical study on the chemical industry, which is one of the most heavily polluting industries.[2] Before proceeding with the empirical test in Section 3.3, we briefly survey the existing theoretical literature on the 'pollution haven hypothesis' (Section 3.2).

3.2   ECONOMIC INTEGRATION, FDI, ENVIRONMENTAL REGULATION AND WELFARE

Let us assume that we have the traditional three-country framework, the typical set-up within the context of the models of economic integration: country 1 and country 2 form a common market and country 3 is the non-member country (or the rest of the world). Along these lines, Rauscher (1992) developed a model whose main results are summarized in this section.

Each country i produces a final good by means of a capital input K, and an environmental good, E, referred to hereafter as emissions. The production function, $y = f^i(K^i, E^i)$, $i = 1, 2, 3$ is concave and exhibits constant returns to scale. A competitive world is implicitly assumed and, in consequence, factor prices are equal to their marginal productivities. The price of the environmental good is exogenously set by the government of each country as a final outcome of environmental policy: in more concrete terms, we assume that a public agency sets an emission tax, t^i.

Let the initial capital endowment of country i be denoted K_0^i and let I^{ij} be the flow of capital that is owned by country i and is exported to country j; we also assume that i and j are the members of the common market and k is the rest of the world. In this situation, the stock of capital in country i is given by the expression

$$K^i = K_0^i - I^{ij} - I^{ik}, \quad i \neq j \neq k \qquad (3.1)$$

I^{ij} may be interpreted as the net foreign direct investment flow from country i to country j and, hence, the following identity should be verified:

$$I^{ij} = -I^{ji}, \quad i \neq j. \tag{3.2}$$

The model is developed supposing that I^{12} is unequivocally positive, which can be interpreted as follows: country 1 is the capital exporter while country 2 is relatively well endowed with the environmental good.

Table 3-1 Countries' typology

Common Market	Relative Scarcity of Environmental Goods	Net Capital Exporter	Country 1
	Relative Abundance of Environmental Goods	Net Capital Importer	Country 2
Rest of the World			Country 3

It should be pointed out that there is not perfect mobility of capital. In fact, the model assumes the existence of barriers to factor mobility by introducing mobility costs; these costs are assumed to be proportional to the amount of capital invested abroad in order to reflect the costs of repatriating the profits earned abroad. This implies that the international allocation of direct investments is optimal if the differences in marginal productivities equal the marginal costs of mobility. The process of economic integration corresponds to lowering the institutional barriers to factor mobility which can be modelled, within this framework, by a reduction in mobility costs.

The model specification assumes the existence of a diffusion process that turns emissions into depositions. It is worthwhile to emphasize that transboundary pollution is taken into consideration since the level of pollution in country k, P^k, is given by the following expression:

$$P^k = a^{ik} E^i + a^{jk} E^j + a^{kk} E^k \tag{3.3}$$

where, a^{ij} is the diffusion parameter measuring the percentage of pollutants emitted by country i that is transported to country j and E^i is the level of emissions in country i.

The study by Rauscher (1992) analyses the impact of economic integration in a context in which environmental externalities are explicitly considered. In more specific terms, the simultaneous effects of creating a common market (decrease of mobility costs) and of imposing a pollution tax[3] are analysed from two different points of view: the relocation of capital and the welfare effects.[4] Rauscher (1992) reaches three main conclusions:

(a) The simultaneous achievement of economic integration (that is, an increase in factor mobility between country 1 and country 2) and environmental policy leads to an increasing flow of FDI from country 1 to country 2, to an increase in emissions by the capital-importing country and to a reduction in the capital-exporting country.

(b) If both countries set optimal (Pigouvian) taxes, then both countries will benefit from integration.
(c) When environmental policy is based on the imposition of suboptimal taxes, the most likely implication from integration is that the capital exporter will be a winner and the capital importer a loser.

Rauscher (1992) discusses capital mobility in the context of a one-sector model. An alternative framework was proposed by McGuire (1982)[5] in which the traditional Heckscher–Ohlin model is extended in order to incorporate environmental resources as inputs. Let us consider the interaction between two countries, Northern (N) and Southern (S), and two industries, X and Y. Let us assume that country N exhibits a relative abundance of capital goods, K, while country S is richly endowed in labour, L; on the other hand, industry X is capital-intensive and industry Y is labour-intensive.

Both countries use the same technologies, which can be expressed by the following production functions: $X = f(L, K, E)$ and $Y = g(L, K)$ where E is the amount of the environmental good used in production.

Now assume that the northern country unilaterally decides to impose a pollution tax on emissions. This policy implies a reduction in the marginal productivities of capital and labour in industry X in the northern country and induces the mobility of these factors to industry Y. Although commodity prices are identical in both countries, the factor returns of capital and labour differ between the two countries; in particular, the relative reward of capital is higher in the southern country than in the northern country, thus implying an outflow of capital from the former to the latter. According to the Rybczynski theorem, the weight of industry X (the dirtier industry) will decrease in country N and its relative market share will increase in country S; the intercountry redistribution of industry Y (the cleaner industry) will follow the opposite adjustment. This movement of capital will continue until factor prices are identical in both countries.

As a consequence of a unilateral environmental regulation in country N, the industry devoted to the production of pollution-intensive goods will move to country S, thus converting this country to a pollution haven.

Table 3-2 summarizes the main conclusions of this survey related to the relationship between FDI and environmental regulations in the context of economic integration:

(a) The process of European economic integration leads to a relocation of capital from the northern to the southern countries. This process tends to be amplified by environmental regulations;
(b) Relative scarcity of environmental goods in northern European countries (higher physical absorptive capacity and environment is presumably a normal good[6]) associated with more strict environmental regulations induces a relocation of pollution-intensive industries from those countries to the southern countries; and

(c) The above-mentioned adjustment processes intertwine and lead to an increase in emission levels in southern countries (the pollution haven hypothesis) and most likely to a reduction of welfare in those countries.

Table 3-2 EU, environmental policy, pollution haven hypothesis and welfare

EU Countries	Flow of FDI	Emissions Level	Welfare Effects	
			Optimal Policy	Suboptimal Policy
Northern Countries	Outflow	Reduction	Positive	Positive
Southern Countries	Inflow	Increase (Pollution Haven)	Positive	Negative

3.3   A MODEL OF FDI WITH ENVIRONMENTAL STRINGENCY

3.3.1 The Model

We propose an econometric model consistent with the theoretical background developed in previous sections. Taking into consideration our earlier discussion, there would appear to be three main factors determining inflows of FDI to a given host country: market size, cost differentials among countries and environmental regulations.

A general specification suitable to represent intercountry flows of FDI is given by the following analytical expression:

$$FDI_{it} = \alpha_0 + \alpha_1 MS_{it} + \alpha_2 CD_{it} + \alpha_3 E_{it} + \varepsilon_{it} \tag{3.4}$$

where

FDI_{it} is an indicator measuring the intensity of inflows of FDI in the sector of chemical industries to country i at year t;

MS_{it} is an indicator reflecting potential market size or economic dimension of country i at year t;

CD_{it} is the average wage level in manufacturing industry in country i at year t;

E_{it} is a quantitative measure of the stringency of environmental regulations in country i at year t;

ε_{it} is a random (white noise) disturbance term.

The intensity of inflows of foreign capital to each country observed in the chemical industry was proxied by two different indicators:

- net inflows of capital (N_FDI) corresponding to the balance between inflows of foreign capital to country i and outflows of domestic capital from the same country; and
- the relative intensity of inflows of FDI calculated using the ratio between inflows of capital in each country and its GDP.

Production costs and market size are two classical explanations for FDI. Foreign capital is driven by international differences in production costs, that is, FDI flows out of countries with high production costs; therefore, a negative sign should be expected for the coefficient, α_2, associated to variable CD_{it}. The market size hypothesis states that, due to scale economies, FDI will not flow into a country until its market reaches a certain size under which production is efficient; in consequence, the expected sign for the parameter related to MS_{it}, α_1, is positive.

To indicate the relative strictness of environmental regulations in each country, we use two different indicators: emissions of SO_2 per unit of real GDP and an aggregate indicator reflecting the per unit of GDP levels of SO_2 and CO_2. The choice between these two alternative variables should be justified and the main shortcomings associated with their use pointed out in order to avoid confusion about the econometric estimates presented in the next section.

The ideal choice for a variable reflecting the stringency of environmental policy should be an aggregate indicator incorporating information related to the different aspects concerning the implementation of environmental policies in each country. However, it is virtually impossible to get a picture of the environmental policy implemented in each country by using a single indicator. On the one hand, environmental regulations are a labyrinth of complex and diversified economic instruments and administrative rules; on the other hand, countries exhibit different enforcement capabilities implying that similar regulations can lead to a wide spectrum of impacts according to the degree of effectiveness of each country.

As it is nearly impossible to get a comprehensive measure of the strictness of regulations, we have adopted indicators that reflect the effective levels of pollution as being the most reliable proxies to measure the stringency of environmental policies. It is not consistent to use absolute-level variables since small, developing and highly polluting countries may exhibit absolute indices comparable to developed and environmentally friendly countries; for this reason, we used relative indices given by the ratio between the level of emissions and GDP for each country. The rationale behind these indicators is the following: a low ratio might be, in principle, associated with tight environmental regulations whereas a high value for the ratio can be interpreted as a sign of a less effective or strict policy.

It is worthwhile to make an additional reference to the aggregate environmental indicator mentioned above. Taking as primary information the ratios SO_2/GDP and CO_2/GDP, we have the synthetic indicator, PC1, as being the first principal component.[7] Since both ratios are positively correlated with PC1, one can conclude that increasing values of PC1 can be interpreted as the result of lax policies while low values correspond to stricter regulations.

Which is the expected sign for coefficient α_3? The basic idea underlying the 'pollution haven hypothesis' is that environmental regulations have a strong effect on industrial location and, in consequence, differential regulations between two countries will lead dirty industries to shift operations from the 'environmentally concerned country' to the 'pollution haven' (which can be either a LDC or a 'material consumption oriented country'). This means that a net outflow should be expected in the former subset of countries while a net positive inflow is more likely in the pollution havens; that is, the occurrence of the pollution haven corresponds to a positive sign for α_3, the coefficient associated to the variable reflecting the degree of strictness of environmental regulations.

3.3.2   Empirical Results

We now turn to the estimation of the model and the statistical results. However, it is worthwhile to start with a brief description of the geographical and sectoral extent of this empirical analysis.

The basic argument against the consistency of the 'pollution haven hypothesis' is the irrelevance of pollution abatement costs when compared with production costs. As mentioned before, numerous studies have estimated the impact of environmental control costs on industry price and output, trade balance and even of macroeconomic variables.[8] A consensual result in most studies[9] is the conclusion that abatement costs tend to be a very small fraction of industry costs on average. According to Tobey (1990)[10] one of the exceptions to this general rule is the chemical industry which spends nearly 3 per cent of its total costs on abatement activities. This was the main reason why we chose the chemical industry for our analysis.

The initial objective of this study was to analyse the inflows of FDI within the countries of the European Union. Unfortunately, the non-availability of data led us to exclude some of those countries and, consequently, our data set only covers seven European countries during the period 1984–92.

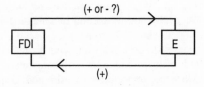

Figure 3-1 The FDI–environment relationship: causality or interaction?

A White test suggested the presence of 'heteroscedasticity'. To correct the biases induced by this problem in the interpretation of estimates, we adopted the procedure described in White (1980), that is, we computed heteroscedasticity-consistent standard errors and *t* values.

We start by using the OLS estimator; however, it is well known that this method is not consistent when, instead of having a causal relationship between the dependent and the exogenous variables, we have at least one independent variable that is jointly determined with the endogenous variable. This is the case, in our model, of FDI and E (see Section 3.3.1):

- on the one hand, for the reasons explained before, we assume that the strictness of environmental regulations tends to have a positive impact on the intensity of the inflows of FDI; and
- on the other hand, the inflows of FDI might have either a positive effect (economic growth associated with the entry of new affiliates will induce an increase in emissions) or a negative effect (multinational enterprises tend to use cleaner technologies when compared with domestic firms).

Because of the interaction between these two variables, we used instrumental variables for E in order to obtain consistent estimates for the parameters.

Table 3-3 Determinants of FDI inflows: OLS estimator (heteroscedasticity-corrected standard errors [a])

	N_FDI	N_FDI	FDI/GDP	FDI/GDP
Const	-267.566	88.324	0.180	0.460
	(-0.740)	(0.290)	(0.253)	(0.678)
GDP	1.234	1.132		
	(5.956)	(5.112)		
GDP/P			0.058	0.102
			(1.350)	(2.097)
SM_IND	-3.192	-7.414	-0.035	-0.054
	(-0.093)	(-0.201)	(-0.443)	(-0.682)
SO_2 /GDP	68.169		0.167	
	(2.013)		(3.148)	
PC1		83.536		0.400
		(0.777)		(2.328)
R^2	0.269	0.233	0.177	0.143

[a] The figures in parentheses denote ratios of the estimated coefficients to their respective White (1980) heteroscedasticity-corrected standard errors.

Scale economies seem to be a relevant determinant of FDI flows since the parameter associated with the indicator reflecting market size is statistically significant and exhibits the expected sign. Although displaying the predicted sign, the variable reflecting cost asymmetries across countries does not seem to influence FDI movements since the estimated coefficient is not significantly different from zero.

Table 3-4 Determinants of FDI inflows: 2SLS estimator (heteroscedasticity-corrected standard errors [a])

	N_FDI	N_FDI	FDI/GDP	FDI/GDP
Const	-267.566 (-0.766)	88.324 (0.303)	0.180 (0.265)	0.460 (0.713)
GDP	1.234 (6.181)	1.132 (5.293)		
GDP/P			0.058 (1.419)	0.102 (2.207)
SM_IND	-3.192 (-0.096)	-7.414 (-0.210)	-0.035 (-0.469)	-0.054 (-0.730)
SO_2 /GDP	68.169 (2.092)		0.167 (3.327)	
PC1		83.536 (0.808)		0.400 (2.445)
R^2	0.269	0.233	0.177	0.143

[a] The figures in parentheses denote ratios of the estimated coefficients to their respective White (1980) heteroscedasticity-corrected standard errors.

The coefficients associated with variables reflecting regulations stringency (SO_2/GDP and PC1) always exhibit the correct sign and are statistically significant in the 2SLS equations. This result is compatible with our expectations and provides empirical support for the pollution haven hypothesis.

3.4   CONCLUSIONS

This paper develops an econometric model that analyses the impact of the strictness of environmental regulations on the location of polluting industries within the European Union (EU). The main issue at stake is the analysis of the so-called pollution haven hypothesis: the relative ineffectiveness of environmental policies promoted by European 'Southern' countries which has stimulated the relocation of 'dirty' industries from the 'Northern' countries; in addition, southern European countries may have purposely undervalued the environment in order to attract new investments.

The empirical study examines the determinants of intracountry flows of FDI (foreign direct investment) promoted by the EU's manufacturing industry. Our empirical model distinguishes two different subsets of explanatory variables for the intracountry flows of capital: we start by mentioning the traditional variables identified in a variety of studies on FDI as being the main determinants of foreign investment (differences in the marginal return to capital, market size of host countries, exchange rate risk, trade impediments, market power, and so on); in a second step we extend the basic Heckscher–Ohlin model by taking into consideration environmental resources as inputs. Different environmental indicators are used to measure the degree of stringency of each country's environmental policy.

Our estimates suggest a significant effect of the strictness of environmental regulations on FDI. Moreover, empirical evidence indicates that lax regulations tend to attract foreign capital, thereby validating the pollution haven hypothesis.

Our theoretical results allow us to conclude that when the pollution haven hypothesis occurs within the context of optimal environmental policies, economic integration generates a positive effect in terms of welfare in every member country. However, this conclusion is not valid when suboptimal environmental policies are implemented; for example, in the case of the European Union, in which the most likely implication from integration is a reduction of welfare in southern countries.

This result suggests that the main factor affecting welfare is not free mobility of capital but the implementation of suboptimal environmental policies. Furthermore, within the context of the European Union, Southern countries are the subset of member states benefiting further from efficient environmental policies.

ENDNOTES

1. See, for example, Walter (1982), Pearson (1987), Leonard (1988), Lucas et al. (1992), Low and Yeats (1992) and Tobey (1990).
2. Tobey (1990) and Low (1992) present empirical evidence on this issue.
3. The author assumes that firms will use the environmental factor of production up to the point where its marginal productivity is equal to the emission tax:

$$f_E^i = t^i \text{ for } i = 1,2,3.$$

4. Welfare in each country is influenced by income and domestic environmental quality. For the sake of simplicity, utility functions are separable in these variables. Country i's welfare, w^i, is given by the following utility function: $w^i = u^i(Y^i) + v^i(P^i)$,where Y^i is the level of income in country i and P^i is the level of emissions in country i. These results assume that environmental policies are exogenously determined in each country. Ambiguous results are obtained when one assumes that each country actively seeks to adjust its environmental regulations to exogenous shocks or new policies undertaken by third countries (cooperative or non-cooperative strategies).
5. For the sake of simplicity, we follow here a more simplified version of this model proposed by Kolstad and Xing (1992).
6. Implying that demand for environmental quality rises with income.
7. The variance explained by the first component is 70 per cent.
8. On this issue see Dean (1992).
9. See, on this subject, Low (1992) and Tobey (1990).
10. Costs reported by this author are referred to the United States and are based on statistics produced by the US Department of Commerce and the Environmental Protection Agency.

REFERENCES

Dean, J. (1992), 'Trade and the Environment: A Survey of the Literature', in P. Low (ed.), *International Trade and the Environment*, World Bank Discussion Paper 159, pp. 15–28.

Kolstad, C. and Y. Xing (1992), 'Do Lax Environmental Regulations Attract Foreign Investment?', *Working Paper*, University of Illinois, Department of Economics.

Leonard, H. (1988), *Pollution and the Struggle for World Product*, Cambridge, UK: Cambridge University Press.

Low, P. (1992), 'Trade Measures and Environmental Quality: The Implications for Mexico's Exports', in P. Low (ed.), *International Trade and the Environment*, World Bank Discussion Paper 159.

Low, P. and A. Yeats (1992), 'Do "Dirty" Industries Migrate?', in P. Low (ed.), *International Trade and the Environment*, World Bank Discussion Paper 159.

Lucas, R., D. Wheeler and H. Herrige (1992), 'Economic Development, Environmental Regulation and the International Migration of Toxic Industrial Pollution: 1960–88', in P. Low (ed.), *International Trade and the Environment*, World Bank Discussion Paper 159.

McGuire, M. (1982), 'Regulation, Factor Rewards, and International Trade', *Journal of Public Economics*, 17, 335–54.

Pearson, C. (ed.) (1987), *Multinational Corporations, the Environment and Development*, World Resources Institute.

Rauscher, M. (1992), 'Economic Integration and the Environment: Effect on Members and non-Members', *Environmental and Resource Economics*, 2, 221–36.

Tobey, J. (1990), 'The Effects of Domestic Environmental Policies on Patterns of World Trade: An Empirical Test', Kyklos, 43, 191–209.

Walter, I. (1982), 'Environmentally Induced Industrial Relocation to Developing Countries', in S. Rubin and T. Graham (eds), *Environment and Trade*, Allanheld and Osmun, pp. 67–101.

White, H. (1980), 'A Heteroscedasticity-Consistent Covariance Matrix Estimator and a Direct Test for Heteroscedasticity', *Econometrica*, 48, 817–38.

4. Environmental Regulations, Firms' Strategies and Market Behaviour: Modelling to Learn

Rui Santos, Luís Jordão, Paula Antunes and Nuno Videira

4.1 INTRODUCTION

In order to cope with growing degradation in environmental quality due to the pollutant emissions generated by a fast growth in business activities, environmental policy has relied on the use of several instruments for pollution control, based on command and control, economic or voluntary approaches. The environmental efficacy of the different instruments and their corresponding impact on firms' competitiveness and market behaviour are matters of debate in theoretical and practical arenas.

Firms have initially reacted to developments in environmental policy, aiming to achieve compliance through pollution control technologies, and adopting more recently a proactive approach, based on changes in production processes, namely through pollution prevention and clean technologies.

The implementation of environmental regulations has often had a differential effect in markets, bringing extra production costs to some firms and competitive advantages to others. Such effects, especially when markets are not competitive, are very difficult to anticipate, due to the high number of interactions that have to be taken into account. This is even more relevant when environmental policy affects different points in a manufacturing chain, introducing combined effects, thus increasing the complexity and dynamics of the problem.

The objective of this chapter is to present tools to help study the effects of environmental regulations on firms' strategic management practices and market behaviour. Due to the dynamic nature and complexity of this problem, a simulation approach based on the use of system dynamics models was adopted.

The potential of system dynamics to address managerial problems is fully recognized, with emphasis being put on the explicit use of both quantitative and qualitative variables, allowing for a description of the system interactions, feedbacks and delays. For this purpose, two simulation models were developed: the Environmental Policy in Oligopolistic Markets (EPOM) model and the ENVironmental MANagement (ENVMAN) model.

EPOM allows us to gain understanding of the effects of different environmental policy instruments in firms' market performance, and of the contribution of R&D strategies to increase firms' competitiveness. This model is also used to study the effects of product-oriented as an alternative to process-oriented environmental policy on market behaviour and its consequences in terms of economic efficiency, equity and environmental quality.

ENVMAN simulates the effects associated with the adoption of reactive and proactive environmental strategies by firms' managers when faced with a new regulation, in this case an emission tax. The model was used to build a learning environment, intending to help managers understand major feedbacks among the firm, the environment and society.

4.2　ENVIRONMENTAL REGULATIONS AND BUSINESS STRATEGIES

Environmental policy instruments, initially based on command and control approaches (for example, emission and environmental quality standards), and later on market-based approaches (for example, emission taxes and tradable discharge permits), are generally aimed at the control and regulation of pollution discharges at the individual firm level, reflecting a process-oriented view of environmental policy. Recently, the implementation of voluntary schemes, namely through the ISO 14 000 series standards, the EC eco-management and audit scheme (EMAS), ecolabelling and voluntary agreements between industry and government, has been increasing in Europe with success, as a substitute or a complement to traditional mandatory approaches.

The concept of integrated chain management has also been introduced recently in the Dutch Environmental Policy Plan, with the aim that substance cycles in production chains are managed in an environmentally, socially and economically responsible manner (Cramer 1996). Such a concept implies that a product must generate as few emissions and consume as little energy as possible during its life cycle, and therefore environmental management transcends the level of the individual company and encompasses the whole product chain, from cradle to grave. This approach considers that all parties in a product chain depend on each other in the search for and implementation of environmental improvements within the chain (Cramer 1996), and can be implemented through the so-called product-oriented environmental policy instruments, namely product standards (such as eco-labels) and product taxes (for example, taxes on products containing solvents) (Oosterhuis et al. 1996; Santos and Antunes 1994).

A relevant issue in the implementation of environmental policy instruments is their effects on markets and on firms' competitiveness, especially when the assumption of perfect competition cannot be accepted, particularly in oligopolistic markets. In many cases, environmental policies contribute to changes in market structure, introducing distortions of competition to the detriment of firms that are less prepared to cope with the new regulations, whose interests have not been represented in the regulatory process, or which have weaker bargaining power (Lévêque 1996). When environmental policy affects simultaneously different points in a product manufacturing chain, the combination of these effects can enhance or attenuate market fluctuations.

Inside the firms, reactive responses are mainly based on the implementation of pollution control technologies at the individual company level. This practice has led firms to adopt research and development (R&D) strategies aimed mainly at the reduction of abatement costs in their efforts to reduce compliance costs. The adoption of a proactive strategy implies that firms direct their R&D efforts to pollution prevention and investment in product eco-design, through innovative practices such as clean technologies, improved housekeeping, materials reuse and recycling, increased energy and resource efficiency and diversification of products. Some authors assert that this strategy can reduce the costs of environmental compliance and bring firms significant operational and competitive advantages (Gabel and Sinclair-Desgagné 1992a, 1993; Starik et al. 1996).

Porter and van der Linde (1995) argue that strict environmental regulation can enhance competitiveness by stimulating innovation. These authors introduce the concept of 'innovation offsets' to describe those situations where 'properly designed environmental standards can trigger innovation that may partially or more than fully offset the costs of complying with them', and present several examples of firms where 'innovation offsets' have occurred (for example, Raytheon, Hitachi, 3M, Robins Company, Ciba–Geigy, DuPont). Through innovation firms can reduce the cost of compliance with pollution control, improve the product itself and improve the process. Other authors, namely Palmer et al. (1995) argue that these considerations are not valid for all firms and sectors, and exemplify this with statements from managers of some companies mentioned in Porter and van der Linde's work, who acknowledge that, although in certain instances a particular regulatory requirement may have cost less than expected, or perhaps even paid for itself, on the whole, environmental regulation amounted to a significant net cost to the company. However, they agree with Porter and van der Linde in that 'regulations have sometimes led to the discovery of cost-saving or quality-improving innovation' and that early estimates of regulatory compliance costs are overestimated, because they did not take into account technological advances in pollution control or prevention.

Higher economic and environmental performances of proactive approaches, revealed in case studies, have led to their encouragement by organizations such as UNEP and the US EPA (UNEP 1994; US EPA 1991, 1992). These practices are referred as bringing up a 'powerful combination of economic savings and environmental improvements having thus been recognized in Agenda 21 as a means of reconciling development and environmental protection' (UNEP 1995).

For developing sustainable environmental strategies a holistic view of the firm's position in society, incorporating economic, environmental, social and behavioural aspects, is required (Madsen and Ulhøy 1996). The lack of such a view, associated with limitations of managers, mental models in processing relevant information, is often referred to as a factor hindering the adoption of proactive strategies. On the other hand, since most environmental management practices are new to many business managers, they may not have integrated them yet in the most efficient way into their planning and decision making processes (Starik et al. 1996). Clearly linked with this is the overall complexity of issues and interactions dealing with corporate environmental management, and the delays between the implementation of environmental measures and their respective effects (Hart and Hauja 1996).

4.3   SYSTEM DYNAMICS SIMULATION MODELS

The models described above study the interactions of environmental regulations with corporate management decisions and market behaviour, intending to be learning tools to help both firms' managers and environmental regulators. Therefore they are mainly concerned with the study of dynamic behaviour patterns for key variables and not with the prediction of values. Although the presented results are dependent on the parameterization adopted in each model, the simulations can contribute to an improved understanding of major relations and delays.

EPOM deals with the effects of environmental regulation on markets and on firms' competitiveness, and on the contribution of R&D strategies. It is also used to study the effects of environmental policy when it affects simultaneously different points in a product manufacturing chain.

ENVMAN focuses on the individual firm level and was developed as a learning tool to help managers understand major feedbacks among the firm, the environment and society. It was developed to compare the adoption of reactive and proactive environmental strategies by firms' managers when faced with environmental regulations exemplified by an emission tax.

System dynamics can contribute to a study of the kind of problems described above, since it allows the development of simple and intuitive models capable of considering:

- the dynamic nature and the complexity of the relations among regulators, firms, markets and the environment, namely to model the interactions, feedbacks and delays among economic and ecological variables for different time horizons;
- an integrated approach to environmental effects throughout the life cycle of a product, and to model reactions to environmental policy when it affects simultaneously different points in a product manufacturing chain; and
- the functioning of the economic system as a resultant of transactions among economic agents based on the goods and services exchange values, supported by a biophysical system where energy and/or mass flows are associated with market transactions.

These features are essential to develop an ecological economics view of the relations between environmental policy, goods markets, resource use, emissions and environmental quality.

4.3.1 Environmental Policy and Oligopolistic Market Behaviour – EPOM Model

EPOM describes the behaviour of two hypothetical companies in a duopoly market. A life cycle analysis approach was adopted, assuming a simple production chain for each product including extraction of raw materials, manufacturing of an intermediate product and production of the final product. Environmental impacts and costs associated with the two products in the stages of distribution, consumption and final disposal were assumed equivalent, and therefore they were not modelled.

The model is organized in sectors, including production, market, environment and research and development (R&D). Figure 4-1 presents a simplified causal loop diagram of the model (for details see Antunes et al. 1995, and Santos et al. 1996).

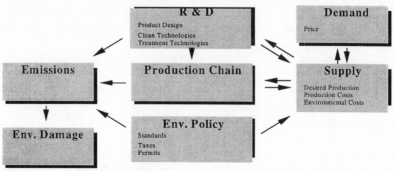

Figure 4-1 Causal loop diagram

4.3.1.1 Production chain sector

In each manufacturing chain a final product is produced, incorporating one intermediate product which uses a raw material. Input–output coefficients are used to represent the number of units of intermediate product obtained per unit of raw material, and the amount of final product per unit of intermediate product. The production of final product is calculated in order to meet the desired production, determined by the market.

4.3.1.2 Duopolistic market

- *Demand* – the two final products are considered perfect substitutes, facing a joint linear demand curve.
- *Supply* – a Cournot model of duopoly was assumed, where both companies are simultaneously trying to choose a profit-maximizing output in each time step, based on a forecast of the output of the other firm.

Without loss of generality a quadratic total production cost function in the produced quantity of final product was assumed for each product. However, the production costs are specifically dependent on the firm's environmental costs and on the cost of intermediate products. Total production costs are given by:

$$TPC = c \times PQ^2 + \left(d + ECF + \frac{PIP}{IC} \right) \times PQ \qquad (4.1)$$

where:

TPC	–	total production cost of the final product
		c and *d* – production costs function coefficients
PQ	–	quantity of the final product

ECF – environmental cost factor
PIP – price of intermediate product
1/IC – input–output coefficient for intermediate product

The environmental cost factor is the average environmental cost in the previous time step. The price of raw materials and intermediate products is assumed constant in each period for any quantity (perfect competition), unless there are environmental costs in the corresponding extraction or production processes which are partially incorporated.

The reaction functions of the Cournot model were calculated in order to accommodate explicitly the environmental costs and the price of intermediate products, given by the following expression for product one:

$$DP1 = \frac{[(a - b \times EP2 - d1 - ECF1) \times IC1] - PIP1}{(b + c1) \times 2 \times IC1} \tag{4.2}$$

where:

DP1 – desired production for product one
EP2 – expected production for product two
a and *b* (slope) – linear demand curve coefficients

4.3.1.3   Environmental sectors
Emissions
Untreated emissions generated at each production stage are computed by applying emission factors (units of pollution/unit produced) to the amounts extracted or produced. Treated emissions for each stage are a function of the amount dictated by the most stringent environmental policy instrument applied at the moment (emission standard, emission tax, transferable discharge permits or product tax) and of the best available technology (BAT), which constraints the maximum treatment allowable in each process.

Tradable Emission Permits
A competitive permits market integrating six agents, one for each production stage, was assumed, with an initial allocation of permits proportional to the untreated emissions at each stage. Permits are valid for a given period, after which a new allocation takes place.

Costs and Environmental Policy Assessment
The average environmental costs for each product are the sum of the treatment, emission tax, permits (negative when the agent is a net seller) and product tax costs, per unit produced. Treatment costs are a function of treated emissions, considering linear marginal abatement cost functions at

all manufacturing stages. The emission tax cost is calculated by multiplying the residual untreated emissions by the unit tax value. The product tax cost is only applied to the final products and is calculated by multiplying the tax value by the emissions generated in the production chain, creating an incentive for the treatment of emissions at all production stages. However, since this tax is applied only to the final products, this incentive is only directed to their producer, and it is assumed that the producers of the final products are willing to finance the treatment costs at the other stages, in order to lower their product tax costs. Thus the treatment costs in the extraction of raw materials and manufacture of intermediate products that are due to a product tax are supported by the manufacturers of the final product. Tax revenues are returned by the government to the community members as lump-sum transfers, ensuring that efficiency losses will not be generated.

Global Efficiency and Environmental Damage
The stock of environmental pollution represents the accumulated emissions generated by both production chains, minus the environmental regeneration, which is modelled as a first-order decay process, with a regeneration rate that decreases with the increase in environmental pollution. Environmental damage is the product of environmental pollution by the average pollution damage associated with it.

The *global efficiency* of the system is also computed by the sum of the accumulated profit in each final product, the accumulated profit reductions in the intermediate products and raw materials stages due to environmental costs, the accumulated consumer surplus and the accumulated emission and product tax revenues minus the environmental damage.

4.3.1.4   R&D policy
Firms faced with environmental regulations have an incentive to invest in R&D, to lower their cost burden. Each manufacturer of final products can reduce environmental costs by adopting three alternative/complementary strategies: (1) invest in improved abatement technologies to reduce treatment costs, (2) invest in cleaner technology to reduce emission factors and (3) invest in product eco-design to reduce the amount of raw materials and intermediate products incorporated. Strategy one corresponds to a reactive approach, while strategies two and three reflect a proactive attitude. This approach is in accordance with Porter and van der Linde's (1995) argument that through innovation firms can reduce the cost of compliance with pollution control, improve the product itself and improve the process.

Final product manufacturers invest a fraction of their profits in R&D, making decisions about the proportion of investment directed to each of the three areas. When the accumulated investment in one area reaches an established threshold value, it is assumed that an innovation occurs. The amount of improvement achieved with each innovation is variable and is a non-monotonic decreasing function of innovations previously attained.

R&D policies for intermediate products and raw materials were modelled assuming that they only invest in abatement technology and cleaner production, and that they allocate their investment equally to these areas.

4.3.1.5   Decision and impact variables

The decision variables of the model are related to the adoption of an environmental policy by the regulator and the firm's response through R&D policy. The impact of decisions in model behaviour is analysed by several variables, including accumulated consumer surplus, accumulated profit and R&D investment for each firm, environmental damage, accumulated treatment costs and tax revenues and the cumulative transacted quantity.

Important steady-state indicators of the system's performance are the price of final products and emissions per unit produced. Other interesting indicators are the values of the emission factors and input–output coefficients, which show, together with the treatment costs, the efficacy of firms' R&D policy.

4.3.1.6   Scenarios and simulation results

The model was first used to simulate the attainment of a Cournot equilibrium when two identical firms are competing in the absence of environmental policy. A series of scenarios were afterwards considered, in order to test the effects on firms' competitiveness of different cost structures and the trade-off effects of environmental policy, as well as the role that the adoption of proactive- or reactive-based R&D strategies can play. These scenarios result from combinations of different assumptions about the following variables, related to firms' performance:

- different production cost function parameters, input–output coefficients and environmental performance (emission factors) for each firm; and
- different combinations of allocation of R&D effort.

On the environmental regulator's side the application of different environmental policy instruments (emission standards, emission taxes, product taxes and tradable discharge permits) was also tested, either in a uniform or progressive (in time) way, allowing also the analysis of different forms of implementation (for example, different types of emission standards, different rules for the initial allocation of emission permits, different criteria for the implementation of a product tax). The instruments were designed so that a similar value of environmental damage was attained at the end of the simulation period.

In the base case (two identical product chains without environmental policy) steady-state conditions are attained after a brief adjustment period, leading to a high level of profits and consumer surplus but an unacceptable level of environmental pollution and damage.

The results obtained with the application of referred environmental policy instruments to this case were in accordance with established theory. For instance: (a) a uniform emission standard results in small direct losses to the market agents' welfare but inefficiencies in the abatement process imply low global efficiency; (b) permits attain a permanent low level of pollution and better results for all agents, due to a more efficient allocation of abatement effort; (c) emission tax attains a more efficient allocation of pollution control than permits, due to delays in the permit transactions process. It is interesting to note that the highest global efficiency is obtained with a progressive product tax, which has a high impact on the final product market but gives a strong incentive for an efficient abatement strategy during the simulation period, resulting in a final low value for the emissions per unit produced, and generating a large amount of tax revenues.

For both emission and product taxes a progressive implementation leads to better results at the end of the simulation period than constant taxes, but these allow a more stringent control of the environmental pollution level (Figure 4-2). Only a high uniform product tax can keep the time path of environmental pollution similar to that obtained with other policies, leading to lower global efficiency. So, an environmental policy which requires a very stringent and continuous control of pollution should not be based on this instrument.

Steady-state market conditions (for example, price and transacted quantity) for the product tax are worse than for permits but, on the other hand, the product tax is easy to implement, since it is applied to a unit of final product, giving also a clear signal to consumers about products' environmental impact.

The allocation of tax revenues raises an interesting equity issue for the welfare evaluation of tax-based policies. The regulator can use these revenues to correct a potential unfair distribution of costs among agents, while for the other instruments the imposition of side-payments can be a solution.

Investment in R&D leads to a general increase in global efficiency and, from the producer's point of view, it is a way to increase profits when faced with environmental policy. Product taxes create the strongest incentive to invest in R&D, followed by emission taxes, and for both instruments the emissions per unit decrease.

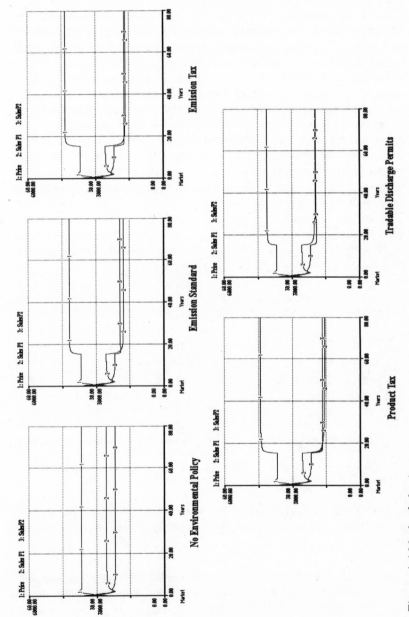

Figure 4-4 Market behaviour

Investment in product design is the strategy that gives better results with this model, implying, however, a reduction in production costs which allows firms to increase sales, thus increasing environmental throughput. This result shows how important it is to integrate scale considerations, as well as economic efficiency and equity, in the evaluation of environmental policy, requiring the adoption of complementary instruments (Daly 1992).

Figure 4-3 shows the results for the case where a firm facing a uniform emission tax only invests in treatment cost reductions (reactive strategy) while the other adopts a proactive strategy. The latter strategy brings competitive advantages to the firm, increasing its sales and profits, even if environmental costs are still higher than those of the reactive firm. This case reinforces the argument presented above regarding the scale considerations, since the environmental regulator must ensure that these advantages do not increase markets transactions, creating an increase in total residual emissions.

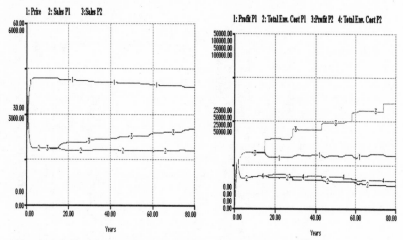

Figure 4-3 Simulation results with alternative R&D strategies

With a reactive R&D strategy, firms can reduce compliance costs. If the policy goal is the achievement of an established environmental damage level:

- a more stringent emission standard must be imposed (when that standard is defined as emissions per unit processed), due to the dynamic increase in the throughput;
- the emission and product taxes can be reduced; and
- the number of permits available should be maintained.

EPOM was also used to test the effects of environmental policy when applied to two different production chains, where one of them has a competitive advantage in the market in the absence of environmental policy, but has more adverse environmental impacts. In this case when the environmental policy is applied the competitive production cost advantage is eliminated by increased environmental costs.

The observed dynamic behaviour (Figure 4-4) shows that the emission standard implies the most significant inversion in market leadership, since it requires the largest effort in emissions reduction in the more pollutant firm. With transferable permits the two firms share equally the market in steady-state, since the difference in production costs is compensated by the small difference in treatment costs plus the cost originated in the permits transactions.

Product and emission taxes cause the most significant decrease in production for both firms, due to the high environmental costs imposed, reducing the market dimension. Nevertheless, they do not create a big difference in firms' market share, since treatment costs are similar and the differences in tax costs, although enough to compensate for differences in production costs, are insufficient to introduce a significant competitive advantage to the other firm.

These results show how changes in firms' competitiveness can be achieved when environmental regulations are applied, leading to increased gains to some firms and losses to others. For the regulator it is important to understand the potential magnitude of these effects before implementation of environmental policy. For instance in some cases regulations can strengthen the monopolistic positions of large firms and this competition distortion can have an indirect negative effect for regulators (Lévêque 1996). The consequences for firms depend on many factors, such as: (a) the market power of firms; (b) the relation between costs of compliance and total production costs; (c) R&D strategy and technological capabilities to react; (d) corporations' attitude, reactive or proactive, to environmental regulation and willingness (or not) to take advantage of lax standards in the short term; (e) differentials between domestic standards and those of the major trading partners.

EPOM is a rich learning environment, which can be further used to test other scenarios, from the regulator's and firm's perspective, and easily expanded to incorporate additional interactions, and test different instruments, namely voluntary approaches. The comments above should be viewed as insights to cover the gap between the often simplified theoretical approach and the complexity of practical implementation of regulations, although some unanticipated results obtained can also be seen as leads for further theoretical work.

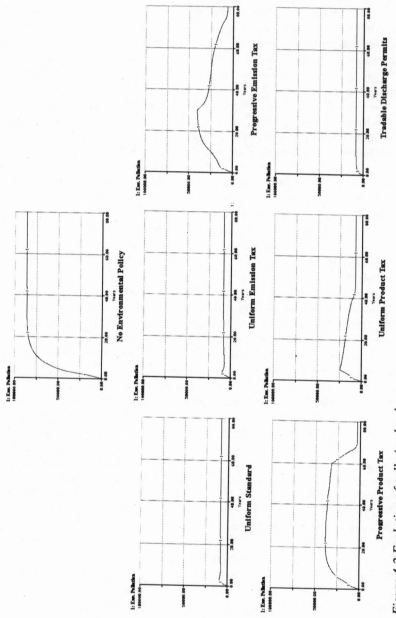

Figure 4-2 Evolution of pollution level

4.3.2 Reactive versus Proactive Management Strategies – ENVMAN Learning Environment

The ENVMAN learning environment was designed to cover the lack of integrated learning tools in environmental management acknowledged by several authors (Starik et al. 1996). Interactive learning environments are increasingly being used in management areas (Isaacs and Senge 1994; Lane 1995) since they provide rapid, unambiguous and systemic feedback on actions taken, and a low-risk setting in which different strategies can be shown, explored and tested. The model underlying ENVMAN was developed to: (1) demonstrate main strategic differences between adopting a reactive or a proactive management strategy in face of environmental policy; (2) allow the user, in an open environment, to test managerial strategies and observe their results.

The model was not built to address theoretical assumptions; rather it aggregates much information that can be found in the literature concerning reactive and proactive environmental management practices. ENVMAN reflects generic interactions, with its conceptualization largely based on the socio-economic model of the firm developed by Tomer (1992). The latter acknowledges explicitly the importance, beyond profit maximization, of other factors in environmental management decision making, namely those concerning environmental opportunities, internal organizational capabilities, 'macro' and 'micro' social influences of extra-firm institutions and infrastructures, and other regulatory influences.

4.3.2.1 Simulation model

The model is divided into four main sectors, linked by interactions, as presented in Figure 4-5. The firm discharges pollution to the environment and delivers goods to society. Environmental quality is a result of the inputs of pollution and of regeneration capacity, and will affect environmental regulation and society's concern for environmental issues. Regulation encourages the firm to reduce pollution, using an emission tax as an example. Finally, society shows through consumer behaviour its needs and/or desires for the firms' products, including the concern for environmental issues. A more detailed description of the model is presented in Jordão et al. (1996).

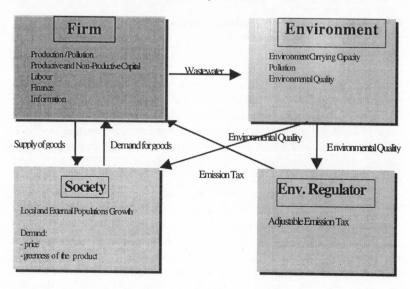

Figure 4-5 Major sectors and interactions of the ENVMAN model

Major assumptions of the model are:

(1) Pollution is related to production, through emission factors, which may be reduced to a given level by investments in pollution source reduction. A reactive end-of-pipe approach can also be adopted through investments in pollution control technologies.
(2) Pollution decay is a function of a regeneration rate, which is affected by average pollution, reflecting the carrying capacity of the environment. An environmental quality index is used as a source of information for the other sectors.
(3) Environmental performance of the firm is controlled by the environmental regulator through an emission tax, adjusted on the basis of the gap between the objective and the current environmental quality.
(4) Demanded quantity is a function of the price and 'greenness' of the product, assuming that consumers have a higher willingness to pay for products with less deleterious environmental effects (Hackett 1995).
(5) A standard Cobb–Douglas production function was adopted, with labour and productive capital as independent variables.
(6) Productive capital is distinguished as standard or 'green', if it is associated with cleaner production processes. Considering the ratio between standard and green capital, an index of 'greenness' of the productive process is calculated, which affects both the emission factors and the 'greenness' of the product. Pollution control capital relates to abatement technologies.

(7) Environmental skills of workers, which depend on investments in environmental training, contribute to enhancing source pollution reduction. This assumption reflects the argument that human resource management, namely commitment of both managers and workers to the environmental strategy, is a crucial issue in introducing an environmental management approach in business (Corbett and Van Wassenhove 1995; Gabel and Sinclair-Desgagné 1992a, 1992b, 1993; Jackson 1993).

(8) Total costs are the sum of operation and maintenance, workforce, regulation compliance, annualized investment and capital adjustment costs. They are deducted from total revenues to compute the accumulated profits of the firm.

The manager's decisions are centred in two areas: (1) environmental management issues, dealing with strategic choices between investments in pollution control or cleaner production, and investments in environmental training; (2) traditional management issues, concerning the firm's productive capacity and response to the market, namely through investments in manufacturing capital and hiring, and information acquisition.

4.3.2.2 Reactive versus proactive strategies

Two endogenous strategies concerning reactive and proactive management are simulated. The reactive strategy is based on investments in pollution control, while the proactive undertakes structural changes in the production chain by investments in green capital. In both, production factors are allocated efficiently, minimizing costs to attain the production level which satisfies demand. Capacity increase is undertaken only while marginal profit is positive.

Initially pollution control and green capital stocks are zero. Adopting a reactive strategy, the firm performs better in the short term, but reaches a limit in capacity increase, due to the high costs associated with regulation compliance. With a proactive strategy the firm is able to simultaneously reduce pollution and maintain its growth capacity.

The limitations on capacity increase of the reactive firm are related to the investment and operation and maintenance costs of pollution control technologies, decreasing the firm's profitability up to a point where it is no longer desirable to increase production. This agrees with the finding of UNEP (1995), that investments in pollution control and payment of emission taxes often turn out to be a financial burden to the reactive firm, bringing additional costs that are never paid back. Investments of the proactive firm are directed to the productive process, and can therefore allow for a payback.

Figure 4-6 shows that compliance costs (emission tax payment, investments and operation and maintenance of pollution control technologies) of the proactive firm remain below those of the reactive firm, even though the former has a higher production. The proactive firm attains a cost advantage from regulation compliance and pollution abatement, as described by Hart and Hauja (1996) in their survey.

After a period of adaptation the proactive firm maintains its marginal profit on the good (Figure 4-6), allowing for additional investments in production capacity. Since these bring simultaneously pollution reduction at source due to process improvements, increasing production can be achieved while pollution load per good is being kept at lower levels than those of the reactive firm (Figure 4-7). As a consequence, cumulative profits and assets of the reactive firm stay lower than those of the proactive firm (Figure 4-7). In the beginning the reactive firm faces a higher growth, due to delays associated with the structural changes undertaken by the proactive firm, while investments in pollution control devices are readily operationalized. In this sense, the reactive firm can react more quickly to environmental regulations, but follow a less efficient strategy in the long term. The results show that the reactive firm approaches the desired environmental quality level from below, whereas the proactive firm moves towards the same objective beyond compliance (Figure 4-7).

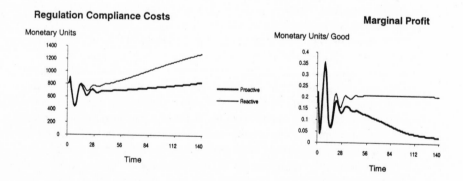

Figure 4-6 Regulation compliance costs and marginal profit on good

Pollution Load per Good

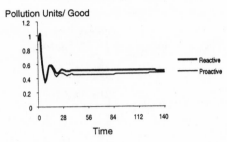

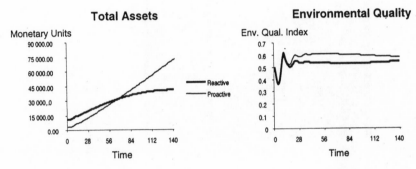

Figure 4-7 Evolution of total assets, pollution load per good, and environmental quality

The proactive strategy leads to higher environmental quality in the region, and has simultaneously a better economic performance, confirming the advantages of this strategy described by UNEP (1995).

4.3.2.3 Interactive learning environment

The endogenous strategies are incorporated in an interactive learning environment, allowing its users to acquire insight into the adoption of reactive and proactive approaches. In this simulator the player can either call for the referred strategies and observe their effects, or play the role of a firm manager, in an open gaming environment, in which decisions have to be taken concerning the issues at stake. Information about the different sectors is retrieved during simulation, allowing for a learning experience in which the user's mental models concerning the role of an environmental manager are expected to be challenged and ultimately enhanced.

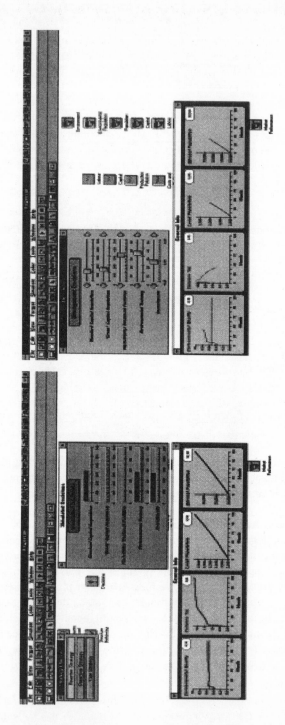

Figure 4-8   Watching the decisions/effects of proactive and reactive practices (first screen) and testing strategies in an open model through the use of slide-bars (second screen)

A major advantage of the developed simulator concerns its capability for effective double-loop learning, due to the possibility for playing in strategic and operational modes: in the first, the player tests his decisions according to a set of assumptions and observes their possible effects; in the second, decisions are effectively used for simulation. With these features, the simulator attempts to address what Isaacs and Senge (1994) describe as the type of learning required for fundamental improvement in organizations: an experience which allows us to discover how established policies are creating problems, and to invent new policies that improve the observed behaviour.

As a final remark, it must be stressed that apart from the simulator itself, associated learning materials were also produced. An overall instructional strategy is proposed, including briefing, gaming and final debriefing, similarly to most management games. It is believed that by implementing such a strategy, one can help the users with what Senge and Sterman (1994) refer to as mapping, challenging and improving mental models.

4.4   CONCLUSIONS

Two system dynamics simulation models are presented to develop understanding about the effects of environmental regulations on firms and markets. This approach can contribute to a study of the relations among environmental regulations, market behaviour and firms' strategies in an ecological economics perspective, that is, allowing the consideration of the dynamic nature and complexity of the interactions, feedbacks and delays among economic and ecological variables for different time horizons. On the other hand it is possible to model the functioning of the economic system as a resultant of transactions among economic agents based on the goods and services exchange values, supported by a biophysical system where energy and/or mass flows are associated with market transactions, and to adopt an integrated approach of environmental effects throughout the life cycle of a product.

EPOM's results showed, for instance, that the implementation of more stringent environmental regulations in oligopolistic markets brings competitive advantages to firms and products that give a better environmental performance in their life cycle. This important conclusion can be used to show managers that, in some situations, the adoption of environmental regulations can increase profits, instead of always being a burden to the firm. The knowledge of changes in firms' competitiveness that can be achieved when environmental regulations are applied is a crucial issue for the regulator.

The model also allowed the identification of instances where an *a priori* desirable environmental strategy, for instance the adoption of investments in product eco-design, can have unanticipated negative dynamic environmental effects due to the increase in the throughput that they allow. These results show how important it is to integrate scale considerations in the evaluation of environmental policy.

ENVMAN demonstrates the main strategic differences between adopting a reactive or a proactive management strategy, in the face of environmental policy; and allows the user to test managerial strategies and observe their results. This kind of learning tool, which allows managers to understand the interactions between the firm, environment and society, can contribute to the adoption of innovative and more efficient approaches to environmental management in firms.

ACKNOWLEDGEMENTS

Partial funding for this work was provided by the Commission of the European Communities – DG XII Environment 1991–94 (II) Programme, contract number EV5V CT940380, by the JNICT/DGA Research Programme, contract number 45/93, and by PRAXIS XXI scholarship BD/5469/95, granted to Luis Jordão.

REFERENCES

Antunes, P., R. Santos and N. Videira (1995), 'Environmental Policy and Oligopolistic Market Behavior: A System Dynamics Approach', final report of the project 'Environmental Policy, Technological Innovation and Firms' Competitiveness in Oligopolistic Industries', DG XII Environment Programme.

Corbett, C. and L. Van Wassenhove (1995), 'Environmental Issues and Operations Strategy', in Folmer, Gabel and Opschoor (eds), *Principles of Environmental Economics: A Guide for Students and Decision-Makers*, Aldershot, UK and Brookfield, US: Edward Elgar, pp. 413–39.

Cramer, J. (1996), 'Experiences with Implementing Integrated Chain Management in Dutch Industry', *Business Strategy and the Environment*, 5, 38–47.

Daly, H.E. (1992), 'Allocation, Distribution and Scale: Towards an Economics that is Efficient, Just and Sustainable', *Ecological Economics*, 6 (3), 185–93.

Gabel, H.L. and B. Sinclair-Desgagné (1992a), 'Corporate Responses to Environmental Concerns', in Folmer, Gabel and Opschoor (eds), *Principles of Environmental Economics: A Guide for Students and Decision-Makers*, Aldershot, UK and Brookfield, US: Edward Elgar, pp. 347–61.

Gabel, H.L. and B. Sinclair-Desgagné (1992b), 'Managerial Systems and Environmental Performance: A Research Agenda', INSEAD Working Paper.

Gabel, H.L. and B. Sinclair-Desgagné (1993), 'Managerial Incentives and Environmental Compliance', *Journal of Environmental Economics and Management*, 24, 229–40.

Hackett, P. (1995), *Conservation and the Consumer – Understanding Environmental Concern*, London, UK: Routledge.

Hart, S.L. and G. Hauja (1996), 'Does it Pay to Be Green? An Empirical Examination of the Relationship between Emission Reduction and Firm Performance', *Business Strategy and the Environment*, 5, 30–37.

Isaacs, W. and P.M. Senge (1994), 'Overcoming Limits to Learning in a Computer-Based Learning Environment', in J.D.W. Morecroft and J.D. Sterman (eds), *Modelling for Learning Organizations*, Oregon, US: Productivity Press, pp. 267–87.

Jackson, T. (ed.) (1993), *Clean Production Strategies: Developing Preventive Environmental Management in the Industrial Economy*, London, UK: Stockholm Environment Institute/Lewis Publishers.

Jordão, L., P. Antunes and R.F. Santos (1996), 'Reactive versus Proactive Corporate Environmental Management: A System Dynamics Learning Environment', *Proceedings of the Environment Society Economics Conference*, Versailles.

Lane, D.C. (1995), 'On a Resurgence of Management Simulations and Games', *Journal of the Operational Research Society*, 46, 604–625.

Lévêque, F. (ed.) (1996), *Environmental Policy in Europe. Industry, Competition and the Policy Process*, Cheltenham, UK and Brookfield, US: Edward Elgar.

Madsen, H. and J.P. Ulhøy (1996), 'Quantitative Techniques and Corporate Environmental Management', *Proceedings of the International Conference on Econometric and Quantitative Techniques for Environmental and Resource Economics*, Lisbon.

Oosterhuis, F.H., F. Ribik and G. Scholl (1996), *Product Policy in Europe: New Environmental Perspectives*, Dordrecht: Kluwer Academic Publishers.

Palmer, K., W. Oates and P. Portney (1995), 'Tightening Environmental Standards: The Benefit–Cost or the No-Cost Paradigm?', *Journal of Economic Perspectives*, 9 (4), 119–32.

Porter, M. and C. van der Linde (1995), 'Toward a New Conception of the Environment–Competitiveness Relationship', *Journal of Economic Perspectives*, 9 (4), 97–118.

Santos, R. and P. Antunes (1994), *Inventory of Product Policy Instruments: Case Study Portugal*, Berlin: IOW-Schriftenreihe 72/94–P of the Institut für Ökologische Wirtschaftsforschung.

Santos, R.F., P. Antunes and N. Videira (1996), 'Environmental Policy and Markets Behaviour: A System Dynamics Approach', *Proceedings of the Environment Society Economics Conference*, Versailles.

Senge, P.M. and J.D. Sterman (1994), 'Systems Thinking and Organizational Learning: Acting Locally and Thinking Globally in the Organization of the Future', in J.D.W. Morecroft and J.D. Sterman (eds), *Modelling for Learning Organizations*, Oregon, US: Productivity Press, pp. 195–216.

Starik, M., G.M. Throop, J.R. Doody and M.E. Joyce (1996), 'Growing an Environmental Strategy', *Business Strategy and the Environment*, 5, 12–21.

Tomer, J.F. (1992), 'The Human Firm in the Natural Environment: A Socio-Economic Analysis of its Behaviour', *Ecological Economics*, 6, 119–38.

UNEP (1994), *Government Strategies and Policies for Cleaner Production*, United Nations Environment Programme, United Nations Publication No. 94–111–D2.

UNEP (1995), *Cleaner Production Worldwide*, Volume II, United Nations Environment Programme, United Nations Publication No. 94–111–D.14.

US EPA (1991), *Industrial Pollution Prevention Opportunities for the 1990's*, United States Environmental Protection Agency Report No. EPA/600/8–91 052.

US EPA (1992), *Pollution Prevention Case Studies Compendium*, United States Environmental Protection Agency Report No. EPA/600/R–92/046.

PART II

Technological Change and Sustainability

5. After the Age of Abatement Technologies? Technological Change for Sustainable Development

Roberto Malaman

5.1 CLEANER TECHNOLOGIES FOR SUSTAINABLE DEVELOPMENT

Usually clean technologies refers to those technical means used to reduce or prevent contaminating emissions from human activities both during production and consumption, through more efficient use of resources, raw materials and energy.[1] No manufacturing process can be perfectly clean. All processes of transformation consume energy and cause the production of liquid, solid or gaseous emissions.

The concept of cleaner technology is thus a relative concept, that is related to the dominant technologies in the period under consideration. In the absolute sense of the word, clean production technologies cannot exist, if for no other reason than that they are all subject to the effects of occupation of territory and energy consumption.

In our analysis we assume a broad definition of cleaner technologies, considering as such all the modifications in processes and products which reduce impact on the environment, as compared to the processes and products for which they have substituted.

Using this kind of approach, many actions taken by companies to reduce energy consumption, cut costs and maximize profits have often led to positive results in terms of conservation of the environment. For the most part, the cleaner technologies introduced by businesses in recent decades were adopted with the prime objective of improving the use of resources and processes. The environmental motivation became explicit only in the face of public policies for safeguarding the environment or in situations where strong external pressures were brought to bear for a reduction in the environmental impact of production processes.

The list of cleaner technologies must, therefore, contain all those examples of a not merely corrective nature which imply reduction of interference with the natural environment, whatever the original motives for their development and diffusion.

Based on the foregoing, it seems inappropriate to speak, generically, of the appearance of a new technological paradigm (see Dosi 1982 and 1988) with regard to cleaner technologies. Each area must be clearly defined, sector by sector, distinguishing one technological trajectory from another, and innovation from innovation. Such a statement can be justified only in those cases where the appearance of an environmental restriction would cause a technological discontinuity, forcing a radical change in the scientific, technological and research principles which are generally employed.

Discussion of the links between technological change, ecological sustainability and industrial competitiveness has been relatively poor up to now (see Faucheux 1997, pp. 132–4). The complex relationship between technology, sustainability and competitiveness requires analysis along several dimensions. Our analysis is aimed at contributing to an understanding of the process of generation and diffusion of cleaner innovative technologies. The focus will be on the behaviour of firms, but the analysis of firms' behaviour will give some insight to the discussion on the instruments to develop an ecological industrial policy.

5.2 THE SUPPLY OF CLEANER TECHNOLOGIES: TECHNOLOGICAL OPPORTUNITIES, MARKET DEMAND AND APPROPRIABILITY

We distinguish three main factors which determine the generation (development) of a technological innovation with the aim of environmental protection: technological opportunities, market demand (including policy-driven demand) and the conditions of appropriability.

Technological opportunities for development of a specific technology for a certain environmental problem differ in each environmental situation, for each sector and for each firm. They are closely related to scientific knowledge and existing technologies, which are commonly referred to as a 'pool of knowledge'. This knowledge is not freely and immediately available. Research and financial investments are required in order to develop these opportunities, and there is always the risk that a project will fail, technically or commercially. The distinction between product innovation and process innovation is significant. Product innovations are usually carried out by the company itself, while process innovations are, for the most part, developed by specialist suppliers.

The propensity to innovate also depends on the sales potential of an innovation. The development of a new cleaner technology for the sole use of a company is not always profitable.

This is another area where it is helpful to distinguish between product and process innovation. The demand for cleaner consumer products can grow spontaneously in the market without intervention by regulatory authorities, therefore stimulating industry to produce such products. Regulation and information to the user (as supplied through the eco-label schemes) helps the diffusion of such products.

On the other hand, demand for cleaner production methods depends on opportunities and on the willingness of polluting companies to acquire cleaner techniques and to incorporate them into their production processes. This demand comes about mainly through environmental regulatory actions.

The maximum stimulus to development of cleaner technologies, rather than the introduction of abatement techniques, is achieved when the objectives of environmental protection are defined and imposed with due advance timing, programming their possible adoption gradually and in the medium term.

The development of an innovation is generally a costly and risky operation for the company involved. Therefore, such innovation is undertaken only when the company foresees sufficient market potential. Imitations produced by competitors weaken this market potential. The risk of copying is often quite high because the knowledge which is incorporated into new technology, from the moment it is marketed, is available to everyone. Knowledge which is easily reproduced drastically lowers development costs for those producing imitations.

The means for protecting oneself from imitators can be summarized as follows: patents, secrecy, maintaining a constant technical advantage over the competition, the effects of the learning curve, construction of a strong market position through a solid reputation, or consolidation of distribution channels.

Detailed research into the conditions of appropriability concerning cleaner technologies has not yet been carried out. It is certain, however, that when these conditions are inadequate, this fact in itself can induce the government to conduct or finance research and stimulate cooperation between companies or laboratories in general and, to an even greater extent, in the area of environment.

5.3   OBSTACLES TO THE DEVELOPMENT AND DIFFUSION OF CLEANER TECHNOLOGIES

New technologies must be integrated into broader technical, economic and social systems and cope with many obstacles. For example, a new production technique must fit into the manufacturing processes of prospective clients and, at the same time, satisfy a multitude of qualitative requirements (performance, user-friendliness, and so on). When a new technology proves lacking in certain qualitative aspects – above all technical – or when the end user's existing production organization must be modified, the spread of new technology usually proceeds quite slowly.

Often such technologies also require different types of training and regulatory legislation. This explains why manufacturers initially concentrated on the development of add-on or end-of-pipe technologies and innovations, which can be easily incorporated into existing production processes and which call for modest changes in the organization of production. In other words, especially in the short term, strategies of adoption or of partial reorientation tend to predominate over those requiring total reorientation.

Additionally, the existing technologies benefit from the dynamic effects of scale and from the phenomena of learning by doing, learning by using and learning by interacting. These translate into price reductions and into a whole series of improvements, such as better performance, wider applications, longer life cycles and increased reliability, which are of great importance for expanding the use of an innovation.

The processes of generation of innovations in the area of cleaner technologies are usually even less smooth than those in other kinds of innovation. Market demand for this type of innovation is generally slack and less easily predictable, especially at the beginning.

This is because:

- the objective of cleaner production is lower on the agenda than that of profits; and because such technologies frequently increase costs, the willingness of industry to commit itself to developing them is modest;
- in the introductory stage, cleaner technologies sometimes feature higher costs and inferior quality, due to low production volume and materials which may have inferior characteristics (not related to environmental impact);
- information problems seem to be greater than in other cases. In fact, there are a multitude of aspects regarding products and processes linked to the environment of which firms, and to an even greater extent, consumers, are not aware; and

- finally, innovations which respect the environment call for more organizational and institutional changes than do other types of innovation.

It is important, therefore, to highlight those factors which go into the decision to develop innovations in cleaner technologies. Literature in this area is quite recent: in particular the works of Freeman (1992), Kemp and Soete (1992), Kemp et al. (1991), Ausubel and Sladovich (1989), Green et al. (1994), and Maltezou et al. (1995).

5.4   CLASSIFICATION OF CLEANER TECHNOLOGIES

Cleaner technologies, though extremely varied and complex, can be classified according to the following typologies:[2]

(1) *Cleaner products*: this includes consumer products which bring about reduced environmental impact generated both by the act of using them and at the moment of final disposal;

(2) *Input reduction*: innovations which bring about a reduction in consumption of raw materials during the production process;

(3) *Input substitution*: used to describe all those cases where innovation results in the substitution of materials whose impact on the environment occurs during the production process, in the use phase or upon disposal of the finished product;

(4) *Energy-saving technologies*: whenever the objective of environmental protection is attained directly by reducing energy consumption – during the production cycle (benefit for the innovator) or at the moment of consumption (advantage for the user);

(5) *Recovery and recycling technologies*: grouped into this category are those cases where the determining factor is that of reduction of residuals obtained directly through readmission into the production cycle (reuse or recycling) of wastes or by-products from the same or other production processes;

(6) *Cleaner production processes*: the concept of clean technology is normally associated with this type. This definition has been used to identify those innovative processes which allow a reduction in residuals and/or in emissions;

(7) *Cleaner products which modify the production processes of other firms*: these are finished products whose positive effects on the environment are expressed at the moment of their introduction into other production processes. The relevance of this category will be explained in the following paragraphs.

5.5 SURVEY METHODOLOGY

Studies focusing on the development and diffusion of environmentally friendly technological innovations have usually been conducted using the case study method:[3] an in-depth examination of some specific cases was made in order to highlight those elements leading both to difficulties and successes, with the aim of drawing conclusions which could then be extended.

A different approach was chosen for our work: rather than an in-depth study of a few cases, the construction of a significant sample was preferred, representative of general phenomena. Mapping of the main processes of innovation and transformation of Italian industry, undertaken with the aim of reducing environmental impact, was conducted taking into consideration a wide variety of sources of information.[4] It was possible to gather a reasonable number of cases of environmentally targeted innovation for a period falling between the mid-1970s and the present.

An information sheet was compiled for each case of innovation surveyed, by using information found in publications or through brief interviews with company representatives.

In all, the database constructed contains information regarding 192 innovations developed by 168 companies, and analysed by means of 28 variables.

5.6 THE OBJECTIVES OF CLEANER TECHNOLOGIES

We classified our sample based on the previously described typologies of innovation. The taxonomy we used makes it possible to distinguish, within the area of production processes, those directly generated by their users from those produced by specialist companies for different users. For those industries which manufacture systems or components for the production processes of others, these are obviously a product, while they are classified as a process by the user. The distinction is relevant to the analysis: processes modified or innovated by the user are generally intended for limited outside diffusion. This is because the company is usually oriented toward directing in-house-generated innovations of process toward improvement of its own competitive position, and does not therefore develop marketing policies geared to the diffusion of the innovation. Usually these firms, although normally of large size, are not even equipped with a sales and marketing organization specifically devoted to the marketing of in-house-generated process innovations.

External diffusion of cleaner production processes manufactured by specialists is, however, much more common, since the company's mission is precisely to maximize the commercial impact of their products. Even

eaner technologies are thus mainly developed where the pressure on
nvironment arising from industrial activities is stronger.
though the commitment by larger companies prevails, even the
est-sized firms are represented in the sample (nearly 10 per cent of
mpanies have fewer than 20 employees, see Figure 5-2). The most
trends which, as we will see, increase the relative importance of
gical products with respect to processes, have evidently broadened
pportunities of small and medium-sized firms in the area of
nmental innovation. The flexibility and high degree of initiative
characterize this type of businesses have aided them in seizing upon
portunities for development in the area of environmental protection.
compared in terms of number of employees, the smaller companies
e less than the larger ones.

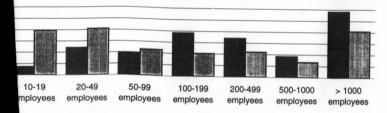

| 10-19 mployees | 20-49 employees | 50-99 employees | 100-199 employees | 200-499 emplyes | 500-1000 employees | > 1000 employees |

Size of innovative companies

TORIAL CHARACTERISTICS OF
IRONMENTAL INNOVATION

wn the various sectors shows the across-the-board nature of
non within the manufacturing industry. To one degree or
onmental innovation is of interest to all industrial sectors and

when the original innovation is created for a particular customer, it is in the
plant designer's best interests to generalize the innovation and to maximize
its diffusion to potential users. The innovation thus created tends to
become a standard of reference and to be offered gradually to all the
potential users, both as a specific investment and during the renovation and
adaptation of production systems.

The innovations in the sample we analysed are highly concentrated in
three of the nine typologies considered in our taxonomy:[5] cleaner products,
cleaner processes and recovery and recycling technologies (Table 5-1).
Included in these three categories, which taken individually contribute
equally to the total, are in fact more than three-quarters of the innovations
considered. Two other categories have considerable significance (8.3 per
cent of the total): energy savings and recovery and specialized components
and products which modify the production processes of other industries.
The reduction and the substitution of production inputs do not generally
constitute priority objectives in the measures taken by firms, while, as we
shall see, they are frequently found as secondary objectives in the
development of clean processes or products.

Table 5-1 Typologies of innovations (principal + max 3 secondary)

	Principal	Principal (%)	Secondary	Total (principal + secondary)
Cleaner products	55	28.6	1	56
Inputs reduction	0	0.0	35	35
Inputs substitution	2	1.0	55	57
Energy-saving technologies	16	8.3	47	63
Cleaner production processes	49	25.5	10	59
Recovery and recycling technologies	45	23.4	22	67
Environmental diagnostic and monitoring	2	1.0	0	2
Add-on or end-of-pipe technologies	7	3.6	8	15
Products which modify production processes	16	8.3	6	22
Total	192	100	184	376

Technological innovations aimed at reducing environmental impact are
often related to complex technologies and therefore fall into more than one

of the categories of innovations in the taxonomy we used. We have attributed up to a maximum of three secondary typologies in all those cases where the innovation under consideration had multiple motivations.

An analysis of the secondary typologies points clearly to the role of reduction and substitution of production inputs and of energy savings, which therefore take on a central role in corporate strategies, but which generally tend to be integrated into broader measures aimed at the improvement of products or processes, from an environmental standpoint. Also taking into consideration the secondary motivations, the production processes developed or modified by the user are by far superior to those worked out by specialists in the supply of complete systems and components to third parties.

Looking at the environmental classification of innovations, the sample appears divided almost equally between air pollution and wastes (26.6 per cent and 26.0 per cent respectively), while reduction of water pollution is the main objective in 19.3 per cent of the cases (Table 5-2). The innovations intended jointly to address more than one environmental problem make up approximately one fourth of the sample (26.0 per cent), in witness of the growing importance of integrated technologies in environmental protection. Air–water, water–waste and air–waste are the main types of combined action, while noise abatement is identifiable as an objective in only 5.2 per cent of the cases, of which only half indicate noise abatement as the sole aim. The abatement of noise pollution is normally carried out concurrently with action upon other environmental media, or through techniques of protection and insulation, which can be classified as end-of-pipe techniques and therefore have not been considered in this study.

Table 5-2 Environmental classification of innovations

	Cases	%
Air	51	26.6
Water	37	19.3
Waste	50	26.0
Noise	4	2.1
Air–water	14	7.3
Air–waste	11	5.7
Air–noise	4	2.1
Water–waste	14	7.3
Water–noise	1	0.5
Waste–noise	1	0.5
Air–water–waste	5	2.6
Total	192	100.0

Even taking into account the innovations w reduction of air emissions and waste remain development and adoption of cleaner technolog reduction of water pollution.

5.7   THE INNOVATIVE COMPANY: SIZE

Figure 5-1 shows the distribution of innova location. Northern Italy plays a leading ro cases studied have been found in the Lombardy alone accounts for 29 per cen located in other parts of the country are le in central Italy and 5 per cent in the south) industrial firms registered in the last cens of cleaner technologies in the north, businesses in the southern part of Italy Lombardy-based companies and those other hand, essentially the same as that i

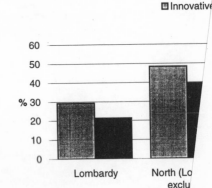

Figure 5-1 Localization of inno

5.8   SEC
        ENV

Breaking do
this phenom
another, envi

firms of all sizes, as we have seen. Table 5-3 highlights the prevalence of the chemical and synthetic fibres industries, which alone represent more than one fifth of the cases. Also widely represented are the areas of machinery and mechanics, electrical materials and the automotive industry. The most significant sectors essentially coincide with those where technological opportunities are large and pollution problems are perceived as a potential obstacle to growth.

Table 5-3 Cleaner technologies breakdown by industry (%)

Oil and gas	3.6
Processing of metals	5.7
Non-metal minerals	5.2
Chemicals and fibres	20.8
Manufacture of metal articles	7.3
Machinery and mechanical	12.0
Office equipment	1.6
Electric materials	8.3
Means of transportation	7.8
Precision equipment	1.0
Food, beverage and tobacco	2.1
Textile, clothing, leather and shoes	4.2
Wood and furniture	1.0
Printing and publishing	2.6
Rubber and plastic	3.1
Other manufacturing	1.0
Construction	1.0
Abatement plants production	4.2
Environmental services	6.8
Others	1.0
Total	100.0

The most environmentally sensitive industrial sector is the chemical industry. In fact, 20.8 per cent of the environmentally friendly innovations fall into that category. This confirms the widespread awareness not only of the inherent risks, but also of the technological opportunities available in the chemical industry.

The strategies of the large chemical companies are, unlike those in other sectors, often proactive with regard both to competitors and to forthcoming regulations. On the other hand, small and medium-sized companies are often simple adopters of the new externally developed technologies. Their strategies are usually defensive, both with regard to regulations and their competitors.

At least 47.5 per cent of the innovations carried out by businesses in this sector were for cleaner products, 25 per cent were innovations of process, 17.5 per cent recovery and recycling technologies, and 10 per cent new products which modify the processes of other businesses. Of the total number of cleaner products studied, a full 34.5 per cent originated in the chemical industry.

A different situation exists for a capital-intensive sector featuring noteworthy economies of scale such as the steel industry (representing 5.7 per cent of the cases we studied). In spite of its size and high level of concentration, the reaction of this industry to the increased influence of environmental restrictions was generally defensive and not proactive, perhaps due to the lack of technological opportunities. Even though the prevailing type of environmental innovations introduced by Italian firms was that of process (36.4 per cent), this should not induce easy optimism about the skills of large Italian companies operating in those sectors which are mature in terms of development of cleaner technologies. In most cases, in fact, what occurred was a simple adaptation of technologies developed in other countries or the introduction of production reorganization, energy savings and recovery measures following the oil crisis of the 1970s.

Innovations carried out in the automotive industry (7.8 per cent of the sample) were 80 per cent cases of new products and 20 per cent innovations of process. The focus on product improvement is obviously influenced by the oligopolistic competition which is characteristic of the automotive market. The strategies employed by Italian firms to combat foreign competition were defensive in 85.7 per cent of the cases. Quite often the introduction of improvements was presented as a necessary condition for survival in the marketplace and the major manufacturers took action using similar timing and methods. Strategies for compliance with regulations turned out to be proactive in 50 per cent of the cases.

The so-called eco-industry (4.2 per cent of the total), including specialized plant design and environmental services, deserves special mention. Innovative activity in this sector is primarily concentrated in end-of-pipe technologies (62.5 per cent) and recovery and recycling (37.5 per cent). Environmental services also originate innovations essentially in the areas of recovery and recycling (84.6 per cent).

Interesting technological opportunities are to be found in the mechanical industry; 12 per cent of the cases examined belong to this sector. The relevant factors for the development and diffusion of cleaner technologies appear to be quite different from those found in the chemical industry. The predominant type of innovation also in the environmental area is the one we have defined as 'product innovation which modifies the production process of another company business'. Not surprisingly, associated with this type of innovation is the expectation to broaden one's market (81.3 per cent). In 43.5 per cent of the cases the market potential is considered to be domestic and in 56.3 per cent of the cases, international. Within this industry, populated by a multitude of small and medium-sized companies, innovative activities are usually of an incremental nature and strongly based on knowledge acquired through interaction with clients (*learning by interacting*).

5.9   DISTRIBUTION OF CLEANER TECHNOLOGIES ACCORDING TO PAVITT'S TAXONOMY

For an in-depth analysis it seemed important to examine the performance of companies using a classification which would allow us to keep track of the methods of implementation of new technologies and of the importance these assume as strategic success factors. For this reason, we reclassified the companies in the sample on the basis of the well-known taxonomy established by K. Pavitt (1984). This identifies four types of sectors with homogeneous features.

1. *Science-based*, where companies are identifiable by their high expenditures on research and development, and often by in-house laboratories and research centres. These are production units wherein most of the innovations in use were created within the company itself. For such sectors, innovation represents the basic success factor, while the high degree of product differentiation greatly limits the role of price competition. In Italy such sectors generate approximately 6.7 per cent of industrial production, while environmental innovations created by this sector make up 7.8 per cent of the total (Figure 5-3). In science-based sectors 42.9 per cent of the cleaner technologies measures were process innovations and 21.4 per cent product innovations.

2. *Specialized suppliers*, where companies, usually manufacturers of capital goods, develop the necessary innovations through systematic collaboration with the users which, often nowadays, takes the form of so-called joint-design activities. These specialized sectors account for 13.3 per cent of industrial production and generate 26.3 per cent of the innovations considered in this study. It is interesting to note how the innovative efforts of these companies are distributed in a uniform manner over the eight typologies outlined. More specifically, 27.7 per cent of the cases considered have to do with product innovations which modify the processes of other businesses, 25.5 per cent recovery and recycling technologies, 19.1 per cent cleaner products and 10.6 per cent process innovations.

3. *Scale-intensive*. In these sectors firms are characterized by high intensity of fixed capital and high production capacity. To have ample and regular demand over time is a key competitive factor. In scale-intensive sectors 32.2 per cent of domestic production is carried out; 35.2 per cent of the innovations originated in this group, 44.4 per cent consisted of product innovations, 25.4 per cent innovations of process and 17.5 per cent recovery and recycling technologies.

4. *Supplier-dominated*, where only rarely are firms capable of in-house production of the necessary innovations, which are mainly introduced by means of externally acquired capital goods and intermediate components. For such firms, the speed of technological innovation represents a strategic success factor, while the limited possibility to differentiate the product places considerable importance on the traditional form of price-competition. In Italy, supplier-dominated sectors contribute 47.8 per cent of overall production. Our study reveals that they originate 30.7 per cent of environmental innovations, where 40 per cent of the cases involve innovations of process, 27.3 per cent product innovations, 20 per cent recovery and recycling, and 10.9 per cent energy savings and recovery.

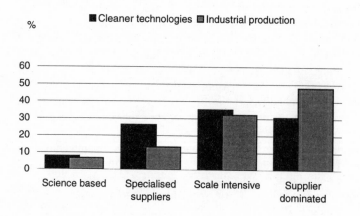

Figure 5-3 Cleaner technologies and Pavitt's taxonomy

5.10   DO CLEANER TECHNOLOGIES SAVE MONEY?

In a significant number (43.8 per cent of the total) of the cases presented, environmental objectives are associated with a reduction in production costs.[6] Excluding those cases related to cleaner products (whose possible cost-reducing effects are tied to consumption more than to the production stage), the share of innovations directly associated with reduction of production costs comes close to 55 per cent of the total.

Conservation of the environment through the development and introduction of cleaner technologies (be it products or processes) appears to be an objective which is frequently integrated into the primary objective of balancing the company budget. This constitutes the main difference, from the standpoint of economic analysis, between cleaner technologies and end-of-pipe technologies, which always imply added costs for business customers who adopt them. The integration of environmental and economic objectives in corporate strategy is therefore a rapidly growing phenomenon, at least in that group of businesses which have adopted a global, integrated approach to the environmental question, abandoning the route of simple application of end-of-pipe technologies. The ability to integrate environmental objectives and profit objectives constitutes a competitive factor of growing importance, especially in those industries having a heavy environmental impact or a great opportunity to introduce innovative products. The importance of the environment as a competitive factor is likely to grow further in the near future.

Market effects arising from the introduction of cleaner technologies are often motivated by the desire to broaden one's market (63.6 per cent) (Table 5-4) and its international dimension (65.5 per cent). On the other hand, process innovations are chiefly tied to in-house use (77.6 per cent) and to the domestic market (65.3 per cent).

In 50.5 per cent of the cases, the expectations of innovator companies are to broaden their market and 54.2 per cent of the innovations are expected to be marketed internationally. In any case, the relationship with the traditional activities of the company is very strong: in 77.6 per cent of the cases a strong link with the core business exists, because of the cumulative nature of all types of technological progress and the importance of technological capacity accumulated over time within the organization.

Table 5-4 The potential customers of cleaner technologies (%)

Typology of innovation	Potential market			
	Internal use	Traditional customers	Market share increase	New market
Cleaner products	0.0	16.4	63.6	20.0
Energy saving technologies	25.0	6.3	56.3	12.5
Cleaner production processes	77.6	0.0	18.4	4.1
Recovery and recycling technologies	26.7	8.9	57.8	6.7
End-of-pipe technologies	14.3	28.6	42.9	14.3
Products which modify production processes	0.0	6.3	81.3	12.5
Total	29.2	8.9	50.5	11.5

5.11   DEVELOPMENT OF CLEANER TECHNOLOGIES AND THE NATIONAL INNOVATION SYSTEM

Firms are only one of the players in the process of technological change. Also included in the system are universities, trade associations, and public and private research centres.

Usually technical change fosters learning phenomena which generate forms of interaction between actors that are much more complex than the mainstream market relationships, involving a different mix of hierarchic organization and/or collaboration among the actors. Technological change thus implies selection, vertical integration, diversification or, more generally, modifications in the division of labour between businesses and other agents.

Our survey indicates that cooperation agreements between businesses, universities and public and private laboratories are the exception rather than the rule in the development of environmentally friendly technologies. In 63.5 per cent of the cases studied, no form of collaboration was in evidence, in 8.3 per cent there were relations between different companies within the national borders, and in 7.3 per cent with foreign businesses. Intragroup collaboration (5.2 per cent) is popular among medium- and large-sized companies belonging to industrial groups included in our sample. The strong international orientation of the collaboration among companies does not depend solely on the presence of some multinational companies in the sample we studied but seems to be a general characteristic of the development of cleaner technologies in Italy. The same phenomenon was seen in the development of end-of-pipe technologies (Malaman and Paba 1993[7]).

Only 2.1 per cent of the innovations were developed in collaboration with universities. Cleaner processes and products are usually intermediate technologies, with a good degree of complexity, but not necessarily developed with a strong scientific foundation nor strong reliance upon basic research.

Both detailed analysis of the case studies examined and some specific characteristics, such as the prevalence of collaboration between firms rather than with universities, generally reduced development times (even for large-sized companies), and limited development costs tend to confirm the above characteristic. Integration and intelligent adaptation of innovations with an intermediate level of technological complexity prevail, and these are generally within the reach of medium-sized companies. Integration between environmental objectives and economic objectives at a company level seems a pursuable goal for most firms through the targeted use of available technologies.

5.12 CONCLUSIONS

Cleaner technologies are frequently complex technologies with multiple objectives: reductions in air emissions and waste production are, however, the main objectives. Cleaner integrated processes are also widespread within industry. This claim must none the less be qualified. We should call attention to a special effort (compared to their share of total national industrial activities) by medium- and large-sized companies, by sensitive industries that have strong specific technological opportunities (the chemical industry creates 20 per cent of cleaner technologies and 34 per cent of the cleaner products), by companies with an international base and market (especially large multinationals), scale-intensive sectors and those identifiable as specialized suppliers. Our analysis also showed a concentration of cleaner technologies in the highly industrialized (and polluted) northern regions of Italy, where pressures on a company's behaviour coming from external pressure groups are stronger.

Cleaner technologies are in general complex technologies, but they are not necessarily developed with a strong scientific basis and tied to fundamental research. Cleaner technologies are generally developed with modest development times and R&D expenditures, through external forms of collaboration which tend to favour relationships between companies over those between companies and universities or outside research centres. Therefore, considerable margins for improvement of environmental compatibility exist within the current technological regimes. The integration between environmental and economic objectives at the company level appears to be a pursuable goal in most cases through the targeted use of available technologies, without changing the dominant technological paradigms. Italian firms move with agility within these bounds.

The great advantage of cleaner integrated technologies against add-on abatement technologies emerge when we look at the economic side. A decrease in production costs has been achieved in half the cases of cleaner technologies analysed. If we add potential abatement cost saving and market expansion potential to direct production cost reduction, the great effort by industry to combine efficiency and environmental protection in an optimum manner stands out even more clearly.

In more than 80 per cent of the cases studied, the influence exercised by legislation on the decision to develop or adopt cleaner technologies is relevant, but the capability adequately to answer to external pressures mainly depends on a company's culture and attitude and the features of environmental policy itself. Companies move towards cleaner integrated technologies (instead of adopting abatement technologies) more quickly when environmental policies are uniform and sound, both in their formulation and application, with clear medium-term goals, making extensive use of voluntary and economic instruments.

Most of the above-mentioned conclusions, even if based on the analysis of the Italian experience, could be easily extended to other industrial countries. The main relevant exception is the intensity of cooperation between companies and universities that is probably much higher in those countries which are technological leaders or first comers in some specific innovative cleaner technology.

ENDNOTES

1. Similar definitions are used, for example, by the Ministère de l'Environnement (1990) and by the European Commission. See also OECD (1987 and 1990).
2. A few cases belonging to two additional classes (environmental diagnostics and monitoring, and add-on or end-of-pipe technologies) were also used in our study, in order to examine their connection with the types of cleaner technologies already mentioned, their link with other objectives, and their relationship with one or more codeterminants or with secondary typologies (see below).
3. Regarding Italy, see the works of the IRS in Dente and Ranci (1992); Ministero dell'Ambiente, GRETA (1988), also cited in Dionisio and Santi (1990) and Gerelli (1994); Federchimica (1992). Similar works were carried out on an international scale; see, for example, BCSD (1992), Willums and Goluke (1992), Maltezou et al. (1995).
4. Collection of cases was made using as main sources of information specialized awards for cleaner technologies, existing surveys of successful cases (Federchimica 1992, Dente and Ranci 1992; Ministero dell'Ambiente, GRETA 1988), company projects submitted in order to benefit from subsidies for technological innovations related to clean technologies, articles in the

major technical journals, information from the most important industrial associations.

5. It should be recalled that the two categories, 'Environmental diagnostics and monitoring' and 'End-of-pipe technologies', are to be viewed as marginal in our analysis, which is focused on clean products and processes. In these two categories, we have taken into consideration only a few interesting cases of add-on or monitoring technologies which also produced reduction or substitution of inputs or had links with the development of clean products or processes.

6. The reduction of production costs recorded by us refers to the past and to the firm which develops the innovative process and not to the user. It therefore excludes phenomena of cost reduction in the stages of use and consumption, and does not take into account the fact that clean technologies are often adopted as an alternative to end-of-pipe technologies or when faced with the risk of plant shut-down or of being driven out of markets. The codetermining cost reduction is therefore referred to the innovator and does not take into account alternative solutions for reaching the same objective.

7. A summary in English of this book is in Malaman and Paba, *The Pollution Abatement Industry in Italy,* IRS Working Paper No. 29, Milan, May 1993.

REFERENCES

Ausubel, J.H. and H.E. Sladovich (eds) (1989), *Technology and Environment*, Washington, DC: National Academy Press.

BCSD (Business Council for Sustainable Development) (1992), *Cambiare rotta. Una prospettiva globale del mondo economico industriale sullo sviluppo e l'ambiente*, S. Schmidheiny (ed.), Bologna: Il Mulino

Dente, B. and P. Ranci (eds) (1992), *L'industria e l'ambiente*, Bologna: Il Mulino

Dionisio, S. and M. Santi (1990), *Le Tecnologie Pulite*, in E. Gerelli (1994), *Applicazioni attuali e tendenziali delle tecnologie pulite: prime indicazioni e politiche per la loro diffusione*, Milano: Quaderni di ricerca dell'Istituto per l'Ambiente.

Dosi, G. (1982), 'Technological Paradigms and Technological Trajectories: a Suggested Interpretation of the Determinants and Directions of Technological Change', *Research Policy*, 2 (3), 147–62.

Dosi, G. (1988), 'Sources, Procedures and Microeconomic Effects of Innovation', *Journal of Economic Literature*, 1120–71.

Faucheux, S. (1997), 'Technological Change, Ecological Sustainability and Industrial Competitiveness', in A. Dragun and K. Jacobsson (eds), *New Horizons of Environmental Policy*, Cheltenham, UK and Brookfield, US: Edward Elgar.

Federchimica (1992), *Processi e prodotti puliti: situazione e strategie di sviluppo nell'industria chimica*, Milano.

Freeman, C. (1992), 'A Green Techno-economic Paradigm for the World Economy, in C. Freeman (ed.), *Economics of Hope*, London: Pinter.

Gerelli, E. (ed.) (1994), *Applicazioni attuali e tendenziali delle tecnologie pulite: prime indicazioni e politiche per la loro diffusione*, Milano: Quaderni di ricerca dell'Istituto per l'Ambiente.

Green, K., A. Irwin and A. McMeekin (1994), 'Technological Trajectories and R&D for Environmental Innovation in UK firms', *Futures*, 26 (10).

Kemp, R.P.M., A.A. Olsthoorn, F.H. Oosterhuis and H. Verbruggen (1991), 'Policy Instruments to Stimulate Cleaner Technology', Paper presented to the EAERE Conference, Stockholm.

Kemp, R. and L. Soete (1992), 'The Greening of Technological Progress. An Evolutionary Perspective', *Futures*, June.

Malaman, R. and S. Paba (eds) (1993), *L'industria verde*, Bologna: Il Mulino

Maltezou, S.P., R. Kögerler and M. Osteraurer (eds) (1995), *Incentives and Policies for Clean Technology, Legislative and Educational Frameworks*, Selected papers from the Third International IACT Conference, Vienna.

Ministère de l'Environnement, Direction de l'Eau et de la Prévention des Pollutions, Service des Technologies Propres et des Déchets (1990), *Les Technologies Propres. Une démarche, Pourquoi? Comment?*, Neuilly-sur-Seine.

Ministero dell'Ambiente, GRETA (Gruppo Esplorativo sulle Tecnologie Ambientali Avanzate) (1988), 'Problemi e strumenti dell'innovazione tecnologica per la tutela dell'ambiente', Rome, mimeo.

OECD (1987), *The Promotion and Diffusion of Clean Technologies in Industry*, Paris.

OECD (1990), *Technology and the Environment*, background report from the Technology Economy Programme (TEP).

Pavitt, K. (1984), 'Sectoral Patterns of Technical Change: Towards a Taxonomy and a Theory', *Research Policy*, 13, 343–73.

Willums, J.O. and U. Goluke (1992), *From ideas to action – The IIC Report on the Greening of Enterprise*, ICC Publications, No. 504.

6. Socio-technological Innovation and Sustainability

Frank Beckenbach

6.1 INTRODUCTION

'Sustainability' is an ambiguous notion: it has a normative as well as an analytical meaning, it combines ecological and economic goals, and it depends on the weighing of ecological restrictions and economic potentials. In this paper the focus will be on the question whether economically caused dynamic ecological constraints can be seen as a reason for a reorientation towards a 'sustainable' reduction of the ecological impacts of economic activities. In answering this question, I will combine elements of three different strands of thought: (i) a system-theoretical view of the ecological conditions of the economy, (ii) the evolutionary perspective on the economy in general and technological change in particular, and (iii) insights from ecological economics as regards the social nature of ecological constraints on economic activity.

In analysing the ecology–economy interaction I will not follow a general framework overarching ecology and economy although such a framework is available in the recent literature on this topic.[1] Rather, I will emphasize the difference between ecological and economic dynamics in choosing different modelling tools. On the level of formal modelling, I will combine a deterministic ecology system (viewed from a macroperspective) and a partly stochastic local search process of firms for technological improvements in the economy (disaggregated into microeconomic entities). In this context, increasing economic order and sophistication is tantamount to ecological disorder. Hence in a rough way perspectives of a quite specific 'coevolution' can be clarified.

In the second section ecological resources are conceptualized as the output of a non-linear dynamic system. Given this, it is not sufficient to define sustainability as a constant total capital stock or future income. Instead, the 'resilience of ecosystems' is suggested as a dynamic notion of sustainability. By assuming an aggregated population model, different 'ecological regimes' can be analysed and the meaning of resilience clarified.

In the third section an evolutionary market model is introduced. The basic idea of this model is to explain economic evolution in terms of technical change. Technical change is shaped by the deterministic market interaction between a multitude of firms and a stochastic process of local search for new technological possibilities in terms of process innovation.

Finally, the fourth section discusses the relation between a decentralized evolutionary process of technical change and the sustainability objective. If there is a social process by which scarcity of ecological resources is effectively signalled, a cyclical process of ecological and economic evolution stabilized by technical change is conceivable. Such a process shows that there is a multiplicity of sustainability options in an evolving society.

6.2   ECOLOGICAL SYSTEMS AND SUSTAINABILITY

6.2.1 Evolutionary Sustainability

It is not sufficient to challenge the neoclassical view on sustainability by simply postulating complementarity between economic and ecological resources as elements of production. Even the requirement that some stocks of natural resources (E) for producing an element of the economic capital stock (K) be taken into account and even acknowledging the multifunctional property of any element of E, there still remains a wide range of substituting 'information and knowledge' for resource elements of production (matter, energy, biomass). Hence the role of technical change in securing sustainability needs to be clarified. From an evolutionary point of view the application of technology is neither simply the outcome of a choice out of a given set of well-known alternatives nor a mysterious switch to a new technology the emergence of which remains unexplained.[2] Rather the 'choice of technique' is the result of a (risky) search process which is by no means led by factor prices alone. Explaining the emergence and the shaping of new technologies is therefore a prerequisite for dealing with sustainability from an evolutionary point of view.

Furthermore, it is not sufficient to postulate 'strong' sustainability rules such as (i) harvesting renewable resources must not exceed the regeneration capacity, or (ii) waste disposal has to remain below the assimilation capacity, or finally that (iii) renewable resources should be substituted for exploited exhaustible resources (Daly 1990, p. 4). The reason for this insufficiency is (i) the systemic interdependence between all these elements (hence they cannot be dealt with separately) and (ii) that they are time-dependent variables in a process with a multitude of dynamic solutions. Hence the question remains: which solution should be aimed at and in what time sequence?

Comparing this dynamic ecological perspective to the conventional static economic point of view reveals a contradiction:

> What characterises ecological systems is that their ability to provide [essential life-support services, F.B.] is a non-linear function of the mix of biotic and abiotic resources which they compromise. There exist threshold values for most resources below which ecosystems cannot function. If certain resources fall below their threshold values, the ecosystem will tend to lose ... productive potential .... The cyclical dynamics of almost all terrestrial and many marine ecosystems, and the tendency for periodic destruction and renewal within the system, are reasons why the biologists focus on the potential of those systems. The economic models behind the key concept of economic sustainability are not characterised by dynamics of this sort. In reality, economic systems behave much like terrestrial ecosystems. They are characterised by strongly cyclic dynamics which also involve creative destruction and renewal of assets, and this is recognised in the most recent literature on non-linear economic systems dynamics ... (Holling 1987, p. 140)

But even if there is some sort of similarity in terms of far-from-equilibrium behaviour a comprehensive notion of sustainability requires a compromise between two systems operating in essentially different ways. Sustainability is a guideline for dealing with ecological economic trade-offs and conflicts. Making these trade-offs and conflicts transparent without losing the systemic and dynamic perspective is the specificity of the notion of resilience.

6.2.2   Resilience as a Dynamic Notion of Sustainability

Generally, resilience can be interpreted as measuring the ability of a given ecological system to absorb exogenous influences and to maintain its character (Holling 1973). Hence resilience touches upon the problem of stability. But then the problem arises that there is an overwhelming variety of stability notions in ecology (Kay 1991). The question is, firstly, in what state variable (or network of variables) should stability be expressed? Secondly, which behaviour of the chosen variable(s) should be the criterion of stability? Whereas the answer to the first question depends on the observer's perspective and research interest, the answer to the second question could be threefold: stability can be distinguished in (i) robustness (or even decrease) in the oscillations of state variables (corridor resilience), (ii) resistance against exogenous shocks (shock resilience) and finally stability as (iii) maintaining the structural solution qualities of the system (structural resilience).[3] These resilience criteria need not overlap and the resilience properties of systems expressed by these criteria may diverge.

The perspective of non-linear far-from-equilibrium systems seems to suggest that there is a positive correlation between complexity (in terms of number of species and type of their relation) and stability. The debate on this point has shown that this is not generally true (Rosser 1991, for a summary). Hence it seems appropriate to distinguish between two different types of complexity: (a) complexity in terms of (increasing) connectedness of the elements resulting in global instability and perhaps in 'creative destruction' (Holling 1987, p. 145, using the famous Schumpeterian term) and (b) complexity in terms of (increasing) variability leading to a multitude of locally stable regions.[4]
The way in which stability is influenced by complexity depends on the type of complexity:

- The higher the (b)-complexity, the higher is the (iii)-stability. Nevertheless the (i)- and (ii)-stability might be low. In ecological systems with a multitude of species and a variety of relations between them the growth rates of the different populations might fluctuate very strongly or shocks might lead to quite a different structure of populations. But the multifunctional role of the populations for the whole system guarantees a high structural stability (low variety in number and types of attractors).
- The higher the (a)-complexity, the lower the (iii)-stability. Strongly related non-linear systems are very sensitive to parameter variations (leading to a change of attractors). Nevertheless the (i)- and (ii)-stability might be high because the attractor basin is large.

This shows that the type of complexity is crucial for the change in stability and resilience properties if complexity is increasing.

Resilience is the ability of an ecological system to maintain its internal order against external influences. Depending on the emphasis placed on a corridor of state variables, on the ruling role of certain attractors or on the structure of attractors, different concepts of resilience are relevant. The common focus of these conceptions is the systemic and dynamic consideration of the impact for the self-organizing capacities of a system given by external influences. Hence resilience is an appropriate candidate for defining a systemic and dynamic perspective for sustainability. Taking into account the distinctions of resilience given above, the use of an ecological system can be called dynamic sustainable:

- if the corridor of a given trajectory is not enhanced;
- if in the case of a sudden change of the parameters the attractor basin remains the same; and
- if the structural patterns of the system's solution are not altered[5].

'Strong' dynamic sustainability means, then, to link these conditions by 'and', whereas 'weak' dynamic sustainability is the case if the link is 'or'.[6]

6.2.3 Model of Ecology

The ecology is depicted by a population model. From an economic point of view a population can be understood as stock of ecological resources (E). For the sake of simplicity a population model with only one population (variable) is taken. Leaving all aggregation problems aside such a model could be thought of as summarizing the main features of a multitude of populations (ecological resources).[7] Hence two constraints of such an approach are obvious: (i) interactions and interdependences between different populations (ecological resources), for example, predator/prey relationships are not captured by such a model and (ii) consideration is confined to resources which are in some way renewable.[8]

Growth population models 'metered' in discrete time distinguish between 'stock recruitment' by the successful part of a newly born population ($f(E)$) and the surviving part of the adult generation ($g(E)$) (Clark 1976, p. 211). Assuming that the lag-structure is only one period, the general form of the dynamic equation for the ecological resources is:

$$E_{t+1} = f(E_t) + g(E_t).$$
(6.1)

The short-term dynamics (operating within one period) are incorporated in the functions on the right-hand side and the long-term dynamics are described by the recurrence formula.

Specifying f as a logistic growth function and g as a square-root function one gets:[9]

$$E_{t+1} = \alpha \left[E_t^{\beta}(1 - E_t) \right] + \vartheta \sqrt{E_t}$$
$$0 \leq \vartheta \leq 1.$$
(6.2)

The parameters α and β define the internal 'connectedness' of the ecological elements ((a)-complexity in the sense of Section 6.2.2).[10]

It is assumed now that the economic impact is given not simply by reducing the ecological resources (economic 'harvest': hE) but also by reducing the survival rate ϑ and by increasing ('heating') the internal dynamics of the ecological system expressed by α. The latter two effects are assumed to be influenced by the residuals (R) resulting mainly from the economic use which is made of the 'harvested' ecological resources (hE) (emissions, waste and so on).

Hence (6.2) is modified to:[11]

$$E_{t+1} = \theta \frac{R}{R+\alpha} \left[E_t^{\beta}(1 - E_t) \right] + (1 - \frac{R}{R+\vartheta}) \sqrt{E_t} - h \cdot E_t$$
(6.2')

Depending on the values for the parameters θ, α, β and ϑ, different types of ecological systems can be 'specified'. The higher the value for θ, the more explosive is the system dynamics for higher levels of E; the lower the values for β the steeper is the curve of the phase space; finally: the higher α and ϑ the less sensitive is the system to an increase or decrease of R (but the lower the absolute influence of a given level of R). According to these (θ–α–β–ϑ) parameters determining the internal ecological dynamics, different 'ecological regimes' can be distinguished.

To illustrate the dynamic behaviour I begin with an ecological regime ('ecological regime I') with internal dynamics on a low level (low value for θ and low value for β) and which is comparatively insensitive to economic impacts (high values for α and ϑ). The starting point is a state of 'equilibrium', that is, $E_t = E_{t+1}$, where no economic use ('harvest') takes place and the impact by residuals is minimal ($h = 0, R \approx 0$) (Figure 6-1a).[12] This is compared with two different levels of R: one where the solution is a cycle (Figure 6-1b) and one where the system behaves in a chaotic manner (Figure 6-1c).

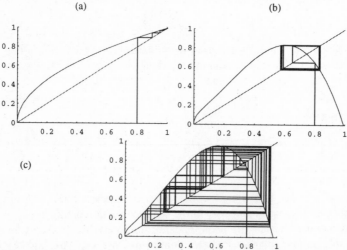

Figure 6-1 Dynamic ecology system ('ecological regime I')

Notes :   (a) globally stable fixpoint solution (θ = 10, α = 30, β = 0.8, ϑ = 80,
             $h = 0, R = 0.1, E(0) = 0.8$),   (b) 2-period cycle ($h = 0.8, R = 25$), (c)
             chaos ($R = 42$).

By contrast, in 'ecological regime II', the internal dynamics is on a high level and the sensitivity to economic impacts is more profound (lower values for α and ϑ). The starting situation ($h = 0, R = 0.1$) is about the same as in 'regime I'. A moderate economic use then leads to a solution with one stable fixpoint (Figure 6-2a). But further increase of the impact of *R* includes a bifurcation into two different types of solutions: the stable fixpoint on one side and a (two-periodic to *n*-periodic) non-stationary solution on the other side. The case of fixpoint and chaos is shown in Figure 6-2b. If *R* continues to rise, the increasing steepness of the declining part of the phase curve implies a 'jump' of the non-stationary trajectory into the attractor basin of the stable fixpoint; what formerly was a chaotic trajectory ends up then in a transient motion towards the fixpoint (see Figure 6-2c).

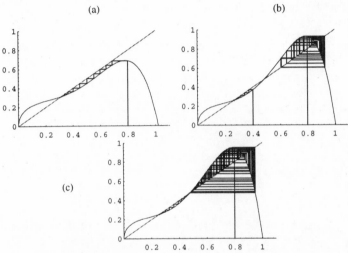

Figure 6-2 Dynamic ecology system ('ecological regime II')

Notes :   (a) globally stable fixpoint solution ($\theta = 18$, $\alpha = 10$, $\beta = 3$, $\vartheta = 70$, $h = 0.8$, $R = 5$, $E(0) = 0.8$), (b) locally stable fixpoint solution ($R = 12$, $E(0) = 0.4$) and local chaos ($R = 12$, $E(0) = 0.8$), (c) globally stable fixpoint solution ($R = 13$).

This regime has two important features: (i) There is an obvious trade-off between stability and activity level of the ecological system and hence between ecological stability and amount of economic harvest;[13] the higher the level of activity is pushed by economic impacts, the more the system becomes unstable and unpredictable; (ii) the starting point is crucial for the type of solution; this indicates the importance of instruments for constraining the activity level in an area which is dominated by a given attractor (avoiding sudden jumps in the activity level).

By combining the cases (a) and (b) of ecological regime II we can illustrate the different meanings of stability/resilience (see Figure 6-3). Given a time period (three time steps) and a starting point ($E(0) = 0.8$) and letting the economic impact (in terms of *R*) increase, the first meaning of resilience (in the broad sense of the term) is expressed by the difference between the minimal and the maximal mapping of the initial value for E (corridor resilience).[14] In Figure 6-3 this is the distance between E_a and E_b. More specifically, resilience is given by the distance between the initial value of E and a point E_c which is governed by an attractor other than the one ruling the starting point (in Figure 6-2 this is the beginning of the attractor basin for the local fixpoint). An exogenous shock (in terms of a sudden change in the initial value) must be strong enough to overcome this distance (shock resilience).[15] If there is no attractor change within a given time period the robustness of the system is only expressed by the corridor resilience.

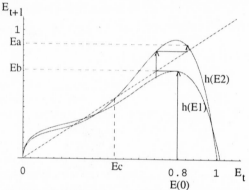

Figure 6-3   *Corridor resilience and shock resilience of the ecological system*

6.3   TECHNOLOGICAL CHANGE IN THE VIEW OF EVOLUTIONARY ECONOMICS

6.3.1 Major Findings

One of the main insights (beliefs) of evolutionary economics is that actions and decisions are shaped by uncertainty (about the environment, about the decisions and actions of others). Firstly, uncertainty gives rise to some sort of additional constraint for choice (patterns of behaviour) and, secondly, uncertainty is the source of a search for new alternatives (innovation) which, if successful, creates the pressure of a more or less deliberate imitation. Hence there is a time-dependent irreversible learning process which gives social systems a specific 'evolutionary' feature. The evolutionary path of such a system is (i) not totally deterministic, (ii) not necessarily optimal and (iii) not homogenizing its elements. This indicates the role of random events, interdependences between actors and initial conditions in such a framework. The microfoundation of such an evolutionary economy is not a maximization rule over a well-known set of clear-cut alternatives under given budget constraints;[16] rather it is about exploring and exploiting alternatives under diverse dynamic constraints. Corresponding to that, coordination in such an evolutionary economy is established not only by prices but also by rules, routines and direct interdependences of the agents.

An important dimension of a firm's coping with uncertainty is technology. Technology is primarily understood as a 'social coagulation' of information and knowledge.[17] According to the basic insights (beliefs) mentioned in the previous paragraph it is assumed that a given technology (i) is not explainable in a deterministic manner, (ii) is not the optimal (most efficient) technology and (iii) is not the same for all firms under similar conditions.

In the case of technology, the pattern feature of behaviour is shaped firstly by cognitive structures like 'technological paradigms' consisting not only of the book of blueprints of the engineer but also of all sorts of tacit knowledge, models of artifacts and systems, rules of thumb as well as knowledge and beliefs about feasibilities. These cognitive structures are incorporated in organizations. The latter are important in forming a non-separable unity of information processing and decision structure, a unity of 'capability and choice' (Nelson and Winter 1982, p. 67). Secondly the application and change of technology is shaped by 'mesoeconomic' order parameters like institutions/intitutional set-up as well as infrastructure and rule systems (for example, appropriability conditions). Normally these elements are combined to form a specific 'regime' of technology in a given place and time.

Taking these two levels of pattern formation into account one can conclude that at each level there is a 'gradualist' (pattern-conforming) path of technological change and 'saltationist' (pattern-eroding) way of change leading to the emergence of a new pattern. But at any time and at any level the dual change (innovation/imitation) is characterized by path-dependence, lock-in and frequency-dependence. Therefore the outcome of technical change is unpredictable.[18]

6.3.2 Model of the Economy

In modelling the economy I follow the suggestions of Nelson and Winter (1982) and the further elaboration by Andersen (1994). The basic idea of this model is to explain economic evolution in terms of technical change. This technical change is shaped by deterministic market interaction between a multitude of firms and a stochastic process of local search for new technological possibilities in terms of process innovation. The firms are characterized by two state variables: the capital stock (K) and capital productivity (A). On one side the states of the firms are inputs for a short-run market process in which market shares, the output price and profits are determined (market module). On the other side the states of the firms are inputs for a process of search for innovating and imitating technological alternatives (in terms of A) (search module). Finally the results of the market operations (in terms of profits) are compared with the findings of the search activities, thus leading to investment decisions (investment module). By these decisions the states of firms in the next period are defined.

Market module: The number of firms, cost per unit of physical capital and total demand are given parameters, where

$i = 1 \dots n$	number of firms;
K_{it}	capital stock; $\mathbf{K}_t = (K_{1t} \dots, K_{it} \dots, K_{nt})$;
A_{it}	capital productivity; $\mathbf{A}_t = (A_{1t} \dots, A_{it} \dots, A_{nt})$;
Q_{it}	output per firm;
Q_t	total output;
P_t	price per unit of output;
D_t	total demand (in real terms);
c_k	cost per unit of capital;
c_{kit}	total capital costs;
ρ_{it}	relation of price to unit costs
KA	capacity utilization

The following relations hold (by definition or by assumption):

$$Q_t = \sum_i Q_{it} \tag{6.3}$$

$$A_{it} = \frac{Q_{it}}{K_{it}}, i = 1 \dots n \tag{6.4}$$

$$D_t = D_0 \left(1 + \frac{Q_t - Q_{t-1}}{Q_t + Q_{t-1}} \right) \tag{6.5}$$

$$P_t = \frac{D_t}{Q_t} \tag{6.6}$$

$$c_k = \frac{C_{kit}}{K_{it}} = \frac{C_{kjt}}{K_{jt}}, i \neq j \tag{6.7}$$

$$\rho_{it} = \frac{P_t}{C_{it} / Q_{it}} \tag{6.8}$$

$$Q_{it} = KA (\rho_{it}) K_{it} A_{it}, 0 < KA \leq 1,$$
$$\left.\begin{matrix} KA = 1 \\ KA < 1 \end{matrix}\right\} if \begin{cases} \rho_{it} > 1 \\ \rho_{it} \leq 1 \end{cases} \tag{6.9}$$

Search module: The search for new technological opportunities takes place in a sequence of two 'lotteries'. In the first lottery a draw with either '1' or '0' is made, that is, it is found whether the expenditures on innovation or imitation respectively were successful or not. The probability of a successful draw is positively correlated with the amount of these expenditures. Because these draws are independent operations, because there are many draws, and because the probability of success is low, a poisson distribution is assumed for these probabilities. If the first draw is successful, a second lottery takes place in which an alternative with a new productivity is discovered. In the case of innovation activities of the firm the probability distribution of these new opportunities is assumed to be normal;[19] due to the coordinating activities of exogenous institutions (for example, research and development undertaken by political administration) the mean value of this distribution is an increasing function of successful attempts to find an innovative alternative within the first lottery. If the new productivity is higher than the one previously realized, the new technology is introduced.[20] In the case of imitation activities of the firm, a successful draw in the second lottery is given, if the capital productivity of the technology which is closest to the mean value is higher than the capital productivity of the technology which is actually in use.

The relevant notations are:

p_{it}^{in} probability of success for innovative search (first lottery);

d^{in} probability of successful innovation per unit of innovative search expenditures (second lottery);

p_{it}^{im} probability of successful for imitative search (first lottery);

d^{im} probability of successful imitation per unit of imitative search expenditures (second lottery);

r^{ink} capital-induced innovative search expenditures;

r^{imk} capital-induced imitative search expenditures;

r_{it}^{in-suc} successful innovative search expenditures;

A_t^{mean} mean value of latent productivity.

The following relations hold by assumption:

$$p_{it}^{in} = p^{in}(d^{in}r^{in})$$ (6.10)

$$\left. \begin{array}{l} \text{if } p_{it}^{in} = \text{true},\\[2mm] \text{then } A_{it}^{in} = \psi(A^{init}, \varphi, in_{it}^{in-suc}, t, A_{it}),\\[2mm] \text{else } A_{it}^{in} = A_{it}\, ; \end{array} \right\}$$ (6.11)

$$A_t^{mean} = A_{t-1}^{mean}(1 + \varphi r_{it-1}^{in-suc})$$ (6.12)

$$p_{it}^{im} = p^{im}(d^{im}r^{im})$$ (6.13)

$$\left. \begin{array}{l} \text{if } p_{it}^{im} = \text{true},\\[2mm] \text{and } A_{it}^{im} < A_t^{mean},\\[2mm] \text{then } A_{it}^{im} = A_{it}^{im\,*},\\[2mm] A_t^{mean} - A_{it}^{im\,*} < A_t^{mean} - A_{jt}, j = i+1...n\\[2mm] \text{else } A_{it}^{im} = A_{it}\, ; \end{array} \right\}$$ (6.14)

$$r_{it}^{ink} = \gamma^{ink}\, \frac{C_{kit}}{C_{it}} P_t A_{it}$$ (6.15)

$$r_{it}^{imk} = \gamma^{imk}\, \frac{C_{kit}}{C_{it}} P_t A_{it}$$ (6.16)

Investment module: We assume that a firm's desire to expand or contract is governed by its price–cost ratio and its prevailing market share, within constraints set by the assumed physical depreciation rate of capital and the firm's ability to finance investment. The larger a firm's current market share the greater must be the price–cost ratio needed to induce a given desired proportional expansion (Nelson and Winter 1982; Winter 1986, p. 212).

The notations of the variables are:

π_{it} rate of profit;

I_{it}^{max} maximum gross investment;

b ratio of external financing to profit;

s_{it} market share;

p_{it} ratio of price to unit costs;

δ physical depreciation per unit of capital;

I_{it}^{des} desired gross investment;

I_{it} gross investment;

η (expected) elasticity of prices.

The following relations hold:

$$\pi_{it} = P_t A_{it} - \frac{C_{it} + r_{it}^{in} + r_{it}^{im}}{K_{it}} \tag{6.17}$$

$$s_{it} = \frac{Q_{it}}{Q_t} \tag{6.18}$$

$$I_{it}^{des} = \delta + 1 - \frac{\eta}{\eta - s_{it}} \cdot \frac{1}{P_{it}} \tag{6.19}$$

$$\begin{aligned} &\text{if } \pi_{it} \leq 0 \\ &\text{then } l_i = 0, \\ &\text{else } l_i = b\pi_{it} \end{aligned} \tag{6.20}$$

$$I_{it}^{max} = \delta + \pi_{it} + l_i \tag{6.21}$$

$$I_{it} = min\ (I_{it}^{des}, I_{it}^{max}) \tag{6.22}$$

$$\begin{aligned} &\text{if } \pi_{it} < 0, \\ &\text{then } K_{it+1} = K_{it}(1 + \pi_{it} - \delta), \\ &\text{else } K_{it+1} = K_{it}(I_{it} + 1 - \delta) \end{aligned} \tag{6.23}$$

6.3.3 Simulations

The following simulations for output, capital stock, capital productivity and profit[21] show clearly that in such an evolutionary economy there is no general tendency toward homogeneity in terms of performance for the microeconomic units (see Figures 6-4 to 6-7). In the given configuration output, capital stock, capital productivity and profits remain different. The reason for this persistence of the inhomogenous performance of the firms is that the differentiating effect of the limited access to innovation knowledge is stronger than the equalizing effect of competition.

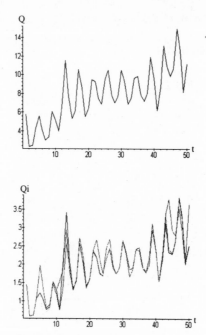

Figure 6-4 Total and individual output

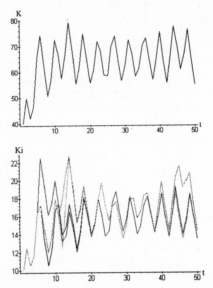

Figure 6-5 Total and individual capital stock

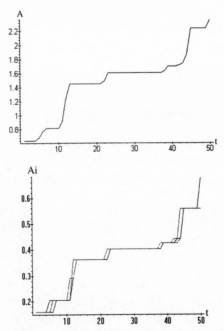

Figure 6-6 Total and individual capital productivity

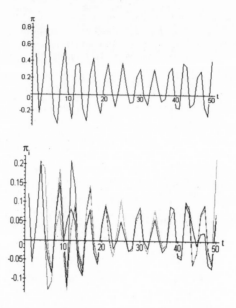

Figure 6-7 Total and individual profit

6.4 TECHNOLOGICAL CHANGE AND SUSTAINABILITY

6.4.1 'Ecologically Sound' Technology in a Market Economy?

Adopting the sustainability perspective sketched in Sections 6.2.1 and 6.2.2 it is not sufficient to define the ecological soundness of a technology as a technology being 'cleaner' in one selected ecological respect.[22] Firstly, all the ecological impacts have to be assessed and secondly, this total impact must be related to the properties of ecosystems, especially to the resilience/stability as defined above (Perrings 1994). Then a technology is ecologically sound if a (chosen) resilience property is maintained. But even given this property for a technology it is important to look at the (ecological) context in which it is applied and the (economic) scale in which it is used (Perrings 1994, p. 314).

   The problem at stake then is threefold: (i) Technological change driven by privately interested firms can be seen as a core factor structuring the 'industrial metabolism' in modern market societies. The propensity either to stick to a given technology or to search for new alternatives is not directly accessible by social or political regulation; even worse, the incentive to innovate/imitate seems to be inversely related to the degree of regulation in many cases. Therefore the question arises: how can ecological scarcity/instability be signalled to this 'private' process in an effective way? (ii) Technological change has a systemic quality. There might be 'good' non-ecological reasons for using a technology: social and economic appropriateness (for example, requirements of mass production), its optimality under a given structure of institutions and law (for example, protection by patents, liability rules). (iii) Technological change has a dynamic quality. Developing a new technology requires a long gestation period: discovery of basic scientific principles, engineering, design, development, prototype construction/testing and finally commercial application; innovation/diffusion as well as learning by using (England 1994). Furthermore in this process lock-in effects are going to happen, including situation-dependent myopic or even random elements instead of appropriate future foresight. Thus the question arises: where is the actor/institution with a long-term and global orientation in figuring out a new technology? There are neither perfect markets anticipating all future costs of new technologies nor impartial political agencies promoting such an orientation; rather myopic rivalry and management of particular interests is the rule and not the exception (see above, p. 762).

Taking all these considerations into account, there seems to be a contradiction between the decentralized/self-organizing nature of the innovating economic process and the global and long-run orientation which is required by 'ecological soundness'. This problem can be solved only by the emergence of a social process of identifying, evaluating and signalling ecological scarcity and hence gathering and feeding back the ecological implications of the decentralized market process.

6.4.2   Ecological Scarcity as a Social Process[23]

The social evaluation process starts by identifying the impacts of the economically motivated use of the ecosystem. Normally this happens by establishing a rough relation between an observed harm, damage or accident, etc. and a man-made emission. Subsequently this relation is refined in two directions: one direction traces the observed emission to specific activities by identifying the individuals, groups or even social structures responsible for this emission; furthermore specific methods of production including special input resources are considered. The other direction is a closer identification of the way in which given (and more or less known) emissions are disturbing, constraining and cost-inducing for economic agents and complementary institutions. Due to the structural features of uncertainty and conflict this evaluation process is not completely separable from focusing and organizing social interests and from corresponding bargaining processes. Hence, such a two-directional evaluation process has informational, organizational and cost-attributing dimensions.[24]

Considering the informational dimension, that is, the gathering and interpreting of information about emissions and their impacts on the economy, the following features have to be noted:

- Scientific controversy on the interpretation of observable ecological facts, on the causes of suggested effects and so on, is normal. Therefore, scientific indecision instead of cumulative creation of a body of eternal scientific truth is the rule and not the exception.
- There is a fundamental asymmetry between the information and knowledge of emission-producing agents and agencies on one side, and the information and knowledge of those suffering from the resulting impacts on the other side.[25] This asymmetry is inversely related to time: the more time is spent debating a specific issue the less relevant becomes the asymmetry. But for every new issue it arises anew.
- Finally, the 'discounting of concern' (Hannon 1987, p. 231) takes place, that is, a devaluation of economic impacts of emissions which are expected in the future (time discounting), of impacts which happen far away (distance discounting), of impacts which are difficult to perceive (sensual discounting), of impacts which are uncertain or risky (uncertainty discounting) and finally, of impacts which are borne by people of other cultural (or value) contexts (interpersonal discounting).[26]

Considering the organizational dimension of this evaluation process, one can assume that despite the mechanism blocking a clear awareness of the economic impact of ecological deterioration, some 'resources of concern' are left which might lead to a more ecologically sound behaviour or a (spontaneous) coalition building to promote such a behaviour and by this to the creation of additional information about emissions and impacts. But such a social learning process is hindered by social dilemmas and high transaction costs whereas such a process is supported by a common interest in preserving institutional legitimacy and by an alarmist and sensation-oriented public.

Finally the attribution of additional 'costs' results from the interaction of information production and information allocation on one side and the bargaining procedure on the other side. These costs consist of perceived damages (for example, destruction of landscape, dramatic reduction of ecological stocks, corrosion of economic stocks, deterioration of product quality, decrease in health quality) and constraints (for example, decrease in spatial and temporal mobility). Corresponding to and compensating for these damages and constraints (which may be partly monetizable by artificial instruments), there are in fact additional monetary expenditures (for example, herbicides, pesticides, fertilizers and irrigation in agriculture to compensate for the increasing instability, evasion costs such as resettlement, recreation and reallocation; repair costs for ecological and economic reconstruction, filter technologies, waste disposal and health expenditures, insurance costs, for example, against crop damage)[27] and opportunity costs (of increasing constraints) which together are called here ecological costs (C_e).

Political regulation can influence the internal conditions of the economy (for example, by redefining property rights, norms of emissions or imposing some additional C_e and by this inducing innovation[28]), the internal conditions of ecosystems (by organizing some recovery activities), the process of information gathering/evaluation (for example, by promoting new/additional information systems, rearranging the access to information), and the social bargaining process itself (for example, by influencing transaction costs). Hence the conclusion can be drawn that ecological impacts/costs are neither objective nor static; figuring out the dynamic range of these impacts/costs requires the analysis of the evolutionary process to identify, to value and to compensate or avoid these impacts or costs.

6.4.3   Ecological Scarcity Influencing Technical Change

To take into account this social process of articulating the scarcity of ecological resources, it is not sufficient to consider the firm simply as an efficiency-oriented entity the existence of which is explained only by market imperfections (for example, incomplete contracts, monitoring advantages and asset specificities). Rather it should be understood as a unique element in a self-organizing network of interdependent relations in organizations, market operations, public awareness and political administration. The threefold feedback loop included in such a network is shown in Figure 6-8.

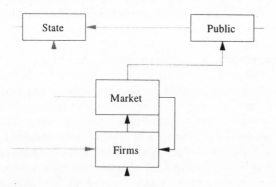

Figure 6-8 Feedbacks of firm's behaviour

Such a network can be seen as a 'selection environment' (Nelson and Winter 1982) for the survival strategies of firms. These strategies are shaped by industry networks, infrastructure, educational systems, norms and standards, public attitudes and so on.

In such a framework of societal evolution firms are seen as a combination of skills and routines in an organizational context (Nelson and Winter 1982).[29] These skills and routines are determining the actions to be taken in a changing environment.

> Firms may be expected to behave in the future according to the routines they have employed in the past. This does not imply a literal indentity of behavior over time, since routines may be keyed in complex ways to signals from the environment. It does imply that it is quite inappropriate to conceive of firm behavior in terms of deliberate choice from a broad menu of alternatives that some external oberserver considers to be 'available' opportunities for the organization. The menu is not broad but narrow and idiosyncratic; it is built into the firms routines, and most of the 'choosing' is also accomplished automatically by those routines. (Nelson and Winter 1982, p. 134)

Compared with the neoclassical conception, firms are understood as a mixture of behaviouralist clumsiness and innovative flexibility. Both features have as common denominator to conceptualize the firm as a 'repository of knowledge. This knowledge in turn, is generated, reproduced and augmented through the application of problem-solving skills and behavioural rules. It is thus social, has a large tacit component, involves both production and organization elements, makes the firm path-dependent and essentially different from other firms'(Foss 1995, p. 133).

According to this difference in firms' behaviour and given an ecological awareness in (parts) of the selection environment there is at least a chance for a self-feeding process of ecological innovation and a corresponding shifting of the selection environment itself. In such a process organizational learning can coincide with a learning process of the public and the political administration.

6.4.4　Combining the Ecological and Economic Model

The ecological model discussed in Section 6.2.3 already includes two constraining elements resulting from the economic use of ecological resources. The first element, the 'harvest' (hE), which simply is a reduction of the available resources at a given time, being a function of physical capital used in the production process. It is assumed that the relation of hE to K is limitational. The second element are residuals (R) resulting from economically induced material transformation (the biophysical side of the economic process of production and consumption). Hence R is assumed to be output-dependent. It has a twofold influence on the availability of ecological resources: given an increase of R, ecological resources are further reduced at a given point of time on one side and their time-dependent development is getting more instable on the other side.

For the sake of simplicity, the results of the social process of scarcity perception are now simply defined as ecological costs. These costs might arise directly out of market competition or might be the result of political regulation such as environmental taxes (taking into account all the intricacies mentioned in Section 6.4.2). In each case they are a little bit 'fuzzy' because they are due to perception and acceptance by the firm. The amount of these costs is assumed to depend on the relation of hE to E and on the (negative) relation of ΔE to E. Then both the h-effect and the R-effect of the economy are depicted: the former influences the numerator and the latter influences the denominator.[30] These environmental costs (in combination with the public pressure, institutional framework and so on) give rise to a different type of technological change: ecology-saving technical change. This means that the expenditures for innovative and imitative search activities are (also) becoming dependent on the relation of environmental costs to total costs. According to the relative weight which is given to capital costs and ecological costs respectively, different regimes of technical change can be distinguished.

The following additional notation is now required:

ε parameter defining the use of ecological resources per unit of capital;

μ parameter defining the residual per unit of output;

C_{eit} ecological costs;

$\Omega_{1,2}$ parameter defining the influence of ecological scarcity on ecological costs;

γ^{ine} parameter defining the influence of environmental costs on innovation expenditures;

γ^{ime} parameter defining the influence of environmental costs on imitation expenditures.

The new relations are:

$$h \cdot E_{it} = \varepsilon K_{it} \tag{6.24}$$

$$R = \mu Q_{it} \tag{6.25}$$

$$C_{eit} = \Omega_1 \frac{h \cdot E_{it}}{E_t} + \Omega_2 \cdot \max\left(0, \frac{E_{t-1} - E_t}{E_t}\right) \tag{6.26}$$

$$C_{it} = C_{kit} + C_{eit} \tag{6.27}$$

$$r_{it}^{in} = r_{it}^{ink} + r_{it}^{ine} = \gamma^{ink} \frac{C_{kit}}{C_{it}} + \gamma^{ine} \frac{C_{eit}}{C_{it}} \qquad (6.16')$$

$$r_{it}^{im} = r_{it}^{imk} + r_{it}^{ine} = \gamma^{imk} \frac{C_{kit}}{C_{it}} + \gamma^{ime} \frac{C_{eit}}{C_{it}} \qquad (6.17')$$

6.4.5   Scenario of Ecological–Economic Evolution

The scenario is a sequence of situations each of which is characterized by a specific parameter configuration. The latter can be seen as the outcome of a particular economic regime which is restricted by an ecological regime. The starting point is a situation of 'ecological regime I' (see Section 6.2.3) including a moderate extraction and emission by the economic system, without ecological costs and hence without technical change. The ecological system (Figure 6-9(a)) as well as the economic system (Figure 6-9(b)) are stable after 20 time steps.

The next situation is one with increased ecological use (extraction, emission) and capital-saving technical change. Because there is no incentive for economizing the use of ecological resources, the latter increases whereas the ecological system becomes unstable and the stock of ecological ressources is depleted within 20 time steps (see Figure 6-10(a)). The absolute scarcity of ecological resource stocks is the main reason for the erratic fluctuations of capital occurring after the depletion point (see Figure 6-10(b)).

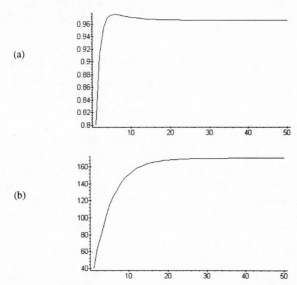

Figure 6-9 Ecological resources and capital in a stationary situation

Notes: $c_k = 0.1$, $\gamma^{ink} = 0$, $\gamma^{imk} = 0$, $\gamma^{ine} = 0$, $\gamma^{ime} = 0$, $\Omega_1 = 0$, $\Omega_2 = 0$, $\varepsilon = 0.001$, $\mu = 0.08$

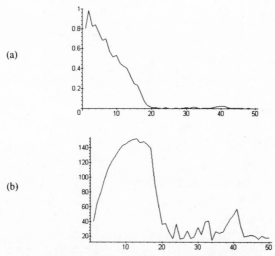

Figure 6-10 Ecological resources and capital in ecological stagnation

Notes: $c_k = 0.1$, $\gamma^{ink} = 0.2$, $\gamma^{imk} = 0.05$, $\gamma^{ine} = 0$, $\gamma^{ime} = 0$, $\Omega_1 = 0$, $\Omega_2 = 0$, $\varepsilon = 0.0025$, $\mu = 0.925$

This physical scarcity is afterwards transformed into socially perceived scarcity (see the process described in Sections 6.4.2 and 6.4.3). Using ecological resources (coupled with capital investment) now becomes a costly operation. Due to the effect of these costs on the profit of firms (and hence on investment) this results in an erractically fluctuating time-path for the ecological resource availability (Figure 6-11(a)) and for capital stocks (Figure 6-11(b)). These fluctuations (and the temporary relative ecological scarcity) are the foundation for an emerging ecology-saving bias in technical change. The corridor of fluctuations (in terms of ecological stocks) is therefore reduced (see Figure 6-12(a)); the time-path of the capital stock also becomes more stable and situated on a lower level (compared with the situation before), indicating that less capital is necessary for satisfying demand (see Figure 6-12(b)). Moreover, the fluctuations of both sorts of stocks become more regular and therefore the possibility of foresight is improved.

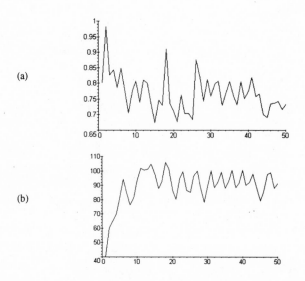

Figure 6-11 Ecological resources and capital asssuming ecological costs

Notes: $c_k = 0.1$, $\gamma^{ink} = 0.2$, $\gamma^{imk} = 0.05$, $\gamma^{ine} = 0$, $\gamma^{ime} = 0$, $\Omega_1 = 15$,
$\Omega_2 = 7$, $\varepsilon = 0.0025$, $\mu = 0.925$

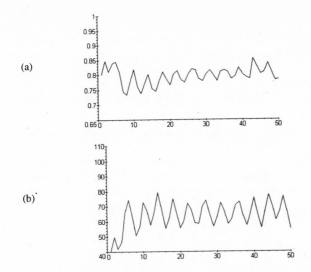

(a)

(b)

Figure 6-12   *Ecological resources and capital with ecology-saving bias in technical change*

Notes: $c_k = 0.1$, $\gamma^{ink} = 0.2$, $\gamma^{imk} = 0.05$, $\gamma^{ine} = 3.2$, $\gamma^{ime} = 0.8$, $\Omega_1 = 15$, $\Omega_2 = 7$, $\varepsilon = 0.0025$, $\mu = 0.925$

Now the process can start again in the same manner but on a higher level of capital and ecology-saving technical change. Assuming a discovery of new possibilities for extracting resources (for example, due to different capital-saving techniques) and assuming that emitted residuals are increasing (for example, due to the discovery of long-run externalities of the ecology-saving techniques), the ecological and economic instabilities can feed each other and, despite a high technological level, the system can collapse again (in Figure 6-13(a) this happens after 50 time steps). Hence – given an adequate social 'ecosensitivity' – ecological costs will be pushed upwards and a new incentive for intensifying the ecology-saving bias in technical change will be established.

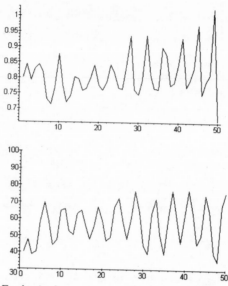

Figure 6-13   *Ecological resources and capital with increasing instability and collapse*

Notes : $c_k = 0.1$, $\gamma^{ink} = 0.2$, $\gamma^{imk} = 0.05$, $\gamma^{ine} = 3.2$, $\gamma^{ime} = 0.8$, $\Omega_1 = 15$, $\Omega_2 = 7$, $\varepsilon = 0.003$, $\mu = 1.2$

Coming back to the core of sustainability in terms of the E-K relationship one might conclude:

- Using (6.2'), (6.21), (6.23), (6.24) and (6.25), the dynamics of E and K, the following difference equations can be deduced:[31]

$$K_{t+1} = \frac{hE_t}{\varepsilon}\left[(P \cdot K_t^2 A_t - \frac{C-r}{K_t})(1+b)+1\right]$$

$$E_{t+1} = \alpha_{max}\frac{\mu K_t A_t}{\mu K_t A_t + \alpha}\left[E_t^{\beta}(1-E_t)\right]+\left(1-\frac{\mu K_t A_t}{\mu K_t A_t + \vartheta}\right)\sqrt{E_t} - hE_t.$$

(6.28)

There is no general analytical solution for this system. Appropriate numerical solutions can only be found by a (social) search process.

- The constancy in the stocks of ecological resources is too ambitious regarding the complexities at stake in both systems, leading to an irregular cycle (see Figure 6-14 corresponding to the relatively stable situation depicted in Figure 6-12 for $t = 10.50$).

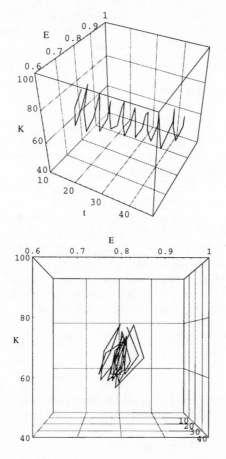

Figure 6-14 (K,E)-cycle

- Instead of being structured by convex isoquants (no cycle possible),
the time-dependent path in the (*K,E*)-space takes the form of an
erratically disturbed cycle. This expresses the divergence in internal
logic between the ecological and the economic system as well as the
unpredictability inherent in both systems.
- Under the given ecological regime and the particular situation
considered here the technical change (in combination with a social
process transforming ecological scarcity to economic costs) can
increase the corridorresilience (in the sense of Section 6.2.3).[32]

If the constancy postulate as regards the sum total of *E* and *K* is relaxed
to an increasing stability postulate or to a constraining of the accessible
corridor, there is not only one option. On what level and to what degree
this stabilizing effect should take place is dependent on the strength by

which the ecological scarcity is articulated by the society and transferred to the markets (macro constraints) and on the type of interactions between the firms in the market (micro relations).

6.5   CONCLUSIONS

In this paper I investigate how ecological macro constraints transform into incentives for microeconomic incentives for innovation. The model and its interpretation indicate that the process of technological innovation cannot be regulated directly. Innovations and imitations are decentralized operations which are shaped by private interests. Due to the risk and uncertainty inherent in these operations their outcome is not foreseeable.

Nevertheless the innovation and imitation activities are bound into a complex system of economic, social and political conditions. Specific constellations of these conditions may induce a self-organizing process towards a more sustainable path of technological change. Making the signalling of ecological scarcities more effective and stabilizing the use of ecological stocks in a sustainable corridor are the main tasks for an evolutionary environmental policy in such a framework.

ACKNOWLEDGEMENTS

Programming help by Esben Sloth Andersen and Steffen Klamt in developing the simulation software is gratefully acknowledged.

ENDNOTES

1.   See, for example, mathematical modelling of non-linear dynamics (Thompson and Stewart 1991), far-from-equilibrium thermodynamics in terms of dissipative structures (Prigogine and Stengers 1985) or portrayal of fitness landscapes stemming from evolutionary biology (Clark et al. 1995).
2.   A prominent example is the 'back stop technology' in neoclassical growth models (Dasgupta and Heal 1979, p. 175).
3.   In formal terms these meanings of resilience can be further specified by using the instruments of non-linear system analysis. Of central importance is the notion of attractor which allows a specification of groups of trajectories. The corridor resilience as well as the shock resilience is defined by the nature of this attractor; the robustness towards parameters determines the structural resilience.
4.   The reduction of variety seems to be a general feature of the modern management of ecosystems. Seeking for gains in ecological productivity is directly or indirectly triggering specialization and by this reducing functional

diversity. Hence resilience is reduced (Holling 1987, p. 144; Perrings 1994, p. 310).

5. Similar considerations are the basis of the concept of 'stability corridor' (Beckenbach and Pasche 1996).

6. This is not the usual distinction between strong and weak sustainability, which is made according to the substitutability of man-made and natural capital as well as to the role of technical progress.

7. Holling (1987, p. 142) gives an example for such an aggregation. Such an aggregation includes intra-ecological substitution possibilities between single ecological elements.

8. The finite supply of abiotic resources can be considered by defining a maximum level of the renewable biotic potential in terms of species beyond which any growth of the latter is impossible.

9. This is the regeneration module of the whole ecological economic system.

10. For $\alpha \leq 4, \beta = 0$ and $\vartheta = 0$, (6.4) reduces to the usual logistic difference equation.

11. h and R are treated as parameters; later on it will be seen that they are variables of the economic system (and hence have also a time index).

12. The impact is only due to natural irregularities (like an eruption of a volcano).

13. For some ecological evidence of this trade-off see Holling 1987.

14. This definition can be refined by relating E_a-E_b to $\sum\limits_{t=1}^{2} R_t$.

15. Note that it is not necessary that the system is already on a stable path. A similar definition is given by Perrings (1995, p. 135) although he does not consider the possibility of a time-dependent change in the attractors of the system.

16. 'In evolutionary theory, substitution of the ''search and selection'' metaphor for the maximization and equilibrium metaphor, plus the assumption of the basic improvability of procedures, blurs the notion of a production function'(Nelson and Winter 1982, p. 227).

17. Hence it is different from the neoclassical 'technical view' as well as from the Marxist 'social interest view' of technology.

18. Recent summaries of an evolutionary treatment of technical change are Nelson (1995), Cimoli and Dosi (1995) and Metcalfe (1995).

19. According to the discrete character of the model the values of this normal distribution are created by a random generator.

20. This technological change happens in a 'disembodied' manner: it takes place by information transfer without requiring a change of the physical capital.

21. Note that the profit here is net of search expenditures.

22. This is done in Agenda 21.

23. This is the evaluation module of the whole ecological–economic model. It is not yet fully endogenized.

24. Different attempts have been made to grasp this complex social interaction process (including institutions, rules, knowledge, and world views) situated between market operations on one side and political regulation on the other: for example, Dryzek (1987, p. 110) calls it 'polyarchy', Berkes and Folke (1994, p. 139) call it 'cultural capital'.

25. Reasons for this asymmetry may be the time needed for the discovery of ecological effects, restricted public access to relevant economic and physical data of the emitting agents and so on.

26. This discounting of concern is a descriptive category (declaring something about how the world is). It has to be sharply distinguished from the prescriptive neoclassical discounting procedure within the usual efficiency framework (declaring something about how the world should be).
27. For a detailed listing of these expenditures see Beckenbach (1994).
28. 'The structure of rights is not only important because of transaction costs and their impact on exchange process, but by also providing an incentive structure for innovations, and hence influencing the evolutionary market process and economic development in general. It is the dimension of 'rights to innovate' rather than ''rights to transact' which is most important from an evolutionary perspective''(Kerber 1993, p. 444). The importance of the ''rights to innovate'' is twofold: (i) as an allowance for negative externalities and (ii) as a definition of the appropriability of the innovation advantage (see Witt 1987).
29. Routines might be differentiated into market routines, organizational routines and search routines. The routines might be more or less different between the firms. Routines cut across the neoclassical notions of 'capabilities' (in terms of feasible technologies) and of 'choice' (in terms of selecting a specific constellation of productive ingredients according to a given goal function) (Nelson and Winter 1982, p. 400).
30. Here again 'ecosensitivity' of firms might differ. For the sake of simplicity this element is excluded from the model. Hence the total ecosensitivity of firms is exaggerated a bit.
31. The innovative and imitative search costs are denoted r and it is assumed that the desired investment is smaller than the maximum investment.
32. Contrary to that for an increase of the attractor resilience, there seem to be more ambitious requirements in terms of information and regulation. This has to be investigated more closely.

REFERENCES

Andersen, E.S. (1994), *Evolutionary Economics: Post-Schumpeterian Contributions*, London: Pinter Publishers.

Beckenbach, F. (1994), 'Social Costs in Modern Capitalism', in M. O'Connor (ed.), *Is Capitalism Sustainable?*, New York: Guilford, p. 91–105.

Beckenbach, F. and M. Pasche (1996), 'Nonlinear Ecological Models and Economic Perturbation: Sustainability as a Concept of Stability Corridors', in S. Faucheux, D. Pearce and J. Proops (eds), *Models of Sustainable Development*, Cheltenham, UK and Brookfield, US: Edward Elgar, pp. 278–301.

Berkes, F. and C. Folke (1994), 'Investing in Cultural Capital for Sustainable Use of Natural Capital', in A. Jansson et al. (eds), *Investing in Natural Capital: The Ecological Economic Approach to Sustainability*, Washington: Island Press, pp. 128–49.

Cimoli, M. and G. Dosi (1995), 'Technological Paradigms, Patterns of Learning and Development: An Introductory Roadmap', *Journal of Evolutionary Economics*, 5 (3), 243–68.

Clark, C.W. (1976), *Mathematical Bioeconomics: The Optimal Management of Renewable Resources*, New York: John Wiley and Sons.

Clark, N., F. Perez-Trejo and P. Allen (1995), *Evolutionary Dynamics and Sustainable Development: A Systems Approach*, Aldershot, UK and Brookfield, US: Edward Elgar.

Daly, H.E. (1990), 'Toward Some Operational Principle of Sustainable Development', *Ecological Economics*, 2, 1–6.

Dasgupta, P.S. and G.M. Heal (1979), *Economic Theory and Exhaustible Resources*, Cambridge: Cambridge University Press.

Dryzek, J.S. (1987), *Rational Ecology: Environment and Political Economy*, Oxford: Basil Blackwell.

England, R.W. (1994), 'Three Reasons for Investing Now in Fossil Fuel Conservation: Technological Lock-in, Institutional Inertia, and Wars', *Journal of Economic Issues*, 28.

Foss, N.J. (1995), 'Evolutionary Economics and the Theory of the Firm: Assessments and Proposals for Research', in Proceedings of the Conference 'Economics and Evolution', Utrecht: Utrecht University.

Hannon, B. (1987), 'The Discounting of Concern: A Basis for the Study of Conflict', in G. Pillet and T. Murota (eds), *Environmental Economics*, Genf: R. Leimgruber, pp. 227–41.

Holling, C.S. (1973), 'Resilience and Stability of Ecological Systems', *Annual Review of Ecology and Systematics*, 4, 1–23.

Holling, C.S. (1987), 'Simplifying the Complex: The Paradigms of Ecological Function and Structure', *Journal of Operational Research*, 30, 139–46.

Kay, J.J. (1991), 'A Nonequilibrium Thermodynamic Framework for Discussing Ecosystem Integrity', *Environmental Management*, 15, 483–95.

Kerber, W. (1993), 'Rights, Innovation and Evolution', *Review of Political Economy*, 5, 427–52.

Metcalfe, J.S. (1995), 'Technology Systems and Technology Politics in an Evolutionary Framework', *Cambridge Journal of Economics*, 19, 25–46.

Nelson, R. (1995), 'Recent Evolutionary Theorizing About Economic Change', *Journal of Economic Literature*, 33, 48–90.

Nelson, R.N. and S.G. Winter (1982), *An Evolutionary Theory of Economic Change*, Cambridge, MA: Havard University Press.

Perrings, C. (1994), 'Sustainable Livelihoods and Environmentally Sound Technology', *International Labour Review*, 133, 305–26.

Perrings, C. (1995), 'Ecological Resilience in the Sustainability of Economic Development', *Economie Appliquée*, 48, 121–42.

Prigogine, I. and I. Stengers (1985), *Order out of Chaos*, London: Fontana Paperbacks.

Rosser, J.B. Jr (1991), *From Catastrophe to Chaos: A General Theory of Economic Discontinuities*, Dordrecht: Kluwer.

Thompson, J.M.T. and H.T. Stewart (1991), *Nonlinear Dynamics and Chaos: Geometrical Methods for Engineers and Scientists*, Chichester, US: John Wiley and Sons.

Winter, S.G. (1986), 'Schumpeterian Competition in Alternative Technological Regimes', in R.H. Day and G. Eliasson (eds), *The Dynamics of Market Economies*, Amsterdam: Elsevier, p. 199–232.

Witt, U. (1987), 'How Transaction Rights are Shaped to Channel Innovativeness', *Journal of Institutional and Theoretical Economics*, 143, 180–95.

7. All Production is Joint Production – A Thermodynamic Analysis

Malte Faber, John L.R. Proops and Stefan Baumgärtner[1]

7.1 INTRODUCTION

Human economic action can be considered to have two components: production and consumption. While traditional economics has focused on the relation between these two phases of the economic process, ecological economics is mainly interested in describing economy–environment interactions. Both production and consumption can be analysed with respect to their interaction with the natural environment. In this paper we wish to contribute to the conceptual foundations of the production side of ecological economics. We will generally neglect aspects of consumption.

Our aim is to employ the fundamental natural science basis of production, the laws of thermodynamics which describe the relationship between energy, matter and entropy, and make these concepts more accessible to economists. The abstract notion of entropy, which is central to ecological economics – as was shown in the groundbreaking works of Georgescu-Roegen (1971), Daly (1977) and Ayres (1978) – will become more accessible in this paper, as it will be supplemented by an additional fundamental concept, that of joint production.

Joint production means that the production of a good (the main product) is necessarily accompanied by the production of one or more by-products. The joint production of mutton and wool is a well-known example. From an ecological point of view, we may note that solid, liquid or gaseous wastes always occur as the joint products of manufactured goods. In particular, by their very nature, chemical processes entail such mostly unwanted joint products.

Apart from the pioneering works of the three authors mentioned above, there have been many other attempts at making economists appreciate the relevance of thermodynamics for describing economic action. The reason why we undertake yet another such endeavour is the following. The study of joint production has played a major role in the development of economic theory from Adam Smith ((1776)1976) to Alfred Marshall ((1890)1925) (see Kurz 1986). But after Marshall the concept of joint production has been given little attention in the economic literature except in the works of von Neumann ((1937)1945/46) and Sraffa (1960). However, the concept of joint production could be made fruitful in economics for two reasons.

First, as will be shown in this paper, the concept of joint production captures essential physical aspects of production. To this end, we want to link the economic concept of joint production to the laws of thermodynamics, and in particular the Entropy Law. In contrast to the complex notion of entropy, the concept of joint production is very concrete and comparatively easy to understand, as well as to apply. Thus the concept of joint production can serve as a pedagogical tool to teach the lessons of thermodynamics about economy–environment interactions to economists who are, after all, far more familiar with the concept of joint production than with the laws of thermodynamics. And second, by describing production in terms of joint production all effects of production are automatically embraced. In particular, the repercussions of human economic activity on the environment are immediately evident.

As a matter of fact, each and every process requires the creation of a 'joint product'. For instance, the growth of a leaf on a tree is accompanied by the 'production' of CO_2. In particular, our statement is important for those activities which are usually called 'production'. Of course, this fact is so obvious and well known among economists, especially among scholars studying environmental effects of economic activities, that it might be considered a waste of time to elaborate on this point. However, the purpose of this paper is to emphasize a non-obvious aspect of the statement that all production is joint production. For it is often argued that joint production of wastes is only an *inefficiency* of production which could, in principle, be overcome by inventing and innovating new techniques or by operating existing techniques efficiently. This is the idea behind process- and product-integrated environmental protection. In contrast, by employing thermodynamic relations we argue that joint production is a *necessary* characteristic of all production.

In the context of the present volume our conclusion is relevant to the question of how to assess the environmental impact of individual products or technologies. Approaches to such an assessment, which are currently being discussed and to some extent employed, are eco-balances, life cycle analyses and eco-auditing. These approaches are usually carried out at the level of individual firms or products. While joint production can easily be dealt with in the framework of materials flow analysis, which is usually carried out at the level of the whole economy, the three approaches mentioned above all encounter more or less serious problems in the presence of joint production (see for example, Mampel 1995). However, as has been shown elsewhere (Faber et al. 1996), the joint production concept is apt to bridge the gulf between valuation at the firm level and at the economy level, as well as between economic valuation and ecological valuation.

This paper is organized as follows. In Section 7.2, we make some general remarks on production. In particular, we comment on the meaningfulness of labour and capital as fundamental, homogeneous factors of production, and relate single production to joint production. We also show how production processes affect the environment. In Section 7.3, production processes in industrial economies are analysed from a physical point of view. The laws of thermodynamics, in particular the Second Law of Thermodynamics, will lead us to the proposition that every process of production is joint production, in that it yields at least two outputs and requires at least two inputs. In Section 7.4, we contrast production processes in agricultural economies with those in industrial economies from the point of view that every production is joint production. Section 7.5 summarizes our conceptual view on production and gives some programmatic conclusions.

7.2 GENERAL REMARKS ON PRODUCTION

Before we present a detailed analysis of production based on the laws of thermodynamics in Section 7.3, we first want to make some general remarks on production from an ecological economics point of view in this section.

7.2.1 The Fundamental Factors of Production

The economics literature has long abstracted from the physical basis of production. The economic process as a whole was described as the exchange of some abstract values. However, a description of economic systems based on monetary measures necessarily neglects real transactions that are not coupled to the transactions of monetized values. In particular, real effects that are not marketed – often associated with the use and destruction of the environment – are excluded from an economic analysis. For that reason, analysing interrelations within the economy, or relations between the economy and environment, based on a thermodynamic description, is a necessary ingredient for building ecological economics (Ayres 1978, p. vi).

Using energy as a central quantity for such a description has a long history among economists and ecologists, briefly surveyed by Kåberger (1991). More advanced from a thermodynamic point of view is the approach pioneered by Georgescu-Roegen (1971) and centred around the notion of entropy. Not only does such an approach allow the consideration of flows of energy and flows of matter, it also allows the linking of transformations of matter to the corresponding need for energy.

While we consider energy and matter as the fundamental factors of production, the classical or neoclassical view on the input side of production is different. In the traditional (neo)classical view, 'labour' and 'capital' are considered as homogeneous factors of production. This description has abstracted from real production processes, which are always transformations of energy and matter.[2] Even the use of a third factor of production, 'land', once made by the classical economists as a reminder that all production relies on a natural basis, has practically been abandoned by the neoclassical economists for a long time.

The reason for this abstraction from the physical reality of production is twofold. First, the choice of labour and capital as the fundamental factors of production reflects the strong interest of the classical economists in the conflict over the distribution of the national income among those social groups involved in its production, namely capital owners and labourers. Second, neoclassical economists neglected the physical reality even more, since they were mainly preoccupied with the question of allocative efficiency in markets. The neoclassical world is a 'model of pure exchange'. With this emphasis, technical details of production did not get the attention they deserve from an ecological economic point of view. As a consequence, production is modelled in the most simple conceivable way, namely by assuming the existence of a production function. It is argued that it is the engineers' responsibility to specify the detailed properties of the respective production functions for the various sectors of the economy. But

> there seems to have been a misunderstanding somewhere because the technologists do not take responsibility for production functions either. They regard the production function as an economist's concept, and, as a matter of history, nearly all the production functions that have actually been derived are the work of economists rather than of engineers. (Dorfman et al. 1957, p. 131)

In contrast to the neoclassical concern, we are interested in describing economy–environment interactions. For that reason we focus on the material basis of all economic action. When we speak of 'production' we always have in mind transformations of energy and matter.[3]

7.2.2 Single Production versus Joint Production

In analysing production, economists prefer to view the process of producing goods or services as *single production*: one or more inputs are conceived to yield exactly *one* product as output. The striving for simple models may be at the origin of focusing on the case of single production which is, strictly speaking, only a special case of the more general case of *joint production*: one or more inputs combined in one process in general yield *more than one* product as output. A general model of joint production would include the description of single production as a special case, as was already remarked by von Stackelberg (1905–1946) in his analysis of production costs:

> Single production is a special case of the joint one. And in fact – and this is decisive – the theory of single production is completely included in the theory of joint production. (von Stackelberg 1932, p. 60; our translation)

Of course, models for joint production are considerably more complicated than those for single production. However, in modern texts on production theory it is argued that all essential features of production can already be studied using models for single production:

> Arguments and intuition developed in the simplest of cases still basically apply, and the economics of a multioutput world, although somewhat more complicated, is for the most part not fundamentally changed. (Chambers 1988, p. 251)

Notwithstanding the fact that economic model-building in our century has focused almost exclusively on the special case of single production, economists in earlier times also acknowledged that in real production processes the case of single production is rather the exception to the rule of joint production. Jevons (1835–1882) noted that

> these cases of joint production, far from being 'some peculiar cases', form the general rule, to which it is difficult to point out any clear or important exceptions. (Jevons (1871)1911, p. 198)

In this paper we do not wish to make an attempt to present a general formal model of joint production. But we shall argue that, if one takes the laws of physics seriously, *every process of production is joint production*. The laws of thermodynamics, which as natural laws apply to every process of transformation of energy and matter, and notably the Second Law of Thermodynamics, the so-called 'Entropy Law', lead us to conceptualize the process of production as joint production. Single production, then, appears as a mere idealization, not existing in the real world.

7.2.3 Production and the Environment

We emphasize that often, when at first glance some production process seems to yield only one product, we are overlooking the joint 'products' because they may not be desired goods, or because effects resulting from their existence might only become apparent much later in time.

Economists usually describe production processes as resulting in *flows* of outputs. The flow of desired products is usually valued on a relatively short time-scale, that is, it is consumed *now* – or, at least, its price is determined on present markets. In contrast, the flow of many undesired joint products is not valued on present markets, but its (environmental) effects only become apparent over time, when this flow of undesired products accumulates and its increasing *stock* causes environmental damage. While we consume *flows* of goods, which are available and thus valued on short time-scales, ecological effects often stem from *stocks* of undesired products which increase over comparatively long time-scales, via accumulation of the respective flows. The perception of the various joint products of some production process on different time-scales might further contribute to the disparity between desired and undesired products.

For instance, CO_2 occurs as a joint product of electricity in the combustion of fossil fuels. While the flow of electricity is immediately available, the flow of CO_2 at first is not perceived at all. It is the accumulation of the flow of CO_2 in the atmosphere as an ever-increasing stock which contributes to the anthropogenic greenhouse effect and has led now, more than 150 years after the beginning of large-scale combustion of fossil fuels, to perceivable climate change. Measurements (IPCC 1990, p. 7) show that the concentration[4] of CO_2 in the atmosphere has continuously increased over the last 200 years from a pre-industrial level of about 280 ppmv to 353 ppmv in 1990. Recent theoretical studies (Cubasch et al. 1995) suggest that, at a confidence level of 95 per cent, the increased concentration of trace gases such as CO_2 in the atmosphere is at the origin of the increase in the global average temperature of $0.7°$ K over the last 100 years.

The joint product CO_2 of electricity is thus brought to our attention only with a time-lag of more than 150 years. Other examples are the increasing stock of waste from wrapping consumption goods, or the accumulation of heavy metals in the sediments of inland waters. In all these cases there is a disparity of the time-scales on which we perceive product and joint product, which at first sight makes joint production look like single production.

It is exactly the unwanted, yet unavoidable, joint 'products', such as CO_2, which cause some of our major current environmental problems. The traditional approach of mainstream economics to describing these problems is based on the theory of public goods and externalities. Joint products which come as unwanted pollutants are considered as special cases, to be treated and eliminated by appropriate regulation or taxation. But, as Ayres and Kneese (1969, p. 282) have stated:

> there has been a tendency in the economics literature to view externalities as exceptional cases. ... We believe that at least one class of externalities – those associated with the disposal of residuals resulting from the consumption and production process – must be viewed quite differently. They are a normal, indeed, inevitable part of these processes.

To what extent the unwanted by-products of desired products are indeed a normal part of current production processes might be illustrated by some empirical data for the situation in Germany[5] in 1990 (Institut der deutschen Wirtschaft 1995). With a GDP of 2425.2 billion DM the overall emissions amounted to 727 million tonnes of CO_2, 1 million tonnes of SO_2 and 2.6 million tonnes of NO_x. In addition, 235.8 million tonnes of solid waste were 'produced'. That makes emissions of 300 kg CO_2, 0.4 kg SO_2 and 1.1 kg NO_x, as well as 'production' of 97.2 kg solid waste per 1000 DM GDP. Considering that, for example, a washing machine represents 1000 DM GDP and weights about 40 kg, it becomes immediately apparent how 'wasteful' production is. From this quantitative relationship one could actually be inclined to interpret the production of desired goods for consumption almost as the side-effect of the production of emissions and solid waste.

Since environmental pollution as a consequence of the process of production is an inherent effect, rather than an 'external' effect, of production, we propose the thermodynamics-based concept of joint production as a general framework for analysing the interaction between human action and nature from an ecological economics point of view. This concept gives a perspective on any kind of production, be it in ecosystems or in economic systems, which eventually will allow us to analyse those systems and their interactions in terms of sustainability. In a similar vein, these interactions have been examined extensively by O'Connor (1993, 1994, 1995) and Perrings (1986, 1994). They study the interrelations between the economic system and the ecosystem which are established by the joint production of economic goods and ecological effects. They both explicitly motivate their respective studies by thermodynamic considerations.[6]

7.3   THERMODYNAMICS AND JOINT PRODUCTION IN INDUSTRIAL ECONOMIES

Following our remarks on production in the previous section, we now turn to a detailed analysis of production based on the laws of thermodynamics. This approach will allow us to understand why joint production is ubiquitous and why the joint outputs of some desired product are often harmful to the natural environment. In this section we concentrate on the production processes typical of modern industrial economies.

7.3.1   The Laws of Thermodynamics

Any process, be it natural or induced by human action, must satisfy the laws of thermodynamics. The two most important laws of thermodynamics make statements about transformations in isolated systems. An isolated system is a system which exchanges neither energy nor matter with its surrounding environment. Briefly, the *First Law of Thermodynamics (Conservation of Energy)* can be stated as follows:[7] 'In an isolated system the total energy is conserved.'

Energy can be neither created nor destroyed. However, it can appear in different forms, such as heat, chemical energy, electrical energy, potential energy, kinetic energy, work, and so on. In an isolated system the sum of energies in their particular forms does not change over time. In any process of transformation only the forms in which energy appears change, while its total amount is conserved.

From a physical point of view, energy and matter are equivalent (via Einstein's famous formula $E = mc^2$). However, the conversion of matter into energy and vice versa is of no practical relevance for the problems under consideration in this paper. As a consequence, the conservation principle stated by the First Law holds separately for both energy and matter: in an isolated system the total energy and the total mass are conserved.

In any process transforming energy or matter a certain amount of energy is irreversibly transformed into heat. This irreversible waste of energy is measured by the variable *entropy*. This is the statement of the *Second Law of Thermodynamics (Degradation of Energy),* the so-called Entropy Law: 'In an isolated system[8] the entropy increases over time or remains constant.'

This is to say that with any process of transformation the proportion of energy in the form of heat to total energy irreversibly increases or remains constant, but certainly never decreases. Consequently, there is a decrease in the proportion of the other forms of energy – the so-called 'free energy' – which could be used to perform useful mechanical work, or which at least could be transformed into heat. In other words, with any transformation of energy or matter an isolated system loses part of its ability to perform useful mechanical work and some of its free energy is irreversibly transformed into heat. For that reason, the Second Law is said to express an irreversible degradation of energy in isolated systems.

Conceiving economic production as the transformation of energy and matter requires taking into account both the First and Second Laws of Thermodynamics. It was a great breakthrough when Ayres and Kneese (1969) employed the First Law to develop what they later called the 'energy/materials-balance-approach'. This concept gave an analytical representation to an insight, which – although being intuitively evident – was not yet explicitly incorporated in economics. It served to come to grips with many important aspects of the use of resources and the related 'production' of environmental pollution. However, the implications of the Second Law, in particular its emphasis on irreversible degradation of energy, were not included in the energy/materials-balance-approach. It fell to Georgescu-Roegen (1971) to stress this point and give an explicit treatment of the very abstract and complex subject matter of the Second Law.

Whereas the First and Second Laws of Thermodynamics have so far been seen as two alternative approaches to describing the thermodynamic basis of economics, we emphasize that these Laws have to be taken together to give a complete description. When analysing joint production from a thermodynamic point of view, later on in this paper, it will become apparent which characteristic properties of joint production are an effect of the First Law and which characteristic properties are an effect of the Second Law.

Despite our conviction that the First and Second Laws of Thermodynamics have to be employed together, the concepts derived in this paper highlight the *qualitative* implications which follow from the Second Law. We note, however, that in order *quantitatively* to describe transformations of energy and matter, one needs to employ indeed both the First and Second Laws. Since we are mainly interested in deriving qualitative results, we shall focus on Second Law considerations. The extensive application of the concept in a quantitative way is beyond the scope of this paper and is left for later study.

7.3.2 A Thermodynamic View of Production

We now develop a description of production which is based on the two Laws of Thermodynamics introduced above. Production can be conceived as the transformation of one or more inputs ($j = 1,2,...$) into one or more outputs ($k = 1, 2,...$). In order to apply the laws of thermodynamics, which refer to isolated systems, the boundary of the system 'production process' has to be chosen such that all inputs and outputs are included in the system.

Each input and each output has a given mass and a given entropy. Let us introduce the following notation:

m_{in}^j – mass of the j-th input
S_{in}^j – entropy of the j-th input
m_{out}^k – mass of the k-th output
S_{out}^k – entropy of the k-th output
m_{in} – total mass of all inputs
S_{in} – total entropy of all inputs
m_{out} – total mass of all outputs
S_{out} – total entropy of all outputs.

The requirement of the First Law of Thermodynamics is that the total mass be conserved in the transformation process. That is, the total mass of all inputs, m_{in}, is required to equal the total mass of all outputs, m_{out}:

$$m_{in} = m_{out}$$

where $\qquad m_{in} = m_{in1} + m_{in2} + \ldots$
and $\qquad m_{out} = m_{out1} + m_{out2} + \ldots$ (7.1)

The Second Law of Thermodynamics requires that in the process of transformation some additional entropy is produced. Thus the total entropy of the outputs is higher than the total entropy of the inputs. The total entropy of the outputs, S_{out}, equals the total entropy of the inputs, S_{in}, plus the entropy generated by the production process itself, $\Delta S > 0$:

$$S_{out} = S_{in} + \Delta S$$

where $\qquad S_{in} = S_{in1} + S_{in2} +$
and $\qquad S_{out} = S_{out1} + S_{out2} +$ (7.2)

In order to make more comprehensible the implications from the thermodynamic description of production, we revert to an interpretation of entropy which is due to Boltzmann.[9] To this end we introduce the specific entropy σ of a piece of matter, which is defined as entropy S per mass m:

$$\sigma := S / m \qquad (7.3)$$

Specific entropy can be interpreted as measuring how ordered or mixed-up different types of material are in a bulk of matter. Low specific entropy describes a heterogeneous and differentiated state of matter, in which different types of material are ordered in a particular way. On the other hand, high specific entropy describes a material which is mixed up and rather homogeneous.[10]

Having laid the thermodynamic basis of a description of production, we can now turn to analyse how the laws of thermodynamics require every process of production to be joint production. For this purpose, we want to distinguish two cases: (i) in most cases it is the Second Law which is the source of joint production; (ii) however, in some cases it is the First Law which is at the origin of joint production.

7.3.2.1   Joint production as a consequence of the Second Law

Let us state the two characteristic properties of industrial production in entropic terms. First, in general, the specific entropy of the desired product is relatively low, since the desired product is usually a very ordered piece of matter.[11] But as the total entropy of the overall output must be relatively high, this requires that as well as producing the required low specific entropy product, we must also produce a balancing by-product, which takes away the large amount of entropy not contained in the desired product.

Second, we can also make a useful distinction concerning the entropic nature of the inputs. Generally, we recognize two categories of these: fuels and raw materials.

- Fuels (for example, oil, coal, gas) serve to provide the energy which is necessary to perform transformations of matter. Concerning their entropic nature, fuels are characterized by very low specific entropy. This is due to the fact that low specific entropy means that they contain a large amount of free energy per mass which can be transformed into mechanical work or heat. This property is based on the very definition of entropy[12]. Of course, it is imaginable that 'pure' energy enters the production process, for example, in the form of sunlight or electrical power. However, it is typical for industrial production processes that the energy is provided by a material fuel which enters the production process as an input and is itself transformed in the course of the process. Thus, we will assume in the following analysis of production processes that energy is provided by some material fuel. From the entropic point of view the distinction between 'pure energy' input and 'energy in the form of material fuel' input does not make a difference.[13] However, from the mass-conservation point of view there is a big difference between the two ways of providing energy for the process. It will turn out that this is one of the key differences between industrial production and agricultural production, to be analysed in Section 7.4.
- Many raw materials (for example, ores such as iron ore, uranium ore), on the contrary, are characterized by relatively high specific entropy. This is due to the fact that most raw materials are used as inputs in rather impure form and still need to be purified and concentrated before they can be used to produce goods.[14]

For example, in iron making the fuel is coke (derived from coal) and the raw materials are iron ore, limestone, and atmospheric oxygen. The combination of coke, which is almost pure carbon, and oxygen has a low specific entropy, while iron ore and limestone are both relatively inert, high specific entropy materials.[15]

Taking an entropic view of production, we can therefore think of the production process as being the shifting of low specific entropy from fuels to desired products, made of initially high specific entropy materials. For example, in the production of iron, we can consider the production process to be that of transferring low specific entropy from the coke to the iron ore, giving the iron as the desired product.

Regarding iron manufacture, the high entropy from the iron ore, as well as the extra entropy generated by the manufacturing process itself, is embodied in the waste materials produced, namely, slag, low-temperature waste gases and waste heat.

Since any production process can only take place if fuel (or pure energy) is used as one of the inputs, and since desired products often have low specific entropy, it follows from our considerations that each production process yields, besides its target product, at least one joint output, namely high entropy. One important form in which this entropy may occur is heat. Another form of high entropy, which is important from the point of view of environmental pollution, is the de-concentration of materials, such as the spreading out of atoms and molecules in the biosphere, via emissions from production and consumption processes.

7.3.2.2   Joint production as a consequence of the First Law

Implicit in our above argument based on the Second Law was the assumption that the desired product is characterized by low specific entropy and high specific entropy characterizes an undesired output. One might also imagine production processes which result in a desired product of high specific entropy, for example, the intentional production of heat for the purpose of space heating, or mixing processes such as the blending of coffee or whisky.[16] In these cases the high entropy which is necessarily produced as a consequence of the Second Law might be entirely contained in the desired product. Of course, in these cases the above entropy consideration does not require a joint output.

As far as the production of heat as a desired product is concerned, it is the First Law – conservation of mass (Equation 7.1) – which reminds us that the entire mass which enters the process as an input also has to appear as an output. The mass of the fuel cannot disappear in the process. Since the desired product 'heat' is massless, there have to be other material joint outputs besides heat. Of course, ashes and CO_2 are well known as the joint products of heat in the burning of fossil fuels. We thus see that, even if the desired product is high entropy heat, the laws of thermodynamics, in particular the First Law, require a joint output to appear besides the desired product.

From what we have said so far it might still seem as if the production of a desired material good by mixing two materials, such as the blending of coffee or whisky, could happen without the necessary existence of joint products. The condition of mass conservation (Equation 7.1) could certainly be fulfilled, and the high entropy produced as required by the Second Law (Equation 7.2) could be entirely contained in the desired product which, due to its mixed-up-ness, is characterized by high specific entropy. However, this is only a theoretical possibility. In reality, in all processes of rearranging matter, heat is necessarily produced and thus always comes as a joint product of mixing processes. In the language of thermodynamics this is to say that reversible processes can only be realized in the theoretical limit of realizing them infinitely slowly. Whenever processes are realized in finite time they are necessarily irreversible in that they yield some waste heat.

7.3.3   A Simple Model of Industrial Production Processes

At this point, we want to conceptualize our view on the production process, which was derived above from thermodynamic considerations, in a simple model of production stripped down to the bare essentials. This model will allow us to formulate the insight from the preceding section, namely that there always exist joint products besides the desired product, in a more formal way. In doing so, we focus on those cases in which the Second Law appears to be the genuine case of joint production. The reason is that this is the only case in which the existence of joint products with repercussions on the environment is not immediately evident. Hence, applying our approach to this case will be most rewarding. The model is depicted in Figure 7-1.

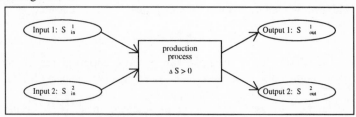

Figure 7-1 The structure of production in a simplified model

Every process of production (based on some material fuel) requires at least two inputs and yields at least two outputs:

- Input 1: fuel (for example, coke), mass m_{in}^1, low specific entropy σ_{in}^1.
- Input 2: raw material (for example, iron ore, lime stone), mass m_{in}^2, high specific entropy σ_{in}^2.
- Output 1: desired product (for example, iron), mass m_{out}^1, low specific entropy σ_{out}^1.
- Output 2: undesired 'product'/waste (for example, slag), mass m_{out}^2, high entropy σ_{out}^2.

The requirement of having at least two inputs and two outputs is due to the entropic nature of the raw material (high specific entropy) and desired product (low specific entropy) on the one hand, and the necessity to fulfil the entropy balance (Equation 7.2) on the other hand. In general, every process necessarily results in one or more of the high entropy by-products. Here, for the sake of simplicity, they are represented by the single output 2.

For every input and output its respective entropy S is determined, following Equation (7.3), by its specific entropy σ, describing its material 'quality',[17] and its mass m. The respective entropies of the inputs and outputs,

$$S_{in}^1 = m_{in}^1 \cdot \sigma_{in}^1$$
$$S_{in}^2 = m_{in}^2 \cdot \sigma_{in}^2$$
$$S_{out}^1 = m_{out}^1 \cdot \sigma_{out}^1$$
$$S_{out}^2 = m_{out}^2 \cdot \sigma_{out}^2$$

have to fulfil the entropy balance (Equation 7.2) as required by the Second Law. In general, the entropy of the inputs is increased by a further ΔS created in the process, as required by the Second Law. In our simple model with just two inputs and two outputs Equation 7.2 now becomes:

$$S_{in}^1 + S_{in}^2 + \Delta S = S_{out}^1 + S_{out}^2 \tag{7.4}$$

The relationship of fuels plus raw materials inputs giving rise to desired products plus wastes is represented in terms of the entropy flow in Figure 7-2. The thickness of the lines represents the amount of entropy.

Having discussed the natural science, that is, thermodynamic, constraints on production,[18] we can also characterize this necessary production structure in economic terms. When the production of one commodity necessarily entails the production of another commodity, we speak of joint production.[19]

Considering the literature, we note that when economists discuss joint production, they generally do so in terms of the joint production of two or more goods, all of which (i) are *desired* to a greater or lesser extent and (ii) are produced (approximately) *at the same time.*[20] Examples include the joint production of wool and mutton, beef and leather, curds and whey, or the joint production of electricity and space heating by cogeneration power stations.

The economic issues discussed in such cases relate primarily to the problem of pricing the two goods and appropriate cost allocation. However, when we take a thermodynamic approach to production, we see that the joint products lack the symmetry of the above-mentioned economic examples, as while both wool and mutton are desired products, iron is desired, but slag and waste gases are not. Nevertheless, we want to term a multioutput production process 'joint production' regardless of whether the various outputs are desired outputs or not.[21]

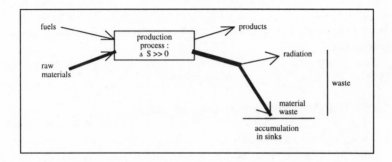

Figure 7-2 Flow of entropy in the industrial production process

Note: The thickness of lines represents the amount of entropy.

By taking a thermodynamically derived joint production approach to manufacturing, it is now clear that external effects from pollutants are not special cases, to be treated and eliminated by special policies, such as appropriate regulation or taxation. Rather, they are ubiquitous and inevitable consequences of the physical nature of producing goods. In that sense the so-called 'externalities' are inherent to every process of production.

7.3.4   The Empirical Relevance of the Model

Taking the above-presented approach to describing production, we learn one important lesson: all desired products have by-products. That means: *every process of production is joint production.* Further, the physical constraints of conservation of mass (Equation 7.1) and increase of entropy (Equation 7.2) imply certain constraints and limits of production processes which, so far, have lacked a clear theoretical underpinning in economic modelling. These constraints and limits are well known to engineers and

economists as empirical facts. However, they have not, so far, been related
to the phenomenon of joint production. The reason for this neglect is, of
course, that the joint products and their corresponding sinks were
considered to be free goods.

Without any clear theoretical underpinning, the relationships implied by
joint production could be modelled only in an *ad hoc* way. Using the
thermodynamic relationships developed above we can now present an
encompassing, coherent scheme of explanation for the various features of
production processes. It is interesting to note that the thermodynamics-
based concept of joint production, as expressed by Equations 7.1
(Conservation of Mass) and 7.4 (Entropy Law), establishes relationships
not only for the output side of production processes, but also for the input
side and for the interrelations between inputs and outputs. Hence, the
concept of joint production developed above in Section 7.3 captures the
essential features of the two laws of thermodynamics and appears to be
much more than just a statement about the number of outputs in some
process of production.

Let us illustrate some of the relations that follow from the entropy
balance (Equation 7.4) by empirical examples.

7.3.4.1   Relationship among the joint outputs

The entropy balance (Equation 7.4) tells us the amount of entropy which,
for given inputs (with specific entropy S_{in}), and given process technology
(increasing the entropy of the inputs by a further ΔS),[22] necessarily has to
be contained in the product and its by-products, S_{out}. Thus the quality of
the product and the quality of the pollution/waste, in the form of the by-
products, are not independent: the higher the quality of the desired
product, that is, the lower the specific entropy of the product σ_{out}^1, the
higher the specific entropy necessarily contained in the by-products σ_{out}^2.[23]

7.3.4.2   Relationship among the inputs

For a given (entropic) quality of the desired product σ_{out}^1, and given
process technology ΔS, S_{in}^1 is the entropy of the fuel input which is
necessary to process a given mass of raw material input of given (entropic)
quality σ_{in}^2. From S_{in}^1 the energy requirement of the process can be
calculated.[24] The higher the difference between S_{in}^2 and S_{out}^1, that is, the
more unwanted high entropy has to be withdrawn from the raw material in
order to produce the desired product, the lower is S_{in}^1, and the more
energy is needed to shift the unwanted high entropy from the raw material
to the waste.

Faber and Wagenhals (1988) present an empirical analysis which
investigates this implication of Equation 7.4. They study copper mining by
analysing data from (1) the Empresa Mineria de Mantos Blancos, Chile's
second largest copper-producing mine, and (2) the total mined copper

production of the United States. The relationship suggested by the entropy balance (Equation 7.4) is indeed confirmed to hold at a macroeconomic level.

Another recent empirical study which supports this relationship is presented by Ruth (1995), who investigates copper and bauxite mining. He uses an entropy framework to model thermodynamic constraints on the process of separating minerals from crude ore, substitution among inputs, and endogenous technical change in mining, smelting and refining.

7.3.4.3   A note on substitutability versus complementarity of inputs
In this thermodynamic view substitutability among the two inputs, raw material and energy, is very limited. While different raw materials of the same entropic quality might be substitutes for each other, as well as different fuels of the same entropic quality, the two distinct classes of inputs defined by their respective entropic quality, high specific entropy raw materials on the one hand and low specific entropy fuels on the other, act as complements rather than substitutes.

In the neoclassical description of production, labour and capital are assumed to be the fundamental factors of production. They are considered to be substitutes for each other to a large extent. In our entropy-based view of production as the transformation of energy and matter, labour and capital fall into the category 'fuel' because they serve to manipulate and transform the other input, namely raw material. Hence, while there might be large substitutability between labour and capital, substitutability between those two 'fuel' inputs on the one hand and raw material on the other hand is limited by the entropy balance (Equation 7.4). They rather act as complements.[25]

Empirical evidence for this complementarity between fuels and raw materials on the one hand, and substitutability among fuels or among raw materials on the other hand, is well known to mechanical engineers. There have been attempts to incorporate this knowledge into economic descriptions of production in the form of so-called 'engineering production functions' (Chenery 1948, 1953). However, this approach received comparatively little interest among most economists.

Ayres (1978) has studied the issue from a slightly different starting point, namely the so-called 'materials/energy balance principle', a purely First Law concept which is based on the conservation of energy and matter (Equation 7.1), but which does not take into account any entropic consequences. He has collected much empirical data and comes to the conclusion

> that the neoclassical concept of a production function is reasonably in accord with the actual state of affairs in the *extraction* sectors and in the *service* sectors. That is to say, either labour or capital can be substituted for the other more or less without a priori limit. On the other hand, a large and important

area of the economy is concerned with processing and/or fabricating materials or material components. In these sectors, material inputs bear a fixed (or nearly fixed) relationship with material outputs, and while labour and capital can largely substitute for each other, they cannot significantly reduce requirements for materials or energy that are 'embodied' in the product; nor can increasing material inputs reduce the need for capital or labour inputs. (Ayres 1978, p. 39)

7.3.4.4   Relationship between inputs and outputs

The entropy balance (Equation 7.4) not only establishes relationships among the outputs or among the inputs of a production process. It also provides some understanding of relationships between the inputs and outputs of a production process. For given inputs (characterized by some entropic qualities σ_{in}^1 and σ_{in}^2) and a given desired product (characterized by an entropic quality σ_{out}^1), the entropy of the unwanted by-products (S_{out}^2) can be lowered by changing the process technology, such that the amount of entropy (ΔS) caused by the production process is reduced. Of course, during the last two decades much technical progress has had just this effect. For example, using car engines with reduced friction results in releasing less heat into the environment.

In real production processes, the amount of entropy increase ΔS due to thermodynamically irreversible process realization is quite considerable. The corresponding increase of entropy by $\Delta S > 0$ in most cases comes in the form of an additional joint product, namely waste heat. For instance, Balian (1991, p. 384) points out that for the production of enriched uranium the actual energy input into real production processes is higher than the theoretical minimum energy requirement by a factor of 70 million! This is entirely due to the additional entropy ΔS added by the process itself, which corresponds to a waste of energy in the form of heat.

7.3.4.5   Summary: interdependence of production and
environmental problems

The main conclusion from this view on production as joint production, and the various relations inherent in this description, is that the quality of environmental pollution caused by the inevitable by-products of the production process is neither independent of the quality of the desired product, nor of the quality of the inputs into the process, nor of the process technology and management. Rather, the thermodynamic relationships (Equations 7.1 and 7.4) suggest various relationships which are important for understanding how undesired by-products, as well as correspondingly created resource and environmental problems, are interrelated and how they relate to the (entropic) quality of the desired products.

To summarize our findings in this section: from applying the laws of thermodynamics, in particular the entropy concept, to the production process we learn two important things. First, all desired products necessarily have by-products. This is to say that every process of production is joint production. Second, as these by-products are of high specific entropy, they will often be unwanted products.

7.4 THERMODYNAMICS AND JOINT PRODUCTION IN AGRICULTURAL ECONOMIES

In the following, by 'agriculture' we mean traditional farming. In contrast, modern agricultural production is highly mechanized and in almost every respect should be classified as 'industrial production'.[26]

As agricultural economics concerns, by necessity, relationships between humans and nature, at first sight it is surprising that environmental economics did not spring from agricultural economics. However, global and intertemporal, as well as severe local, resource and environmental problems first arose from industrial production processes. For this reason, we surmise, thinking about economy–environment interactions also started in the context of conventional general economics. Concerning agricultural production, there just did not seem to be any problems with respect to the natural environment, besides local and instant ones.

Taking a thermodynamics approach, one immediately sees that the energetic and entropic processes in agricultural economies are very different from those in industrial economies, so that there is little interface between them. Traditional agricultural economies are based on non-exhaustible energy sources, that is, solar radiation. This energy is directly applied to the agricultural production process. Fuels as energy-providing inputs do not play an important role. On the sink side, the material waste is such that it can be, and is in general, used by agriculture itself, or by other organisms (see Figure 7-3).

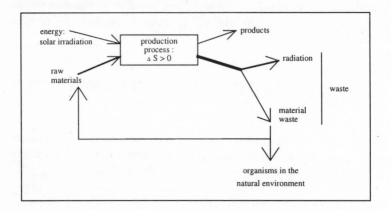

Figure 7-3 Flow of entropy in the agricultural production process

Note: The thickness of lines represents the amount of entropy.

Hence the waste in agriculture is of a non-damaging nature to the environment, and is even beneficial. In Figure 7-3, the thickness of lines again represents the amount of entropy. In general, the entropy of the inputs is increased by a further ΔS created in the process as required by the Second Law. One should note that, in general, in agricultural production processes this increase of entropy by the process itself is not as much as in industrial processes (see Figure 7-2).

In contrast, modern industrial economic activity is almost completely based on fossil fuels and uranium for the production of usable energy. The energy released is used to transform raw materials into the target products, which exhibit generally low specific entropy, and into waste, which has high specific entropy. Due to the First Law of Thermodynamics (Equation 7.1), the mass of the fuels has to appear in the outputs. Typically, this increases considerably the amount of waste which is produced. Agricultural production, which is not based on material fuels but directly on (solar) energy, does not have this problem.

In both industrial and agricultural production, the waste serves as a carrier for the unwanted entropy. However, there is a great difference concerning the entropic quality of the wastes. Waste can be of two distinct types. First, there is material waste (solid, liquid or gaseous). Second, there is immaterial waste, which is radiative heat. While radiative heat can leave the earth for space, which constitutes a limitless sink, material waste accumulates on earth. In agriculture the unwanted entropy is mainly radiated away from the earth; in the industrial processes, the unwanted aware not only of one's goals, but of unintended but inevitable consequences. At the same time, it makes evident that the case of external effects, which neoclassical environmental economics builds upon, is not a case which only occurs in some cases of production and consumption, but is of a ubiquitous nature. Second, since at least one of the by-products of an industrial production process has to be an unwanted waste product, as discussed in Section 7.3, one sees immediately that all production has repercussions on the environment.

At first sight, there might arise the impression that our paper has a pessimistic message because of the *necessary* occurrence of joint products. However, for two reasons we do not consider this to be the case: (i) being aware of the ubiquity of joint production, society may undertake increased efforts to avoid wastes by means of process- and product- integrated environmental protection. As noted in Section 7.3.4, we see a great potential for reduction, even though there will always remain a certain amount of joint products due to thermodynamic reasons; (ii) in addition, the awareness of the necessary existence of joint products may make society reconsider the composition of the set of desired products and the absolute amount of production in such a way that less entropy and fewer undesired joint products are produced. We believe that this reconsideration does not necessarily lead to a reduction in welfare.

For further study we see two fields of application for our approach to describing production:

- First, the thermodynamic view of production, in particular the consequences of the Entropy Law, will allow the limits of the substitutability between different factors of production to be analysed. This idea is already outlined in Section 7.3.4.
- Second, since the concept of joint production is a unified approach to describing production both in economies as well as in ecosystems, it is especially apt for describing and analysing economy–environment interactions with special regard to sustainability. Further analysis in this direction could be based on previous work by Faber et al. (1995a).

In summary, thermodynamics and joint production are important conceptual tools for describing economy–environment interactions. The notion of joint production captures essential physical aspects of production.

ENDNOTES

1. We are grateful to Shmuel Amir, Harald Dyckhoff, Manuel Frondel, Bernd Klauer, Reiner Kümmel, Reiner Manstetten, Georg Müller-Fürstenberger and

entropy is materialized, and thus accumulates as potentia
wastes (see Figure 7-2).

7.5 CONCEPTUAL FOUNDATIONS FOR THE
PRODUCTION SIDE OF ECOLOGICAL
ECONOMICS

At this point we shall attempt to summarize the results we ha\
in this paper. In doing so we shall try, at the same time
foundations for the production side of ecological economi
interrelationship of production with nature. Our comments \
programmatic nature. We argue that thermodynamics and join
are two fundamental concepts to be used. They are employe
unifying treatment in several respects.

The thermodynamic concepts of energy and entropy are
science basis for all processes in the economy, the environm
interactions between these two. Thus energy and entropy a
notions for the economy and nature, and this recognition is a
step for the development of ecological economics.

However, using the notion of entropy, in particular, gives
separate difficulties. First, employing this notion is imp
developing the essential questions to be analysed in the field o
economics, but the notion itself, in general, helps little in givi
solutions to practical problems. Second, the notion is so difficu
natural scientists have, more often than not, problems in \
correctly. This holds, of course, even more for social scien
therefore expedient to supplement the entropy concept by a noti
more concretely applicable, and easier for others to come to
and use.

We consider the notion of joint production to be a fundamen
this purpose. The notion of joint production captures the essen
of the entropy concept: irreversibility. In that sense, once
understood the entropy concept, joint production appears to
obvious. As the above examples in Section 7.3.4 illustrated, the
joint production has the advantage of being concrete and com
easy to understand, as well as to apply. The reason why we stres
of understanding so much is that we consider it important that
issues can be made understandable to the public at large, an
applied to everyday problems by the public at large.

The notion of joint production is fundamental in two respect
makes clear that one always gets more than one wants, because o
obtains, besides the main product, at least one by-product, and
many of these. This shows that in taking action, one should a

Armin Schmutzler for critical reading and valuable comments on an earlier draft.

2. One should note that both labour and capital, when reduced to their material and energetic basis, appear as 'extremely heterogenous aggregates (which) have all the scientific validity of the medieval elements of earth, air, fire, and water', as Boulding (1981, p. 28) puts it.

3. The production of services (for example, hair-cutting, or consulting) nevertheless falls within the scope of our analysis in so far as the production of services always requires a material basis and thus has to obey the laws of thermodynamics.

4. 'Concentration' here denotes the share in volume and is measured in ppmv = parts per million by volume.

5. The data refer to the situation in the former (pre-1990) Federal Republic of Germany.

6. A quite different aspect of joint production has been studied by Cornes and Sandler (1984). They formalize the idea that public goods (or bads) are provided jointly with private goods. While this seems to be unrelated to our thermodynamic considerations it is nevertheless certainly relevant to the question of how joint products of desired goods affect the natural environment. This idea has been further analysed by, for example, Cornes and Sandler (1994) and Vicary (1997).

7. For a comprehensive treatment see, for example, Reif (1965).

8. This statement holds only for *isolated* systems which exchange neither energy nor matter with their surrounding environment. An introduction to the entropy concept, its meaning in systems which are not isolated, and a discussion of its application in ecological economics can be found in Baumgärtner et al. (1996a, b). Atkins (1984) and Faber et al. (1995b) give an extensive introduction to the entropy concept for the non-physicist, while Reif (1965) presents a more technical introduction for the reader with a physics background.

9. For a detailed explanation see, for example, Atkins (1984).

10. It is important to note that this is a purely statistical interpretation, making a statement about the arrangement of elements of an abstract system, which are assumed to be indivisible and not subject to chemical reactions among each other. However, the entropy of real material substances, as defined above in a thermodynamic context, is not only about material homogeneity or heterogeneity, but also about how chemically reactive or unreactive these substances are. From the latter point of view, high entropy would indicate a low tendency for chemical reaction and thus homogeneity in the energy potential of the substances. For example, a mixture of hydrogen and oxygen in the ratio 2:1 might be completely homogeneous with respect to spatial distribution but nevertheless possesses very low entropy due to its high potential for chemical reaction. The two aspects of entropy, distribution of matter and distribution of energy potential, might have an opposite influence on the entropy of a system. In order to determine whether the entropy of a mixture of substances is high or low one would actually have to calculate quantitatively the two aspects of entropy. However, this distinction has no effect on the argument in the paper.

11. See Endnote 10.

12. Engineers and physicists prefer energetic terms over entropic terms as the more fundamental ones. As a matter of fact, free energy F and entropy S are related by $F = U - TS$, where U is the internal energy and T is (absolute) temperature. For given U and T a decrease in S is equivalent to an increase in F. Hence, speaking of low entropy S is equivalent to speaking of high free energy F.

13. A pure energy input is characterized not only by *very low* specific entropy, but even by *negative* entropy. Thus the logic of our argument applies also in the case of pure energy inputs.

14. See Endnote 10.

15. See Endnote 10.

16. Another example is the use of high specific entropy iron slag as a desired input in the construction industry. Generally, the long-lasting infrastructure elements of an economy (or organism) are made of high specific entropy materials, for example, concrete, brick, shell, bone.

17. 'Quality' here refers to the homogeneity of some material. As described above, specific entropy can be interpreted as measuring this 'quality' of the material. The lower some material's specific entropy, the more heterogeneous is its material structure. On the other hand, the higher the material's specific entropy, the more mixed up is the material. From the point of view of industrial production, this is equivalent to a statement about the material quality as an input or output of production. However, one should bear in mind the qualification of this statement in Endnote 10.

18. We again remind the reader that for a meaningful quantitative application one has to integrate the First and the Second Laws of Thermodynamics. However, in this paper we concentrate on qualitative aspects and thus stress the Second Law's implications. For that reason we take Equation 7.4, which is purely in entropy terms, as the analytical representation of our simple model.

19. It is an essential property of joint production that not only two or more outputs are produced, but that they are *necessarily*, from a technical point of view, produced together in one process. This may be caused by some laws of nature, for example, in chemical reactions, or as a consequence of the above-presented thermodynamic relationships.

20. One notable exception is the work of Sraffa (1960), who considered the existence of durable capital goods as a special case of joint production. In this case the joint outputs appear over time. For Sraffa this is the most important aspect of joint production: 'The interest of Joint Products does not lie so much in the familiar examples of wool and mutton, or wheat and straw, as in its being the genus of which Fixed Capital is the leading species' (Sraffa 1960, p. 63).

21. In that sense we use the neutral term 'joint product' as distinct from the terms 'by-product' or 'side-product' which already imply that the joint product is not a desired one. For a systematic description of the different notations in use see Müller-Fürstenberger (1995, Chapter 2) or Dyckhoff (1993). An encompassing approach to describing joint production, which may also include the production of bads, has been developed by Dyckhoff (1996). He defines 'joint production' with regard to (i) the system of production, that is the set of all available techniques, (ii) the desired product, whose production is the ultimate goal of the employed process or processes of production, and (iii) the recognition of the various outputs. Such an approach is especially apt

in discussing the repercussions of (joint) production on the environment. However, in contrast to Dyckhoff we are of the opinion that joint production is an objective characteristic of every process of production, regardless of the recognition of the various outputs.

22. Entropy may serve as a measure of how wasteful production is. The higher the extra entropy ΔS created in some process of transformation, the more waste (heat) is produced in that process.

23. This might be illustrated by the example (given in Balian 1991, pp. 383–5) of the enriching of uranium by isotope separation. However, in order to perform a quantitative analysis of this example, which properly relates the respective entropies and specific entropies, one needs to take into account First Law considerations as well. This is beyond the scope of this paper. We will present elsewhere a detailed study of this example.

24. We should qualify this statement in the sense that (i) for a proper calculation the respective masses have to be known, and (ii) the relation between entropy S and free energy F (see Endnote 12), $F = U - TS$, is unique only for given internal energy U and (absolute) temperature T. In this case, the free energy is indeed completely determined by the entropy.

25. We note that this structure of substitutability corresponds to the one of so-called 'nested' neoclassical production functions.

26. It is interesting to note that Hannon et al. (1993), who study sustainability based on physically measurable evidence, namely the rate of entropy formation on a given area, find 'that the Amish farm is sustainable and the modern farmer is not' (p. 264). The crucial difference between the two is identified as the use of fossil fuels.

27. For an overview of 'entropy, information and confusion in the social sciences' see Proops (1987). An analysis of the often misleading 'use of the entropy concept in ecological economics' is given in Baumgärtner et al. (1996b).

REFERENCES

Atkins, P.W. (1984), *The Second Law,* New York: Scientific American/W.H. Freeman.

Ayres, R.U. (1978), *Resources, Environment, and Economics – Applications of the Materials/Energy Balance Principle*, New York: John Wiley & Sons.

Ayres, R.V. and A.V. Kneese (1969), 'Production, Consumption, and Externalities', *The American Economic Review*, 59, 282–97.

Balian, R. (1991), *From Microphysics to Macrophysics – Methods and Applications of Statistical Physics I,* Berlin, Heidelberg, New York: Springer-Verlag.

Baumgärtner, S., M. Faber and J.L.R. Proops (1996a), 'Entropy: A Unifying Concept for Ecological Economics', in M. Faber, R. Manstetten and J.L.R. Proops (eds), *Ecological Economics – Concepts and Methods*, Cheltenham, UK and Brookfield, US: Edward Elgar, Chapter 6.

Baumgärtner, S., M. Faber and J.L.R. Proops (1996b), 'The Use of the Entropy Concept in Ecological Economics', in M. Faber, R. Manstetten and J.L.R.

Proops (eds), *Ecological Economics – Concepts and Methods*, Cheltenham, UK and Brookfield, US: Edward Elgar, Chapter 7.

Boulding, K.E. (1981), *Evolutionary Economics*, Beverly Hills: Sage.

Chambers, R.G. (1988), *Applied Production Analysis – A Dual Approach*, Cambridge: Cambridge University Press.

Chenery, H.B. (1948), 'Engineering Production Functions', *Quarterly Journal of Economics*, 63, 507–31.

Chenery, H.B. (1953), 'Process and Production Functions from Engineering Data', in W. Leontief (ed.), *Studies in the Structure of the American Economy*, Oxford: Oxford University Press.

Cornes, R. and T. Sandler (1984), 'Easy Riders, Joint Production, and Public Goods', *The Economic Journal*, 94, 580–98.

Cornes, R. and T. Sandler (1994), 'The Comparative Static Properties of the Impure Public Good Model', *Journal of Public Economics*, 54, 403–21.

Cubasch, U., B.D. Santer and G.C. Hegerl (1995), 'Klimamodelle – wo stehen wir?', *Physikalische Blätter*, 51, 269–76.

Daly, H.E. (1977), *Steady-State Economics: The Economics of Biophysical Equilibrium and Moral Growth*, San Francisco: W.H. Freeman.

Dorfman, R., P. Samuelson and R. Solow (1957), *Linear Programming and Economic Analysis*, New York: McGraw-Hill.

Dyckhoff, H. (1993), *Betriebliche Produktion. Theoretische Grundlagen einer umweltorientierten Produktionswirtschaft*, Heidelberg: Springer-Verlag, second edition.

Dyckhoff, H. (1996), 'Kuppelproduktion und Umwelt: Zur Bedeutung eines in der Ökonomik vernachlässigten Phänomens für die Kreislaufwirtschaft', *Zeitschrift für Angewandte Umweltforschung*, 9, 173–87.

Faber, M., F. Jöst, R. Manstetten, G. Müller–Fürstenberger and J.L.R. Proops (1996), 'Linking Ecology and Economy: Joint Production in the Chemical Industry', in M. Faber, R. Manstetten and J.L.R. Proops (eds), *Ecological Economics – Concepts and Methods*, Cheltenham, UK and Brookfield, US: Edward Elgar, Chapter 13.

Faber, M., R. Manstetten and J.L.R. Proops (1995a), 'On the Conceptual Foundations of Ecological Economics: a Teleological Approach', *Ecological Economics*, 12, 41–54.

Faber, M., H. Niemes and G. Stephan (1995b), *Entropy, Environment and Resources – An Essay in Physico-Economics*, Berlin, Heidelberg, New York: Springer–Verlag, second edition.

Faber, M. and G. Wagenhals (1988), 'Towards a Long-term Balance between Economics and Environmental Protection', in W. Salomons and U. Förstner (eds), *Environmental Management of Solid Waste - Dredged Materials and Mine Tailings*, Berlin, Heidelberg, New York: Springer-Verlag.

Georgescu-Roegen, N. (1971), *The Entropy Law and the Economic Process*, Cambridge, MA: Harvard University Press.

Hannon, B., M. Ruth and E. Delucia (1993), 'A Physical View of Sustainability', *Ecological Economics*, 8, 253–68.

Institut der deutschen Wirtschaft (1995), *Zahlen zur Wirtschaftlichen Entwicklung der Bundesrepublik Deutschland*, Köln: Deutscher Instituts-Verlag.

IPCC (1990), *Intergovernmental Panel on Climate Change – The IPCC Scientific Assessmen,*. R. Houghton, G.J. Jenkins and E. Ephraumes (eds), Cambridge: Cambridge University Press.

Jevons, W.S. (1871), *The Theory of Political Economy*, reprint of the fourth edition (1911), London: Macmillan.

Kåberger, T. (1991), 'Measuring Instrumental Value in Energy Terms', in C. Folke and T. Kåberger (eds), *Linking the Natural Environment and the Economy: Essays from the Eco-Eco Group*, Dordrecht: Kluwer Academic Publishers.

Kurz, H.D. (1986), 'Classical and Early Neoclassical Economists on Joint Production', *Metroeconomica*, 38, 1–37.

Mampel, U. (1995), 'Zurechnung von Stoff- und Energieströmen – Probleme und Möglichkeiten für Betriebe', in M. Schmidt and A. Schorb (eds), *Stoffstromanalysen in Ökobilanzen und Ökoaudits*, Berlin and Heidelberg: Springer, pp. 133–45.

Marshall, A. (1890), *Principles of Economics*, reprint of the eighth edition (1925), London and Baltimore: Macmillan.

Müller-Fürstenberger, G. (1995), *Kuppelproduktion – Eine theoretische und empirische Analyse am Beispiel der chemischen Industrie*, Heidelberg: Physica-Verlag.

Neumann, J. von (1937), 'Über ein ökonomisches Gleichungssystem und eine Verallgemeinerung des Brouwerschen Fixpunktsatzes', *Ergebnisse eines mathematischen Kolloquiums,* 8, 73–83; English translation (1945/46), 'A Model of General Economic Equilibrium', *Review of Economic Studies*, 13, 1–9.

O'Connor, M. (1993), 'Entropic Irreversibility and Uncontrolled Technological Change in Economy and Environment', *Journal of Evolutionary Economics*, 3, 285–315.

O'Connor, M. (1994), 'Entropy, Liberty and Catastrophe – the Physics and Metaphysics of Waste Disposal', in P. Burley and J. Foster (eds), *Economics and Thermodynamics: New Perspectives on Economic Analysis*, Dordrecht: Kluwer Academic Publishers, pp. 119–82.

O'Connor, M. (1995), 'Cherishing the Future, Cherishing the Other: A "Post-Classical" Theory of Value', in S. Faucheux, D. Pearce and J. Proops (eds), *Models of Sustainable Development*, Cheltenham, UK and Brookfield, US: Edward Elgar, pp. 321–44.

Perrings, C. (1986), 'Conservation of Mass and Instability in a Dynamic Economy–Environment System', *Journal of Environmental Economics and Management*, 13, 199–211.

Perrings, C. (1994), 'Conservation of Mass and the Time-Behaviour of Ecological–Economic Systems', in P. Burley and J. Foster (eds), *Economics and Thermodynamics: New Perspectives on Economic Analysis*, Dordrecht: Kluwer Academic Publishers, pp. 99–117.

Proops, J.L.R. (1987), 'Entropy, Information and Confusion in the Social Sciences', *Journal of Interdisciplinary Economics*, 1, 224–42.

Reif, F. (1965), *Fundamentals of Statistical and Thermal Physics*, New York: McGraw-Hill.

Ruth, M. (1995), 'Thermodynamic Constraints on Optimal Depletion of Copper and Aluminium in the United States: a Dynamic Model of Substitution and Technical Change', *Ecological Economics*, 15, 197–213.

Smith, A. (1776), *An Inquiry into the Nature and Causes of the Wealth of Nations*, reprinted in W.B. Todd (ed.) (1976), Oxford: Clarendon Press.

Sraffa, P. (1960), *Production of Commodities by Means of Commodities*, Cambridge: Cambridge University Press.

Stackelberg, H. von (1932), *Grundlagen einer reinen Kostentheorie*, Wien: Verlag von Julius Springer.

Vicary, S. (1997), 'Joint production and the Private Provision of Public Goods', *Journal of Public Economics*, 63, 429–45.

PART III

Sustainable Development as a Social Partnership between Firms, Citizens and Government

8. The Company Environmental Scheme[1]

Valérie Martin and Françoise Garcia

In the wake of growing public attentiveness to the quality of life and conservation of the natural heritage, regulatory and competitive pressures today work together, forcing businesses to integrate environmental concerns into their strategies. Once an imposed constraint, environmental action is progressively, increasingly, perceived as a factor contributing to progress, and is becoming an indispensable strategic advantage. Respecting environmental legislation is thus becoming a sign of enhanced competitiveness.

> The internalization of environmental challenges into the framework of economic activity imposes a 'double loop' learning period on all members of the organization. The strategic and operational targets set must reflect the nature and scope of environmental challenges. It is not a matter of drawing up specific standards for integrating environmental concerns into the organization's activities, but rather a question of radically overhauling the entire set of standards, assumptions and frames of reference used by all the actors involved, by linking the conventional economic dimensions of their activities to the environmental dimension. (Llerena 1996)

As a result businesses are moved to improve their corporate image and strengthen their legal position by implementing public information policies that ensure greater transparency regarding the company's environmental performance and intentions.

Businesses are also working to develop employee responsibility, so that the notion that the environment is everyone's business can make headway. Businesses are thus showing their willingness to seek solutions to environmental problems on their own, but in a context and conditions that they feel are realistic and compatible with management constraints. Public authorities draw up environmental strategy and objectives, but the methods and solutions for attaining these goals remain a corporate prerogative.

Environmental management is thus considered to be a fully valid tool in business quality management, even if at the outset these two approaches are grounded in different interests (satisfying collective aims in the one case, customer–supplier contractual relationships in the second). By reducing environment-related costs, environmental management remains an economic goal in and of itself: appropriate consumption of raw materials, mastery of production costs, improved product quality, greater efficiency and reliability of the productive apparatus, optimal management of risk insurance contracts. Furthermore, in terms of standardization, satisfying environmental criteria constitutes a significant advantage for obtaining product quality labels and/or company certification.

At that level, we can consider that most of the businesses are regarding environmental management as a strategic tool for gaining competitive advantage (Shrivastava and Scott 1992, Shrivastava 1995). Then, based on what Welford and Barghava (1996) demonstrated from the ecological economics literature, businesses behaviour could be described at the intersection of three main environmental strategies:

- 'Excellence' and 'leading edge': this implies moving beyond compliance, viewing environmental management as good management seizing environmentally based opportunities that have arisen as a result of the environmental challenge and striving towards state-of-the-art environmental management (Roome 1992).
- 'Incorporation of the environmental management strategy into the overall corporate strategy': this implies giving due weight and importance to issues during the planning process and not including them as an afterthought. Welford and Gouldson (1993), Taylor (1992) and Newman and Breeden (1992) feel that the organization's environmental policy programmes and practices should be incorporated into all the activities of the business. Each and every aspect of an organization's environmental impact should be taken into consideration.
- 'Effective communication': communication, as explained by Buhr (1991) and Grayson (1992), plays a significant role in maintaining good public relations and in achieving competitive advantage.

A number of paths have been envisaged to respond to this challenge, via regulatory frameworks and standards (eco-audit regulations, environmental management standards), partnerships between public authorities and businesses (for example voluntary agreements), or the development of assistance tools for environmental management (for example guidelines for self-diagnostics, waste management audit). But, perhaps more importantly, many of the more recent initiatives on the environment have been market driven and are voluntary. Collectively their impact is to demand that businesses take more responsibility for the environmental damage which they create and to approach corporate environmental management in a more proactive way. (Welford 1996)

None the less, the multiplicity of approaches offered today brings into sharp focus the question of the needs and wishes of industrialists, and particularly small and medium-sized enterprises in this domain.

This paper aims to highlight the role of Company Environmental Schemes in the French context, contributing to the promotion of a global approach and facilitating integration of environmental awareness with business strategy. It also will show how the Company Environmental Scheme developed in France by ADEME (Agency for Environment and Energy Management) is a suitable response to industrialists' needs, and particularly those of small and medium-sized enterprises.

8.1   FROM REGULATION TO VOLUNTARY ACTION

Since the mid-1980s, the French government strategy concerning the environment has evolved. The emergence of the precautionary principle in legislation presented by Environment Minister Barnier in February 1995 was the real consecration of this new kind of regulation based essentially on voluntary schemes, rather than on regulatory negotiations (that is, set in a specified framework between public authorities and industrialists). This section focuses exclusively on the French method entitled 'Company Environmental Scheme' and the European Eco-Management and Audit Scheme. Other standards applicable to sites or products and environmental management will be not discussed here.

8.1.1 Regulatory Background

Since the passage of legislation (French law dated 19 July 1976) regarding the classification of installations in order to protect the environment, the European Community and the French state have added obligations to the load borne by businesses, including impact studies, requests for permits, and so on. Up to now, environmental legislation has been dominated by a 'command and control' principle.

At the European level, the European Commission has extended its role since 1993, and the White Paper on 'Growth, competitiveness and employment' refers explicitly to the 'demand for a new model of sustainable development'. Likewise, the fifth Action Programme focuses on this concept. The Commission's role, in keeping with the institutional dynamics of the European Union, is one of initiative, as well as that of monitoring the application of this legislation by the member states. The limitations of this mode of functioning have led the Commission to develop other instruments that underpin environmental legislation in order to guarantee its efficacy. Two new tools, among others, are set to change the EU regulatory context applicable to the environmental impacts of industry. These are the EMAS Regulation adopted 29 June 1993 and the Integrated Prevention Pollution Control directive adopted 24 September 1996.

The surveillance of compliance with the measures prescribed in regulations and permits has led to the application of many penalties in France. In addition, an ordinance adopted on 1 March 1993, commonly called the 'integrated ordinance', sets forth minimum national standards, guided by principles based on the best available technology at acceptable cost. These standards may be tightened at the local level if necessary, by prefectural ordinance regarding permits. The aims of the 'integrated ordinance' are to ensure a high degree of protection for the environment and for residents. This benchmark is intended to: enhance the clarity of regulations; ensure legal security of operators by avoiding unfair competition; protect natural sites and habitats, and keep waste, risks and noise under control; and lastly, limit the transfer of clean-up responsibility from industrialists to local authorities. Furthermore, joint schemes supported by public authorities and industrialists have been set up regarding products and production sites. To be precise, it is important to note that this ordinance has been annulled by the Council of State on 21 October 1996; but the spirit of this integrated ordinance will be preserved any way.

8.1.2   The Approach and Contents of the Company Environmental Scheme set up by the French Environment Ministry

Legislative advances made during the 1990s signal a gradual transition from a regime of repairing of environmental damage to a regime aimed at preventing harm to natural surroundings. This is why the Environment Ministry, seeking to supplement its regulatory functions, felt the need to monitor French companies in their approach to environmental performance and started to promote an action based on cooperation in order to arouse debate, rebuild the social link, and change ways of thinking.

This approach began in 1990, following up the thinking which had contributed to the elaboration of the National Environment Plan. The Company Environmental Scheme constitutes the main instrument of this policy. The new approach is that it addresses businesses in general, covering all companies regardless of their status, sector of activity, or size, and all corporate functions.

The voluntary process proposed by the Environment Ministry targets essentially large corporate groups, first because they possess the technical, human and financial resources that will allow them to take the leap and join the scheme quickly, and secondly in order to create momentum that will draw in other companies later. The basic principle is simple: there are no contractual ties between the company and the ministry, which simply validates the company's plan, and then the company does as it likes. Methodological support measures are provided by the ministry and a consultant (SKL Conseils); they constitute aids for thinking about the issues, and scientific back-up. An outline for drawing up the plan is also suggested: (1) internal and external factors that influence the company's environmental performance; (2) a balance sheet summarizing the company's environmental action; (3) the objective of the company and its commitment to the environment.

Company Environmental Schemes are by nature intended to introduce a degree of coordination into the handling of environmental issues: identification of problems, definition and planning of actions, estimation of information costs and involvement of personnel. The aim is to allow the company to carry out the process without the pressures of a crisis. The Company Environmental Scheme can thus be presented as a tool for the elaboration of a business strategy and information and communication policies. As a consequence, the decision to draw it up can only be taken at the highest level of the company, that is the level of chief executive officer, because it involves a full overhaul of the company's strategy. This condition seems essential; operational departments are not all equally receptive to environmental issues, and the contents of the plan involve the core strategy of the company. In short, as Tibor and Feldman (1996) noted, 'environmental management has gone from an add-on function to an integral part of business operations'.

At present some fifty companies have joined this initiative, including Aéroports de Paris, CIBA, EDF, Elf Atochem, Gaz de France, GSM, McDonald's France, Sanef and SNCF who have already published their Company Environmental Scheme.

GSM is an example; it is a major producer of granulated products (subsidiary of Arena, Ciments Français group) which started work in 1992 on a rolling environmental plan that sets out numeric targets in 15 sectoral plans. These plans focus in particular on resource conservation through reduced uptake of water-borne alluvial matter (10 per cent less over five years), better working conditions and high-quality plant improvements. The application of the plan is overseen by environmental monitoring committees made up of employees and outside stakeholders (community groups, elected officials, government authorities, and so on).

According to G. Winter,[2] the Company Environmental Scheme provides three main phases, allowing businesses to: identify and quantify the company's impacts on the environment; find and adapt the best solution to medium-term problems (in general a three- to five-year horizon); integrate environmental action into site management, product design and manufacturing, and even into the company's relationship with other partners; and plan the steps to be taken to reduce environmental impacts.

As a strategic methodological tool, dynamic and global, for integrating the environmental dimension into overall business management, the Company Environmental Scheme includes the specific feature of setting strategic targets, and emerges as an advanced and broad-based level of environmental thinking: the scheme covers not just one plant site, but encompasses the whole company or corporate group. The Environmental Scheme thus includes several approaches: the product approach, the site approach, and an approach by branch of activity. In this respect all the other narrower decision making tools that the company uses can be integrated under the Company Environmental Scheme. The elaboration of a scheme addresses all corporate functions, and all lines of activity should be allowed to make their contribution, notably through active participation in work groups. This broad implication has a double effect: for one, it makes it easier to collect data and draw up a balance sheet; for another, it reinforces the personal involvement of executive management and employees. The Company Environmental Scheme thus emerges as a structural framework enabling industrialists to go much further than just defining environmental action. It is without a doubt a reflection of executive management's desire to make a commitment to an environmental policy that extends beyond minimal regulatory compliance. The Company Environmental Scheme provides the chief executive officer with both an environmental performance chart that is as complete as possible, and a management tool.

There are two limits to this approach. First, dissemination of the scheme in small and medium-sized enterprises poses problems. These firms have neither the time, the human resources nor the financial means to undertake such a task on their own. In addition they need much more methodological support and even on-site help than do large groups. Secondly, for certain companies, this form of industrial code of conduct is clearly tenuous and problematic. It can be observed that their attitude has a tendency to be limited to charters that formalize and harmonize trade practices, rather than overhauling them altogether and placing some restrictions on prerogatives that hitherto had been unquestioned. It seems plausible that the commitments contained in these charters are all the more easily displayed as there is no serious verification of their actual application – Duclos (1991). The limitations of the Company Environmental Scheme (as of all environmental management schemes relying on voluntary action) are to be found particularly in this area: the question of effective control via the market and various stakeholders involved, outside of any coercive regulatory framework, is thus highlighted.

8.1.3 The Eco-Audit Regulation

The European Commission has undertaken to put into place the elements needed to establish and implement a veritable environmental management and audit scheme, on the strength of the Commission's role, laid out in the Single Act and the Maastricht Treaty, in promoting sustainable development, and the role of the industrial sector. After much debate, the European regulation EEC/1836/93 was adopted in full on 29 June 1993, allowing for the voluntary participation of industrial businesses in an EU-wide environmental management and audit system. It is applicable only to industrial companies and will be soon extend to the transportation, banking, and tourism sectors.

The main characteristics of this system are summarized below.

This regulation rests upon a requisite Europe-wide harmonization in the environmental domain, and particularly in the area of environmental management, for at least three reasons:

- pollution does not recognize boundaries;
- some countries are active on the scale of Europe, others are more broadly international; and
- market distortions may occur between different companies.

The companies that adopt this system are required to conduct an initial environmental review of their site(s) studied, set up an environmental management system and write a site-specific environmental statement each year. This statement is published after validation by an independent accredited certification body which first scrutinizes the environmental review and the environmental management system. On the condition that applicable environmental regulations are respected, the sites that are thus 'certified' will obtain the right to include a distinctive logo on corporate documents (but not on products or packaging), and will be listed in a register published in the Official Journal of the European Communities.

The aim here is not to shield the chief executive officer from any eventual liability, but to enable the company to manage both its environmental impacts and its environmental image. The eco-audit thus emerges as an integrated corporate management tool, whereby periodic use of environmental audits can contribute to the company's overall identity. The eco-audit has furthermore a leveraging effect, allowing companies to anticipate national and European regulations. The commitment to this approach leads companies to set up technology and regulatory intelligence services of national and international scope.

The environmental audit can provide significant opportunities for industrialists.

- Like any audit, the environmental audit should help a company highlight its strengths and weaknesses, and anticipate measures to be taken, without any outside pressure. In this framework, however, the publication stipulated by the regulation is a constraint industrialists cannot avoid.
- Industrialists must often work hard to obtain community acceptance of their plant. Participating in an eco-audit approach can help a plant or an industrial zone resolve some problems of relations with the community, notably through the development of better communication.
- With an audit the industrialist becomes aware of dysfunctional aspects of its site, and can save, even make money, by saving water, raw materials or energy.
- An audit also gives industrialists a better position for negotiating insurance premiums, because an environmental audit constitutes a sort of pledge to limit uncertainties and risks of negative environmental impacts.

This European regulation thus provides for reconciliation of voluntary action with a regulatory process. In several European countries this was the first attempt to introduce an environmental policy instrument on a voluntary basis. In fact the success of EMAS must be relativized, especially in France, because if we make a quick comparison between Germany and France, figures are as follow: 530 German sites are already 'certified' while only 9 French sites are in that situation; furthermore there were 116 German verifiers and only 10 French ones. One explanation could be the following: businesses, and particularly small and medium-sized enterprises, are in need of stimulation and monitoring but also of 'interpretation guidelines' so as to be able to implement an environmental management system into their organization. The Company Environmental Scheme proposes an answer to these industrialists.

8.2   ADAPTING THE COMPANY ENVIRONMENTAL SCHEME FOR SMALL AND MEDIUM-SIZED ENTERPRISES, AS PROPOSED BY ADEME

ADEME is a state industrial and commercial body established by the law of 19 December 1990. Under the joint responsibility of the French Ministries of the Environment, Industry and Research, ADEME is involved in energy conservation and energy renewable sources, air pollution, soil pollution, waste and noise. Then, ADEME plays its role of public expert, for example, by helping companies to anticipate market change and new standards in order to build environmental concerns into their development strategies.

Given its missions, ADEME has adopted a global and cross-disciplinary approach in the field of energy, air and waste. The agency develops this approach in liaison with businesses, especially small and medium-sized enterprises, because unlike large groups, these companies usually do not possess the information, knowledge base and implementation capacities needed to fully integrate environmental concerns. ADEME, working with the firms Coopers and Lybrand Consultants and SKL Conseil, has thus drawn up a Company Environmental Scheme approach that is complementary to the Environment Ministry Company Environmental Scheme. ADEME published its Company Environmental Scheme in October 1995, in liaison with the Environment and Industry Ministries. We will show how this approach is particularly well suited to the needs of small and medium-sized enterprises.

8.2.1 Background

In France, small businesses and industries make up a large part of the country's economic fabric (36,000 on record in 1992), and therefore constitute a prime target for environmental management. And yet, concern for environment seems to have become a significant issue for small and medium-sized enterprises mainly because of pressure exerted by large groups, for whom the argument of environmental competitiveness has taken on great importance.

Paying closer attention to the targeted small and medium-sized enterprises meant that adjustments have to be made to make the Company Environmental Scheme concept more accessible, for at least three reasons:

- businesses are not all at the same stage of development in terms of environmental management;
- inadequate information and stimulation of awareness within small and medium-sized enterprises on issues of environmental management; and
- various initiatives in this domain.

Among other initiatives, ADEME has undertaken since 1993 the development of a partnership approach to environmental management, targeting small and medium-sized enterprises. The agency's work in this domain is based on:

- the reference document on Company Environmental Schemes issued by the Environment Ministry;
- the eco-management working group made up of specialists from ADEME, including sectoral divisions and regional delegations;
- the in-depth analysis of work already carried out by ADEME; and
- experience garnered by the two consultants (Coopers and Lybrand; SKL Conseil).

These introductory remarks reveal the set of different tools that are available, embedded in the broader framework designed to accommodate a global environmental approach, that is the Company Environmental Scheme. Furthermore, the great many tools developed, regulatory and others, in the field of environmental management can no longer be submitted to industrialists as distinct processes. These tools constitute a coherent set of instruments to be given a new focus in the context of a broader policy framework, in which businesses will gradually build up a full range of managerial practice. The Company Environmental Scheme is not intended to replace standards or labels; it does, however, facilitate compliance with standards and label criteria via a flexible and pragmatic approach that businesses can apply themselves, using in-house resources.

8.2.2   A Method that Meets Industrialists' Needs

ADEME's goal is to help actors in the economy foresee changes in regulations, make well-informed decisions and improve the efficacy of their environmental management. To ensure the best possible dissemination, ADEME has sought to make the method more accessible for industrialists by taking their wishes into account.

Nevertheless, the main features of the scheme have been preserved:

- the broad scope of the environmental assessment and management tool;
- integration of environmental analysis as far upstream as possible in each of the company's functions;
- a dynamic office which gives the company a medium-term vision of its environmental strategy, and not just a snapshot of the action already undertaken;
- internal mobilization, which is to a certain extent a warranty for the scheme's success; and
- setting an example: publication of the Company Environmental Scheme (if the company so desires) has a major impact as an example for other companies and creates a significant push for emulation.

ADEME has also sought to give more consideration to various aspects that take on even greater importance for small and medium-sized enterprises. These are:

- development of a methodological approach that closely follows industrial concerns: benefits, costs, quality, improved performance;
- progressive implementation of the scheme: ADEME's goal is to see small and medium-sized enterprises as a whole gradually become aware of the importance of environmental issues and at least take the initial steps towards a Company Environmental Scheme by conducting an assessment of the company's position; and
- development of a training scheme to stimulate demand, which could take the form of partnerships for promotion of the scheme; these partners would act to relay information efficiently to small and medium-sized enterprises, notably at both local and sectoral levels.

Two requirements were imposed for the elaboration of the methodology:

- compatibility with actors' needs: it was very important that the actors in the economy were able to appropriate the tools, regardless of the rank, size or sector of activity of the company involved; and
- the widest dissemination possible: as it is not ADEME's role to take the place of engineering firms, it was important that businesses, as well as consultants and trade organizations, were able to use the method, either in its generic form or by adapting it to a particular sector.

8.2.3   Presentation of the Method Proposed by ADEME

The method is intended for businesses in all sectors to pursue activities that will enhance their performance, and become active and responsible in protecting the environment. The conditions *sine qua non* for the success of this method are: the unwavering commitment of the head of the company throughout the process; the motivation of all the company's personnel for the environmental cause; a strong commitment on the part of all involved, so as to achieve solutions that are quite the opposite of environmental alibis. To take all these dimensions into account, the course of action proposed was an approach that establishes links between all the functions in the company.

The method is presented in two separate manuals. The first is a methodological manual which constitutes a reference framework for the company's executive officer, allowing progress to be monitored and new phases of work to start up. This manual lets the executive take hold of the

Company Environmental Scheme and make it his or her own project. Next comes the operational manual, a practical guidebook intended for the environmental manager which contains specific guidelines for carrying out various tasks. It is very important to note that all the suggested tasks can be carried out either directly by in-house staff, or in collaboration with an outside consultant. The method allows the company to monitor closely the work contracted to a consulting firm. The duration of each of the phases described below is variable, depending to a large degree on the executive officer, previous experience with this sort of work, availability of information, and so on. In addition, given the rolling nature of these plans (a three- to five-year horizon), the Company Environmental Scheme emerges as a recurrently useful tool.

The first phase is *Achieving Awareness*; in this phase the company gathers readily available information and carries out a first series of immediate improvements. Internally this phase marks the company's commitment to the Company Environmental Scheme.

The chief executive's first task is to appoint an environmental manager, who thus possesses an official assignment, and an *ad hoc* working group comprising, if possible, representatives from all of the company's activities. Next in this phase, the working group gathers available information in order to draw up an initial assessment of the environmental risks and opportunities for the company. A first set of improvement goals can be set at this point. The expected results are identification and realization of immediate improvements without major financial implications or mobilization of personnel. At the close of this phase the head of the company must decide whether to pursue the scheme or not.

The second phase, *Knowing is Growing*, aims to enable companies to design and implement an environmental management system that fosters continual improvement of the companies' overall and environmental performance.

In the course of this phase the company evaluates in greater detail the environmental impacts of its activities, notably to better assess the proportional share each activity contributes to the impacts observed. On this basis, the working group under the leadership of the environmental manager identifies further improvements to be made, and sets short- and medium-term objectives by ranking the measures to be taken. The group also sets up and monitors the environmental programmes, and after evaluation makes adjustments to the existing systems as necessary. The expected results from this phase are principally the integration of environmental concerns with the regular activities of the business, the creation of mechanisms for anticipating regulatory changes and market trends, and a growing motivation for innovation on the part of the personnel. It is also important to note that cost/benefit analysis constitutes the core of this second phase.

When this work has been completed, the chief executive officer must decide if further external communication is desirable, thus leading into the third phase, *Gaining Recognition*.

In any event, and this is a crucial point, a recognition must exist internally, prior to the first two phases. This recognition is in fact the main engine driving the appropriation (and therefore the success) of the process by the company's entire personnel. In all cases the prime objective is to have the company's efforts recognized by its partners, and to distinguish the company from its competitors. The main results expected here are the enhancement of the company or its products, better integration into the fabric of the local community and greater customer fidelity.

8.2.4 Dissemination and Evaluation of the Method

The dissemination of the Company Environmental Scheme method is based on a range of actions. Today, dissemination is more specifically based on increasing awareness of the Company Environmental Scheme through ADEME participation in training for companies, partners and service providers.

8.2.4.1 A regional focus

A concern for the area's ecology has taken a central place in the local political debate – Levett (1996). The regional delegations of ADEME play a crucial role in disseminating agency policies; they are responsive at the local level to various key issues and their ability to mobilize local partners in an effort to build environmental quality and energy efficiency into local projects and actions made them a major actor of the dissemination of the Company Environmental Scheme. For this reason the Agency plans to launch a training and education programme aimed at various actors in the local economy (chambers of commerce and industry, technical consultants, and so on) so that the company's development can contribute to the economic development of the region. Furthermore they can play a significant supporting role (humanly and/or financially) for companies by helping them to implement their environmental process step by step. Today a few regional offices (Poitou–Charentes, Bretagne, Provence Alpes–Côte d'Azur, for example) have already launched the Company Environmental Scheme process in their respective regions, with companies drawn from a range of sectors. To describe succinctly the ECOLIA operation led by the Poitou–Charentes Delegation, we can say that its objective is to monitor 30 companies (in the agro-food sector) according to the first phase of the Company Environmental Scheme and to stimulate a need to pursue the action in phases two and three for at least three to five companies. After this test, it will be decided if ADEME will extend the operation to companies from other sectors. For a wider dissemination, one difficulty can be seen: we are in a very competitive sector where many actors, like public authorities and service providers, have already developed their own tools; the risk in giving businesses an unstructured vision of the action is so very high. ADEME's answer is to promote collective operations including Regional Council, DRIRE – Regional Representation of the Ministries of Industry and Environment– and local service providers to allow synergy.

8.2.4.2   Sectoral versions

The sectoral approach is designed to give partners easy access to experts with specialist knowledge about complex systems. In fact, it can be summarized as follows: companies' priorities, in terms of strategic management and environmental protection, vary from sector to sector. The tool offered to industrialists from different sectors should not be a general one, but should use the technical requirements for processes and pollutants relative to each activity, and in addition should highlight specific regulatory constraints. Industrialists who participated in the early stages of validation of the Company Environmental Scheme, aware of the importance of an integrated approach, also expressed the desire that ADEME should publish Company Environmental Scheme tools adapted to each sector of activity, working closely with the relevant trade organization and technical centres. Adapting a Company Environmental Scheme does not imply changing the foundations of the method but it will mean replacing general information by data or questions relevant to the sector under study. Advanced contacts have already been established in the areas of mechanical manufacturing, foundries, leather working, textiles, pulp and paper, as well as with various branches of the agro-food sector. In this last sector, about fifty small and medium-sized enterprises, from various branches (canned goods, beverages, animal food, delicatessen specialities etc.), some of which are already certified under ISO 9000, have volunteered to participate in a programme of dissemination of the Company Environmental Scheme. This programme has been launched jointly by ADEME and the Agriculture Ministry (Directorate Direction of Foodstuffs); the technical coordination is provided by ACTIA (Association for Technical Coordination for the Agro-food Industry) and ADEME.

ADEME and the French Plastics Convertors' Federation are partners in a joint pilot project which started up in 1994 and is slated to be terminated at the end of 1997. After a survey of close to 1,200 companies, aimed at identifying typical forms of pollution engendered in this sector, the federation decided to draw up a manual of environmental management for its industrial site. The Company Environmental Scheme was to serve as the working tool. In addition, ADEME and Coopers and Lybrand Consultants helped create environmental coordinators specialized in plastics. Implementation in the field has started, with the goal of enrolling about one hundred companies from this sector in an eco-audit process.

After training the technical centres' engineers in the method, the work is carried out in three phases: (1) realize a preliminary sectorial version; we will study the opportunities and constraints induced by the environment for the companies and survey the environmental impacts related to the sector; (2) validate this initial proposal through pilot projects in the framework of a training programme for some selected industrialists; (3) draft the final proposal, taking into account the information collected during the pilot operations.

8.2.4.3   Training and evaluation

A training programme is still being drawn up; it forms an indispensable complement to the promotion and dissemination of the Company Environmental Scheme method. Training is first of all ensured internally at ADEME; the Agency's engineers are well armed to effectively monitor and assist companies with their environmental plans because they have themselves fully integrated this method. Then comes outside training, first of all for companies and relay links, and then for technical consultants. The aim here is for companies to have access to enough information to set up their Company Environmental Scheme on their own if they so desire.

ADEME is now carrying on an evaluation study of current Company Environmental Scheme activities, covering not only the methodological tool and its innovative content, but also its dissemination. The Agency will thus possess:

- activity indicators;
- indicators regarding the adoption of the method by companies;
- feedback to be drawn on in the future; and
- information on the method's strong points and drawbacks.

The evaluation of the action undertaken constitutes a strategic aspect of the promotion and dissemination of the Company Environmental Scheme concept. This evaluation should enable ADEME and its partners and service providers to adjust to changes in the handling of environmental issues.

8.3   CONCLUSIONS

All the changes that we are now observing show that businesses are increasingly asserting an active and responsible role in their communities. Judged by their effectiveness, some think that businesses should take on a greater social and educational role alongside other institutions. This is the direct result of a social change, 'another way' of conceiving relationships with others. The desire to integrate environmental protection within a company will in general proceed down from the highest level of management, but the key to its success lies in the involvement of all stakeholders: employees, suppliers, customers. This 'top–down' approach would seem to offer the best chance for success, because it reduces uncertainty and broadens the rational action of the actors involved. Centralizing decision making at the highest hierarchical level allows an effective information system to be installed, offering strong incentives.

Lastly, all these instruments are dependent on a voluntary act on the company's part, that is to say the company decides, in light of its own needs and objectives, whether one or more of these instruments should be integrated into its strategic outlook.

Does all this mean that concerns for the environment provide a source of competitive advantage for businesses? Yes, even if it is still necessary today to break down the assumptions in many companies, notably in small and medium-sized enterprises. Protection of the environment carries non-negligible costs, and existing environmental regulations seem a heavy load to bear in the current economic context. And yet, the companies that have accepted the environmental challenge are for the most part companies that seem to be basically healthy, and which have successfully reconciled economic development and ecological progress. The Company Environmental Scheme should thus be useful in helping an increasingly large assortment of companies adopt as their own the concept of sustainable development. But the Company Environmental Scheme cannot be seen as an end in itself. Even if businesses follow this methodology, it will be only an internal reference, not an alternative to other references like the EMAS regulation or the ISO 14001 standard, just a way to go through these ones, as we have shown in this paper. Nevertheless, especially in France, there is a real debate between 'implementation versus certification'. Some large corporate groups would like to point out these internal reference they have developed, especially for cost reasons. The French Ministry of the Environment disagrees with this strategy because even if the results of such procedures were good from an environmental point of view, who would be able to certify it? And if we go further, in the context of the globalization of the economy, how would French businesses be able to extricate themselves? Environment appears today as a factor of differentiation in this context. How would they be able to point out these internal reference when even developing countries (South America and East Asia, for example) throw themselves into the ISO 14001? Beyond this set of problems, the real question is to know which forces are driving the market. The recognition of an official standard which corresponds to some precise environmental criteria? The recognition of a company and a name which can be seen as a synonym of quality and environmental respect? Either, does certification offer a real choice for businesses?

ENDNOTES

1. 'Company Environmental Scheme' constitutes the English translation of the French methodology 'Plan Environnement Entreprise', C. Avert.
2. German Winter is a German businessman, author of *Business and the Environment: A New Synergy, and advocates of an integrated environmental management.*

REFERENCES

Buhr, N. (1991), 'The Environmental Audit: Who Needs It?', *Business Quarterly*, Winter, 27–32.

Duclos, D. (1991), *Les Industriels et les Risques pour l'Environnement*, Paris: L'Harmattan.

Grayson, L. (1992), *Environmental Auditing*, Oxford: Technical Communications.

Levett, R. (1996), *Business and the Environment*, in R. Welford and R. Starkey (eds), *Business, the Environment and Local Government*, London: Earthscan Publications Ltd, pp. 251–268.

Llerena, D. (1996), *Internalisation de l'Environnement et Apprentissages dans les Organisations*, PhD in Sciences of the Economy, BETA, Université Louis Pasteur, Strasbourg.

Newman, J.C. and K.M. Breeden (1992), 'Managing in the Environmental Era', *The Columbia Journal of World Business*, Fall and Winter.

Roome, N. (1992), 'Developing Environmental Management Strategies', *Business Strategy and the Environment*, 1 (1), 11–24.

Shrivastava, P. (1995), 'Environmental Technologies and Competitive Advantages', *Strategic Management Journal*, 16, 183–200.

Shrivastava, P. and H.I. Scott (1992), 'Corporate Self-Greenwall: Strategic Responses to Environmentalism', *Business Strategy and the Environment*, 1 (1), 11–24.

Taylor, S.R. (1992), 'Green Management: the Next Competitive Weapon?', *Futures,* September, 669–80.

Tibor, T. and I. Feldman (1996), *ISO 14000, a Guide to the New Environmental Management Standards*, Irwin Professional Publishing.

Welford, R. (1996), *Corporate Environmental Management*, Earthscan Publications.

Welford, R.J. and A.P. Gouldson (1993), *Environmental Management and Business Strategy*, London, UK: Pitman Publishing.

Welford, R.J. and Barghava (1996), 'Corporate Strategy and the Environment: the Theory', in R. Welford (ed.), *Corporate Environmental Management*, Earthscan Publications.

9. The Use of Regulatory Mechanism Design in Environmental Policy: A Theoretical Critique

Matthieu Glachant

9.1 INTRODUCTION

For twenty years, the traditional question of the efficiency of the different instruments of environmental policy has been closed. On theoretical grounds, the superiority of economic instruments over regulatory ones has been established since the 1970s. Many economists consider that, on this point, the only remaining task of the profession is to persuade reluctant policy makers to expand their use. But, today, we are at a turning point and a new debate on policy instruments becomes increasingly necessary for two reasons. First, in the practitioners' world, an increasing number of new policy approaches are being designed and tested, such as voluntary agreements, eco-auditing schemes, informational approaches and so on. In this respect, it can be claimed that policy makers are much more imaginative than theorists. These novelties clearly require additional economic analysis. Secondly, in the academic world, a major innovation in standard microeconomics, the normative theory of incentives, is being extended to the field of environmental economics. In particular, it proposes truth-revealing mechanisms, solving information asymmetry problems between the regulator and the regulated firms (see, for instance, Segerson 1988, Loehman and Dinar 1994, or Laffont 1993). Such mechanisms appear as new and sophisticated policy options which could compete in the future with existing regulatory or economic instruments. This paper focuses on this theoretical invention. It presents the principles of mechanism design and discusses its potential for efficiently meeting environmental goals. It is argued that, despite its elegance, the normative power of mechanism design is dramatically weakened by the implicit assumption of zero administrative costs.

In the next section, we explain how mechanism design theory solves the strategic problem of information asymmetry between the regulator and regulated firms. In the third section, we discuss the use of such mechanisms in environmental policy. We argue that they require communication between each firm and the regulator. To the extent that communication costs are not taken into account in the analysis, it weakens their normative power, in particular when the number of regulated firms is high. In the fourth section, we show that our criticism is, in fact, similar to the criticism by Coase in 'The problem of social cost' of the Pigouvian tradition. Finally, we propose ways to bypass the problem. One route can be qualified as a pragmatic Pigouvian strategy whereas the other clearly breaks with the traditional analysis by developing the so-called neo-institutional project of Coase and others.

9.2   THE PRINCIPLES OF MECHANISM DESIGN

To make efficient environmental policies, the regulator needs information. In particular, he needs information about pollution abatement costs and this is true whatever the instrument used.[1] For instance, the regulator needs this information to select the adequate level of an emission tax. But these pieces of information are initially owned by the firms. This is the key question of the mechanism design literature: how can we design policies able to cope efficiently with information asymmetry between regulated agents and the regulator?

To collect this information, the trivial solution which consists in requesting information of firms raises a basic strategic problem initially identified by Hurwicz (1973): the firms know that information will be used by the regulator to design a policy which will affect their profits. Hence they have an incentive to manipulate reported information in order to influence the content of the policy. More explicitly, they have an incentive to announce overestimated pollution abatement costs in order to get a less ambitious policy. This result is in fact very general and can be stated as follows: communication between agents is subject to strategic manipulation if (i) the objectives sought by the emitter and the receptor differ and (ii) the receptor's decisions influence the emitter's gains.

To cope with the strategic communication problem, the theory of incentives considers the interactions between the regulator and the firms as relationships between one principal and n agents. In this framework, the goal is to design incentive schemes which render truth-telling profitable for firms. Such incentive schemes are called 'mechanisms' or 'implementation mechanisms'. To present how such mechanisms work, let us consider a simple example of environmental policy aimed at reducing the emission of pollution by an industry of n firms. The private pollution abatement cost of the firm i is C_i and the social benefit due to avoided external costs is B. Additionally, q_i is the private pollution abatement objective to be met by the firm i. Concerning benefit and cost functions, we made the following classical assumptions: $B''(Q) < 0$, $C_i''(q_i) > 0$, $C_i(0) = 0$ and $B'(0) > C'(0)$. Finally we assume that B is known by everyone and that C_i is only known by the firm i.

The goal of the regulator is to design a policy which allows the efficient allocation of private objectives $A^* = (q_1^*,..., q_n^*)$ with:

$$C_1'(q_1^*) = ... = C_i'(q_i^*) = ... = C_n'(q_n^*) = B'(\Sigma q_i) \qquad (9.1)$$

In mechanism design theory, we say that the regulator wants to implement a social choice function f that associates to each n-tuple $R = (C_1, ..., C_n)$ the desirable social state $A^* = (q_1^*,..., q_n^*)$.

We have seen that he cannot implement f directly since he does not know R. To get this information, the only solution is to request the information about C_i of the firm i. We have m_i, the message sent by i concerning the value of C_i. Of course, the message can be false or true. M is the space containing all the messages which can be sent by whatever firms.

To solve the strategic problem, the basic principle of mechanism design is that the regulator commits *ex ante* to using a result function which associates each n-tuple $(m_1,...,m_n)$ of messages sent by the n firms, with a particular policy represented by the allocation A:

$$F : (m_1,..., m_i,.. m_n) \longrightarrow A = (q_1,... q_i,... q_n) \qquad (9.2)$$

F is a function of M^n mapped into the allocation space.

The commitment of the regulator into F now provides each firm with an accurate view of the pollution abatement costs it will face, given the n-tuple of messages. In this situation, the incentive to manipulate information is stronger that ever: F directly indicates to the firm the effects of its message. Nevertheless this is the beginning of the solution since firms' communication strategies now depend on F. In this respect, the regulator is able to influence the firms' communication behaviour through this *ex ante* commitment. The problem is to identify the function F for which truth-telling communication strategies are profitable for the firms.

To characterize this function, we need to predict firms' communication behaviour. As explained by Palfrey (1992), each firm will define its communication strategy taking into account its expectations regarding not only the regulator's action (defined by F) but also the way the other firms will strategically behave: the adopted policy depends on the messages sent by all firms.

The situation is represented in Figure 9-1. The firms define their message within a strategic game $G(\mathbf{R})$ where $\mathbf{R}$ is the vector of the n private pollution abatement costs. Then, the regulator implements the allocation of private objectives A via the application of F on m, the n-tuple of messages.

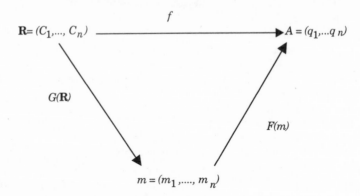

Figure 9-1 Principle of mechanism design

Source: Adapted from Laffont (1988, p. 113)

$G(\mathbf{R})$ is a game in which:

- The firms are the n players.
- The individual firm's strategy consists in sending m_1. M_n is thus the strategies combination space.
- P_i is the gain of the firm i associated with the combination of strategies $m = (m_1,...m_n)$.

The problem of the regulator is to know if he can commit himself to a function F which renders truth-telling profitable for the n firms. In formal terms, does a function F exist given the combination of strategies $m^* = (m_1^*,..., m_n^*)$ holds:

$$\begin{cases} F(m^*) = A^* \\ \forall \mathbf{R}, m^* \text{ is the equilibrium of the game } G(\mathbf{R}) \end{cases} \quad (9.3)$$

The general answer of the theory of incentives to this question is affirmative. The incentive mechanism F is a menu of linear contracts. Each contract associates a message with a regulation including an emission quota and a lump-sum payment to the regulator. Each individual firm has to choose from the menu the contract it wants to undertake, that is, its level of pollution and the associated monetary payment.

The level of the monetary payments is defined to render truth-telling profitable. For instance, reporting a high pollution abatement cost is profitable for a firm because it results in a low private pollution abatement objective. To thwart this incentive to report overestimated costs, the menu will associate the message 'my pollution abatement cost is high' with a higher monetary payment to the regulator than payments incurred by firms reporting a weaker cost. Of course, the difficulty lies in the setting of the appropriate level of payment. If the payment is too high, it leads the firm to report an underestimated cost.

In the menu, some payments are negative, that is, firms reporting low costs will be subsidized. In this respect, one key property of the mechanisms is that the budget neutrality constraint at the level of the regulator does not hold. This means that the sum of all the payments of the firms is always negative. The fact that the use of the mechanism results in public deficits reflects the informational rents enjoyed by the firms in their interactions with the less informed regulator. As a consequence, mechanisms are only second-best optimal.

9.3 THE NORMATIVE POWER OF MECHANISM DESIGN THEORY FOR ENVIRONMENTAL POLICY

For 15 years, such theoretical tools have been extensively applied to problems of economic regulation. The vast majority of these contributions have dealt with natural monopoly questions (for a survey, see Caillaud et al. 1988) whereas, concerning environmental policy, contributions were limited until recently (however, see Kwerel 1977; Segerson 1988). But the situation is quickly changing and such theoretical investigations are growing rapidly. In an environmental policy context, the models are built considering n firms with a continuity of possible types and the existence of information asymmetry between firms which leads to Bayesian equilibria (Laffont 1993).

At first glance, mechanism design theory proposes new and sophisticated policy instruments differing from the traditional emission standards, tradable permits and emission taxes. In fact, these traditional instruments are still present in the menu. In the example developed in the previous section, the regulations of the menu were based on emission quotas associated with lump-sum payments. The regulation can also be based on an emission tax. In this case, the menu is a linear tax schedule including the traditional Pigouvian tax and a lump-sum payment or subsidy. Thus each firm selects a particular taxation system. If the regulation is based on a tradable permit system, permit prices remain set by the market but a system of lump-sum payments is associated with the market transactions.

Hence the proper innovation of mechanism design is to associate these classical instruments with lump-sum side payments in menus of regulation. Menus and lump-sum payments play a unique role: to make the firms reveal their true pollution abatement costs. It follows that mechanism design needs to be assessed for what it is: a normative theory of information collection by the regulator.

In this respect, the normative power of such a project is dramatically weakened by an implicit assumption of zero communication costs. Indeed, mechanisms require from the firms, and much more from the regulator, an intense activity of communication and computation. The use of mechanisms allows the completion of the following tasks:

(1) The design by the regulator of the menu of regulations. The complexity of such a task will depend on the quality of information initially owned by the regulator.
(2) The communication of the menu to firms.
(3) The assessment by each firm of the menu, which leads to the definition of the messages to be sent to the regulator.
(4) The message collection by the regulator.
(5) The computation of the definitive regulation to be implemented.
(6) The implementation of the regulation which is tailored to each firm.

This process requires two ways communication between the regulator and each regulated firm. In this framework, the zero communication costs assumption is particularly heroic for environmental policy problems which are characterized by a high number of regulated firms. We can notice that, given the centralized nature of the mechanism (that is, it entails a dialogue between each firm and the regulator), this assumption is particularly unrealistic at the regulator level.

9.4   MECHANISM DESIGN AND THE NIRVANA APPROACH

The old debate between Coase and Pigou can illuminate this criticism of mechanism design. Let us briefly recall the traditional interpretation of 'The problem of social cost' of Coase (1960). If market transaction costs are nil and if property rights are non-ambiguously assigned, public intervention is not required to solve externalities: decentralized bargaining between polluters and pollutees will lead to a Pareto-optimal outcome. Moreover, and this is precisely the Coase Theorem, the allocation of property rights does not affect the outcome of such negotiations. It is now recognized that this traditional interpretation is rooted in a deep misunderstanding of the Coasean project. As a matter of fact, we can quote Coase himself (1988, p. 15):

I showed in 'The nature of the firm' that, in absence of transaction costs, there is no economic basis for the existence of the firm. What I showed in 'The problem of social cost' was that, in absence of transaction costs (...), the institutions which make up the economic system have neither substance nor purpose (...). What my arguments suggest is the need to introduce positive transaction costs explicitly into economic analysis so that we can study the world that exists. This has not been the effect of my article. The extensive discussion in the journals has concentrated almost entirely on the Coase theorem, a proposition about a world of zero transaction costs.

According to Coase, it is necessary to integrate transaction costs into economic analysis because they are inherent to an economic systems.[2] It is then as absurd to consider a world of zero transaction costs as it would be to consider a world of zero production costs. The 'Coase Theorem' helps to demonstrate this point: without any positive market transaction costs, decentralized bargaining prevents the emergence of any externalities and thus no environmental policies are required.

The Pigouvian tradition is especially criticized by Coase and his followers because it assumes that transaction costs related to public intervention are nil. Regarding mechanism design, we have in fact developed this argument. We criticized the fact that the normative analysis of mechanism design did not take into account the transaction costs incurred by the use of the mechanism. Demsetz (1969) wrote of the 'Nirvana approach'. According to him, the basic problem of welfare Pigouvian economics is the reference which is used to define externalities (or market failures in general). The externalities are deviations from a Pareto optimum defined in the ideal Walrasian world without any positive transaction costs. The Pigouvian tradition advocates public intervention to fill the gap between such ideal and real situations. It gives birth to a constant normative willingness to reach perfection (Nirvana). As we say in French 'le mieux est l'ennemi du bien' ('better' is the enemy of 'good') and beyond a certain level, the policy arrangements which are designed exhibit higher administrative costs than the resulting welfare increase. Concerning mechanism design, our point is that such a level is reached.

The alternative project of Coase is proposed in section VI of his article. Three types of transaction are distinguished and hence three kinds of transaction costs: (i) the market transaction costs, (ii) the administrative costs of organizing the transactions within a firm, and (iii) the administrative costs of organizing the transactions by the government, that is the administrative costs of central planning. Additionally, Coase qualifies the government as a super-firm given that its coercive power allows it to organize transactions in every part of the economic system. He then proposes the following prescriptions to cope with externalities:

- A reallocation of property rights through decentralized bargaining is better when market transaction costs are lower than the administrative costs of organizing the transactions within the firm or by the government.
- A long-term cooperation between polluters and pollutees or the merging of these agents into a single firm is better when its costs are lower than market transaction costs and administrative costs of public intervention.
- Public intervention is preferred when its administrative costs are lower than market and the firm's administrative costs.
- Finally, it could be better to do nothing if all the transaction costs of the above options are higher than the resulting increase in welfare.

The different options proposed by Coase are not necessarily the relevant ones. In particular, the merging of polluters and pollutees seems quite rare. But the core of the Coasean project is elsewhere: his approach is based on the comparative assessment of the sum of the transaction and production costs of alternative options (including the *status quo*).

9.5　CONCLUDING COMMENTS: THE ROUTES TO OVERCOME THE OBSTACLE

The criticism of mechanism design developed in this article does not signify that incentives theory is useless in designing new efficient policy instruments. While keeping the theoretical building blocks of incentives theory and the zero communication cost assumption, a solution is to develop a second-best approach (or a third-best one, in fact, since incentive schemes are only second-best optimal!) consisting of analysing the properties of more simple mechanisms embodying less stringent communication requirements. Nevertheless, this approach is fundamentally pragmatic since these less information-demanding mechanisms are not designed using theory (it will require coping with information costs): they are proposed and assessed. In fact, it consists in following a similar way to that of Baumol and Oates (1988) who have simplified the traditional theory of policy instruments with their second-best approach which considers a social pollution abatement objective exogeneously given.

Another route consists in explicitly taking into account information costs into the analysis. If we recall that information costs are in fact transaction costs, it leads to a completely new theoretical orientation initiated by Coase (1960) and Demsetz (1969): a neo-institutionnal analysis of the efficiency of environmental policies. This route is more ambitious and thus inevitably more difficult.[3]

Finally, another radical and obvious way to escape the Nirvana illusion is to invest analytical efforts in the evaluation of the existing policy instruments which are still waiting for economic analysis (such as voluntary agreements and eco-auditing schemes).

ENDNOTES

1. He also needs information about environmental external costs. The goal of the monetary valuation techniques of environmental damages is typically to provide the regulator with this information.
2. There is no commonly accepted definition of transaction costs (see Allen 1991). In this paper, transaction costs are the costs of organizing a transaction (on a market, in a firm and so on.). They are, *inter alia*, information costs, negotiation costs and monitoring costs.
3. For a theoretical work on this line, relaxing the zero administrative costs assumption, see Glachant (1996a, 1996b).

REFERENCES

Allen, D.W. (1991), 'What are Transaction Costs?', *Research in Law and Economics*, 14, 1–18.

Baumol, W. and W.E. Oates (1988), *The Theory of Environmental Policy*, Englewood Cliffs, NJ: Prentice Hall.

Caillaud, B., R. Guesnerie, P. Rey and J. Tirole (1988), 'Government Intervention in Production and Incentives Theory: a Review of Recent Contributions', *Rand Journal of Economics*, 19 (1), 1–26.

Coase, R.H. (1960), 'The Problem of Social Cost', *The Journal of Law and Economics*, 3, 1–44.

Coase, R.H. (1988), *The Firm, the Market, the Law*, New York: University of Chicago Press.

Demsetz, H. (1969), 'Information and Efficiency: Another Viewpoint', *Journal of Law and Economics*, 12 (1), 1–22.

Glachant, M. (1996a), 'Efficacité des Politiques Environnementales et Coûts d'Information: une Approche Coasienne', PhD dissertation, CERNA, Ecole des Mines de Paris.

Glachant, M. (1996b), 'The Cost Efficiency of Voluntary Agreements: a Coasean Approach', paper presented at the International Conference on the Economics and Law of Voluntary Approaches in Environmental Policy, Venice, 18–19 November.

Hurwicz, L. (1973), 'The Design of Mechanisms for Resource Allocation', *American Economic Review*, 63 (2), 1–30.

Kwerel, E. (1977), 'To Tell the Truth: Imperfect Information and Optimal Pollution Control', *Review of Economic Studies*, 44, 595–602.

Laffont, J.J. (1988), *Fundamentals of Public Economics*, Cambridge: MIT Press.

Laffont, J.J. (1993), 'Regulation of Pollution with Asymmetric Information', Annual Conference of the European Association of Environmental and Resource Economics (EAERE), Fontainebleau, 17–18 June.

Loehman, E. and A. Dinar (1994), 'Cooperative Solution of Local Externality Problems: a Case of Mechanism Design Applied to Irrigation', *Journal of Environmental Economics and Management*, 26, 235–56.

Palfrey, T.R. (1992), 'Implementation of Bayesian Equilibrium: the Multiple Equilibrium Problem in Mechanism Design', in J.J. Laffont (ed.), *Advances in Economic Theory, Sixth World Congress*, Cambridge: Cambridge University Press, pp. 283–323.

Segerson, K. (1988), 'Uncertainty and Incentives for Non Point Pollution Control', *Journal of Environmental Economics and Management*, 15, 87–98.

10. Environmental Privatization and Technological Norms

Martin E. Diedrich

10.1 INTRODUCTION

In recent years a number of countries have adopted policies aimed at giving a greater role to private ownership in the natural resource sector. For example, in Britain the regional water companies have been privatized and have been given a considerable degree of control over the exploitation of the nation's regional water resources; similar policies have been followed in France and other European countries; see Buller (1996) for a survey and NRA (1994) for a detailed document on the British framework. Typically such privatization is accompanied by a whole range of new regulatory instruments such as technological standards on water treatment plants, minimum standards on drinking water quality, price controls and maximum withdrawal quotas. While some of these instruments address problems of monopolistic behaviour and other forms of imperfect competition, the bulk of regulatory measures are concerned with establishing 'good practices' aimed at maintaining the quality of the newly privatized resources; as a shorthand, we may refer to these measures as 'technological norms' imposed on water producers.

The present paper provides a novel theoretical justification for the need to impose regulatory measures on the privatized water industry. We argue that technological norms are a necessary response to a certain type of *inflationary pressure* that emerges in connection with privately owned water resources. This inflationary pressure is not due to any form of market failure but is a natural consequence of the arbitrage behaviour of water producers. If a nation's water resources are transferred into private ownership, the government has to keep the associated inflationary pressure in check, and the only way to do this is by imposing technological norms on water producers.

Our argument is based on an analysis of the *price implications* of unregulated water privatization. We establish a fundamental intertemporal price condition that has to be satisfied if unregulated water companies are to adopt a water extraction policy that is sustainable in the long run. This price condition is similar to the Hotelling Rule (1931) familiar from the theory of exhaustible resources. Indeed, our condition may be interpreted as a generalization of the Hotelling Rule from the case of *exhaustible* resources (oil) to the case of *renewable* resources (water). As a shorthand, we refer to our price condition as the 'Modified Hotelling Rule'.

The Modified Hotelling Rule shows that in the absence of technological norms, the only mechanism by which water owners will be induced to adopt a sustainable water extraction policy consists of a continual *rise* in the price of water, in a manner similar to the rising price of oil under the original Hotelling Rule. If resource prices do *not* rise as prescribed by the Modified Hotelling Rule, private resource owners will be induced to reduce maintenance work and to withdraw more water than is environmentally sustainable, thereby destroying the nation's water resources. The unregulated privatization of natural resources thereby creates *inflationary pressure*, requiring ever rising water prices to ensure the maintenance of the nation's water resources. This inflationary pressure threatens the long-term viability of the economy by eroding the incomes of those households who do not own water resources; we refer to this process as the 'Hotelling Dynamics'. Closer inspection of the Modified Hotelling Rule reveals that technological norms are the only way to eliminate this inflationary pressure; government regulation serves to 'tame' the Hotelling Dynamics. In this light, government regulation has the function of making private resource ownersip *compatible* with stable prices and with a viable income distribution.

Our results follow from very basic assumptions on competitive behaviour and do not rely on any specialist features of the model; the Modified Hotelling Rule holds for every economy where water resources are privately owned by profit-maximizing water companies. We stress that the inflationary pressure of the Hotelling Dynamics is *not* caused by any form of market failure; it will be in force even if future demand and future prices can correctly be anticipated and if all markets are perfectly well-behaved. Thus, rather than being a response to *market failure*, technological norms act as a fundamental *precondition* for the normal operation of markets if water resources are in private ownership.

The analytical insights from our investigation of the Modified Hotelling Rule have powerful policy implications. By identifying the inflationary pressure associated with unregulated water production, we provide a fresh perspective on the intimate link between government regulation of water *prices*, on the one hand, and government regulation of water *quality*, on the other hand. In the light of the Modified Hotelling Rule, we can show that any attempt to control the pricing policies of private water producers by government regulation has to be accompanied by suitable technological norms; price regulation without quality regulation would result in undesirable resource destruction.

The paper is organized as follows. Section 10.2 discusses the physical and institutional background of the water problem. Section 10.3 outlines the underlying economic problem and presents a simple example that encapsulates the basic idea of this paper. Section 10.4 sets up the analytical framework. Section 10.5 derives the Modified Hotelling Rule and establishes the Hotelling Dynamics. Section 10.6 interprets the Modified Hotelling Rule by contrasting the case of renewable resources with the case of exhaustible resources. Section 10.7 discusses the policy implications.

10.2 PHYSICAL AND INSTITUTIONAL BACKGROUND

This section briefly surveys the key physical properties of water resources and sketches the regulatory framework for privatized water companies in Britain.

Water resources are renewable but potentially destructible resources. A nation's water system comprises a complex network of interrelated local and regional water cycles whose behaviour depends heavily on the surrounding geographical and climatic conditions. Only a very small part of the circulating water is directly accessible for human withdrawal, typically while passing through lakes and rivers or while being stored in aquifers. Moderate amounts of withdrawal do not affect the nature of a local water system as underground acquifers slowly replenish themselves from surface water and lakes receive inflows from rainfall and contributing rivers. However, if human extractions are very high, the accompanying changes in the geographical and climatic conditions supporting the regional water cycle will reduce the regenerative capacity of the regional water system, meaning that the potential for sustainable future withdrawals declines. For example, if the withdrawals from an underground aquifer exceed inflows for a long time, the walls of the aquifer may dry out and become inpenetrable for the surface water from above, and excessive withdawals of surface water may change the local soil, resulting in a reduced capability of the soil to absorb local rainfall and hence in a reduced rate of water replenishment. Very often, the degradation of a water resource cannot easily be reversed; in many cases, recovery from degradation will be very slow or even impossible. For introductory surveys of various physical aspects of water resources and water management, see Leopold (1974), Goudie (1990) or Kluge and Schramm (1988).

Both the supply of water and the demand for water are highly inflexible. On the demand side, household demand is characterized by minumum consumption requirements for each individual person while industrial demand exhibits strong complementarities in many agricultural and manufacturing processes; as a result, society's overall demand for water exhibits a very strong downward rigidity. To a certain extent water demand can be reduced by preventing unnecessary leakages and by recycling industrial water, but the scope for such measures is limited and realistically one cannot expect to reduce the total demand for water below a certain minimum level without adversely affecting the welfare of society. On the supply side, sustainable water extraction levels from local water sources are finite and typically not much larger than those required by current demand levels. In countries with access to the sea, water supplies can be increased by using desalination processes on sea water, thereby allowing in principle unbounded water supplies. However, desalination is extremely costly and not a desirable alternative to supplies from local freshwater sources. Currently most countries experience various degrees of water shortages. For example, in Britain in 1994 four of the ten regional water companies in England and Wales were faced with water resources whose long-run supply potential exceed current demand by less than 15 per cent; any further increase in demand would require unsustainably large extraction rates (see NRA 1994). Countries with non-trivial water shortages include India, China, South Africa, Poland and Israel (in ascending order of severity); see WRI (1986, 1992).

The adverse effects of current water extractions on the future quality of the water resource can be moderated by a policy of active resource management involving deliberate human maintenance activities. A typical example would be a reforestation programme that increases the capability of the soil to absorb local rainfall and thereby reduces the local water loss due to natural water outflows. Other maintenance activities alter the quality of the water resource by embedding various forms of man-made capital equipment in the natural environment (dams, pipelines). Active resource management makes it possible to maintain the quality of the water resource while increasing the level of annual water extractions; however, such increases in sustainable annual water supplies will always remain within certain strict bounds that are set by the natural characteristics of the regional water system.

As a background for our theoretical discussion of technological norms, we now briefly review the regulatory framework imposed on the privatized water industry in Britain; see Buller (1996) and NRA (1994) for further details. Privatization of all regional water companies was instituted by the Water Act from 1989. Under the Water Act, financial responsibility for water abstraction, purification and delivery lies entirely with these private companies. Water companies are supervised by three separate regulatory bodies that are responsible for price control, drinking water quality and resource management, respectively. The body responsible for resource management is the National Rivers Authority (NRA); the body responsible for price control is OWFAT.

The 1989 framework has been modified by the Environment Protection Act from 1990, the Water Resources Act from 1991 and finally the Environment Act from 1995 (see Water Law 1995). The Environment Act led to a closer integration of the various aspects of water regulation; in particular, the National Rivers Authority has been replaced by a more powerful body called the Environment Agency. Despite these changes, the basic institutional structure under the new Act is very similar to the previous structure; in either case, private regional water producers are supervised by a government body responsible for maintaining the quality of regional water resources. Here I outline the institutional arrangements under the 1989 Act, as these are more fully documented; similar arrangements can be found under the 1995 Act.

Under the 1989 Act, the National Rivers Authority (NRA) acts as a *licensing authority* for water abstraction and sets various targets as regards the quality of water resources (leakage reduction, balanced water flows in rivers etc.). The NRA grants abstraction licences to companies that pursue a satisfactory policy toward meeting these targets and has the right to withhold licences from companies violating these policies; see NRA (1994, pp.11–14). Apart from the right to grant or withhold licences, the NRA has only very limited control over the concrete activities or development plans of the private water companies. In particular, the NRA is *not* meant to 'play a significant role in financing, developing or operating future new resources. (...) It needs to act independently in assessing proposals or monitoring developments, as opposed to becoming an agent or operator arguing for a particular water resource option' (NRA 1994, p. 54). This statement explicitly excludes the NRA not only from *financing* proposed new resource management schemes, but also from *developing* or *promoting* such schemes; the NRA is reduced to playing a mere *supervisory role*. The Environment Agency that has replaced the NRA under the 1995 Act plays a similar role with regard to the private water companies.

The *quality supervision* exercised by the National Rivers Authority after 1989 and by the new Environment Agency after 1995 is closely linked to the *price supervision* exercised by the OFWAT body. Typically, improvements in resource management as required by the Environment Agency will be combined with a relaxation in the price restrictions that OFWAT imposes on water companies. Our discussion of the Modified Hotelling Rule in the remainder of this paper will shed new light on this intimate link between price and quality control.

10.3 THE ECONOMIC PROBLEM

This section previews our main argument by studying a very simple example. Sections 10.4–6 will present the argument in a more general formal framework.

Consider an economy that has a fixed number of regional water resources ('plots'). For simplicity, assume that all plots are identical. Water resources are privately owned by profit-maximizing investors and can be traded on markets. At the end of year t, the price of a plot is v_t. Water is extracted during the period and sold at the end of the period at market prices, y_t. For simplicity, assume that extraction is costless. The amount of water extracted from the plot during year t is f_t. Each plot is capable of generating a sustainable output of 5 units of drinking water per year; by restricting the annual water extraction to 5 units per year, the owner of the plot ensures that the quality of his plot remains intact so that in the following year the same plot will once again be capable of generating 5 units of water. However, it is possible for the owner of a given plot to extract more than 5 units, say by tapping sensitive layers of the aquifer. Let's suppose that the maximum extraction level per year is 105 units of water. Overextraction will result in quality degradation; for simplicity, assume that any extraction in excess of 5 units will result in a complete destruction of the resource, implying that the potential for future extractions from the given plot will drop to zero. Water is an essential commodity, in the sense that, in any one year, a certain amount of drinking water has to be supplied. If all resource owners were to extract more than 5 units per plot in any given year, all plots would be destroyed and next year's demand for water could no longer be satisfied. Thus, for society to survive, some resource owners have to restrict their annual extractions to sustainable levels of 5 units per plot. Under what conditions will a private, profit-maximizing resource owner refrain voluntarily from overextraction? The answer to this question will yield the Modified Hotelling Rule.

Each resource owner treats his plot as an investment project. The owner can choose between two possible extraction policies. Either he restricts annual extractions to 5 units, thereby maintaining the original quality of the plot, or he extracts the maximum amount of 105 units, thereby destroying the plot. Which of these two options is chosen depends on the associated costs and revenues. Consider a given year, say year t. For any given plot, the initial capital outlay needed to obtain the plot at the beginning of year t is v_{t-1}, the market price of a plot. The opportunity costs per unit of investment are given by the interest rate, r; by investing v_{t-1} at the beginning of year t into his plot, the owner of the plot loses rv_{t-1} in interest earnings during the year. Thus, the total costs of running the plot during the year are $(1 + r)v_{t-1}$, comprising the initial capital outlay and the opportunity costs of that outlay. These total costs will be the same for all resource owners, regardless of the extraction policy adopted. By contrast, revenues depend on the choice of extraction policy. At the end of year t, the resource owner has two potential sources of revenue from his plot. On the one hand, he sells the water f_t extracted during the year at price y_t, giving revenue $y_t f_t$. On the other hand, if the plot is still intact at the end of the year, he can also sell his plot at price v_t, giving revenue v_t per plot. We assume that, at the end of the year, the plot will have no value if it has been destroyed due to overextraction. Only if the annual harvest f_t was restricted to 5 units can the plot be sold at price v_t at the end of the year.

We can now compare the costs and revenues of the two possible extraction policies. Costs are $(1 + r)v_{t-1}$ in either case, revenues are $5y_t + v_t$ in the case of sustainable extractions and $105y_t$ in the case of overextraction. Profit-maximizing owners will never adopt an extraction policy where costs exceed revenues. Thus, if resource destruction is to become unprofitable, the revenues from overharvesting must be smaller than total costs, yielding the following price condition for sustainable water extraction:

$$(1 + r)v_{t-1} > 105y_t \tag{10.1}$$

Suppose that condition (10.1) is in fact satisfied. Condition (10.1) ensures that no resource owner will adopt the unsustainable extraction policy. But (10.1) in itself does not ensure that the sustainable policy will in fact be adopted. To make sustainable extraction profitable, the revenues of the sustainable extraction policy must be large enough to cover all costs; in equilibrium, revenues will be exactly *equal* to costs (otherwise there would be a pure profit, inducing further capital movements into the water industry). Thus we obtain our second condition:

$$(1 + r)v_{t-1} = 5y_t + v_t \tag{10.2}$$

In a competitive economy, both conditions must be satisfied if resource owners are to abstain from overextraction. Combining (10.1) and (10.2) yields:

$$y_t < (1/(105 - 5))v_t \tag{10.3}$$

Substituting (3) into (1) yields:

$$(1 + r)v_{t-1} > (105/(105 - 5)) y_t \tag{10.4}$$

Denote the term $(100/(100 - 5))$ by $(1 + g)$; in our example, $g = 5\%$. The number g is called the *natural productivity rate* of the water resource; it measures the rate at which the the sustainable extraction level (5 units) can compete with the unsustainable extraction level (105 units). Rate g will drop to values close to zero if the unsustainable extraction level is much larger than the sustainable level. Using g, we can rewrite (10.4) as follows:

$$v_t > (1 + r)/(1 + g) y_{t-1} \tag{10.5}$$

Condition (10.5) is a special case of the Modified Hotelling Rule developed in Section 10.4 below. It gives an intertemporal condition on the price of the water resource; the price of the water resource in any given year must be larger than $(1 + r)/(1 + g)$ times its price in the preceding year if sustainable harvesting is to be profitable when compared with unsustainable harvesting. Typically, we expect the unsustainable harvest levels to be very large compared with the sustainable levels, meaning that the natural productivity rate g will be close to zero. Rate g therefore is likely to be smaller than the interest rate r; condition (10.5) then implies that the price of the water resource has continually to grow in every single year. This identifies the inflationary pressure resulting from unregulated private ownership of natural resources.

Our example was based on a number of very strong assumptions. In particular, we assumed zero extraction costs and a very limited number of potential extraction policies. Sections 10.4 and 10.5 derive the Modified Hotelling Rule in a much more general context.

10.4 ENVIRONMENTAL TRANSFORMATIONS

In this section, we generalize the ideas from Section 10.3 within a more general framework, allowing for an arbitrary number of competing extraction policies where each extraction policy may be costly in the sense that it requires various commodity inputs and labour inputs. All the vectors and scalars defined in this section are non-negative.

Each 'environmental transformation' (or 'extraction policy') is equivalent to a production process that transforms inputs into outputs. The water system enters the transformation process as an input at the beginning of the period and leaves the transformation process as an output at the end of the period, possibly in a different quality. The water supplies that have been extracted from the resource during the period are treated as a joint output of the resource transformation. Embedded man-made capital equipment is treated as an inseparable part of the water resource; a regional water system containing a dam is considered to be of a different quality than the same water system without the dam. Altogether, there are M distinct qualities (or 'types') of water resource. There is one type of water and one type of labour and there are m types of reproducible commodities other than water. Formally, the jth environmental transformation is represented by the quintuple $(q_j, k_j, l_j, h_j, f_j)$, with the following temporal structure between inputs and outputs: $(q_j, k_j, l_j) \rightarrow (h_j, f_j)$.

The $M \times 1$ vector q_j identifies the water resources that enter into the transformation at the beginning of the period, while the $M \times 1$ vector h_j identifies the water resources that leave the transformation at the end of the period. Scalar f_j identifies the maximum permissible water extractions under policy j. The $m \times 1$ vector $\boldsymbol{k}_j$ gives the commodity inputs (including durable capital goods) required by the jth extraction policy for maintenance purposes; scalar l_j gives the associated labour inputs. Each environmental transformation uses exactly *one* unit of one particular type of water resource and transforms it into exactly *one* unit of another (possibly identical) type of water resource. Hence, vectors $\boldsymbol{q}_j$ and $\boldsymbol{h}_j$ are both *unit vectors*. If $\boldsymbol{q}_j$ is the kth unit vector $\boldsymbol{e}_k$ and $\boldsymbol{h}_j$ is the zth unit vector $\boldsymbol{e}_z$, then the jth extraction policy transforms one individual water resource of quality k (at the beginning of the period) into a one individual water resource of quality z (at the end of the period).

An extraction policy that maintains the water resource at quality k while providing positive annual water supplies is called *k-sustainable*. Formally, the jth environmental transformation is called k-sustainable if $\boldsymbol{q}_j = \boldsymbol{h}_j = \boldsymbol{e}_k$ and if $f_j > 0$. If the jth extraction policy is k-sustainable, we also say that the corresponding water extractions f_j are k-sustainable. By contrast, if $\boldsymbol{g}_j = \boldsymbol{e}_k$ and $\boldsymbol{h}_j = \boldsymbol{e}_z \neq \boldsymbol{e}_k$, policy j is called *k/z-degrading*.

Suppose policy j is k-sustainable and policy i is k/z-degrading with $f_i > f_j$. We define the *natural productivity rate* of policy j relative to policy i as $g_{ji} = (f_i/(f_i - f_j)) - 1$; by construction, $g_{ji} > 0$. Intuitively, the natural productivity rate measures the degree to which k-sustainable water extractions f_j approach the extraction potential f_i that *would* be feasible if the owner were to accept a resource degradation from quality k to quality z. Rate g_{ji} is very large if the sustainable annual extraction level f_j is very close to the larger but unsustainable level f_i; it is close to zero if the sustainable level is negligible relative to the unsustainable level.

The reader will note that our framework is very general and that we impose hardly any substantial restrictions on $\boldsymbol{q}_j$, $\boldsymbol{k}_j$, l_j, $\boldsymbol{h}_j$, and f_j; the framework thereby enables us to capture a very broad class of patterns of environmental change within the context of production theory. An alternative representation of environmental change was given in Diedrich (1995). The current framework is more flexible than our original approach and lends itself more easily to an investigation of the deeper structural features of environmental change; see the path-breaking study of Erreygers (1996) for a detailed discussion.

10.5 PRICE DYNAMICS

This section identifies a fundamental price condition that has to be satisfied if private resource owners are to abstain from resource destruction. This condition is a natural extension of the Hotelling Rule for exhaustible resources; we call it the 'Modified Hotelling Rule'. All the price vectors defined in this section are non-negative.

We wish to abstract from any form of market imperfection and assume that all water resources are privately owned and traded on competitive markets. There is a resource market at the beginning and at the end of each period; the market at the end of period t is identical with the market at the beginning of period $t + 1$. The $1 \times M$ vector v_t gives the resource prices at the end of period t (at the beginning of period $t + 1$); the kth component of v_t is denoted by $v_t^{(k)}$. Typically, investors will not trade resources at every date but will maintain resource ownership for more than one period; in such cases we assume that the owner evaluates his non-traded water resource by using internal accounting prices that accurately reflect competitive market prices. The market price of an individual water resource reflects its value as a potential source of water extractions.

By convention, water bills are paid at the end of the period; scalar y_t gives the price of water at the end of period t. We assume that water is an essential commodity and that its price is positive. For each of the m reproducible commodities other than water there is a market at the end of each period; the $1 \times m$ vector p_t gives the commodity prices at the end of period t (at the beginning of period $t + 1$). The nominal wage rate in period t is w_t; wages are paid at the end of the period, out of the incoming revenue. In each period, there is a money market in which money can be borrowed and lent at nominal interest rate r_t; we think of r_t as the intertemporal opportunity cost of committing money to real investment projects. For simplicity, we assume that w_t and r_t are constant over time. To avoid considerations of uncertainty, we assume that investors can accurately predict all future prices.

In period t, extraction policy j requires initial capital outlays $p_{t-1}k_j + v_{t-1}q_j$, covering the required commodity inputs k_j and the required water resources q_j during the period. These capital outlays give rise to (actual or notional) interest payments $r(p_{t-1}k_j + v_{t-1}q_j)$ during the period. Labour inputs during the period are l_j and result in wage payments wl_j at the end of the period. Thus, at the end of period t the total costs of the jth extraction policy are $(1 + r)(p_{t-1}k_j + v_{t-1}q_j) + wl_j$. The total revenues of policy j are $v_t q_t + y_t f_j$, where $v_t q_t$ gives the remaining value of the resource at the end of the period and $y_t f_j$ gives the revenues from water sales.

In a competitive economy, no extraction policy must yield any extra profits. Thus:

$$(1 + r)(p_{t-1}k_j + v_{t-1}q_j) + w_t l_j \geq v_t q_t + y_t f_j \qquad \text{(for all } j\text{)} \quad (10.6)$$

If the weak inequality $\geq$ in (10.6) is replaced by an equality $=$, policy j *breaks even*; if $\geq$ is replaced by a strict inequality $>$, policy j makes *losses* and is said to be *unprofitable*. Profit-maximizing investors will not pursue an extraction policy that is unprofitable; they would rather sell the resource at the beginning of the period and let their money capital yield interest earnings in the money market. Thus, for a extraction policy j to be adopted, we must have:

$$(1 + r)(\mathbf{p}_{t-1}\mathbf{k}_j + \mathbf{v}_{t-1}\mathbf{q}_j) + w_t l_j = v_t q_t + y_t f_j \tag{10.7}$$

10.5.1 Modified Hotelling Rule

Consider k-sustainable extraction policy, policy j, and let policy i be a k/z-degrading policy with $f_i > f_j$. For policy j to be competitive relative to policy i, prices $\mathbf{v}_{t-1}, \mathbf{p}_{t-1}, \mathbf{v}_t, \mathbf{p}_{t-1}, y_t$ must satisfy condition (10.7):

$$v_t^{(k)} \geq \left(\frac{1 + r}{1 + g_{ji}} \right) v_{t-1}^{(k)} + \left(\frac{1}{1 + g_{ji}} \right) v_t^{(z)} + \Omega_{ji} \tag{10.8}$$

where

$$\Omega_{ji} = (1 + r) \left[\mathbf{p}_{t-1} \mathbf{k}_j - \left(\frac{g_{ji}}{1 + g_{ji}} \right) \mathbf{p}_{t-1} \mathbf{k}_i \right] + \left[l_j - \left(\frac{g_{ji}}{1 + g_{ji}} \right) l_i \right] \tag{10.8a}$$

In particular, if $\Omega_{jh} > 0$:

$$v_t^{(k)} \geq \left(\frac{1 + r}{1 + g_{ji}} \right) v_{t-1}^{(k)} \tag{10.9}$$

Proof Apply (10.6) to i and (10.7) to j and shuffle.

Term Ω_{ji} in (10.8) measures the degree to which the costs of the maintenance activities of the sustainable policy j exceed the costs of the maintenance activities of the unsustainable policy i, where the latter are discounted by the factor $(g_{ji}/(1 + g_{ji}))$. Factor $(g_{ji}/(1 + g_{ji}))$ is always smaller than unity; if the unsustainable extraction level f_i is much larger than the sustainable level f_j, $(g_{ji}/(1 + g_{ji}))$ will be very small. Thus, for the reference policy h, Ω_{jh} is likely to be positive and we expect that inequality (10.9) has to be satisfied for policy j to be competitive.

Condition (10.9) shows that the price of the water resource must *rise* if the interest rate r is larger than productivity rate g_{ji}. If $r > g_{ji}$ but $v_{t-1} \leq v_t$, the sustainable policy j will not be able to compete against the unsustainable policy i and profit-maximizing resource owners will follow an extraction policy that leads to a decline of the quality of the water resource. To prevent such a decline, the value of the water resource must *appreciate* during the period in order to compensate the resource owner for the earnings they lose by abstaining from the increased water extractions associated with the unsustainable policy i. Since the physical quantity of the resource is given by nature and cannot be increased, resource prices have to rise to achieve the required appreciation of resource values. Condition (10.8/10.9) really is a generalization of the Hotelling Rule from the case of exhaustible resources to the case of renewable but depletable resources; in the limiting case of $g_{ji} = 0$, the water resource is in fact reduced to an exhaustible resource.

For brevity, we refer to (10.8/10.9) as the *Modified Hotelling Rule*. We note that the Modified Hotelling Rule must be satisfied in *every* period of the growth path if the sustainable extraction policy is to be economically viable. We also note that inequality (10.8) has to be satisfied for *every* extraction policy i that competes with j. In the rest of the paper, we shall assume that $g_{ji} < r$ and $\Omega_{ji} > 0$ for some unsustainable policy i.

We note that the Modified Hotelling Rule is based on arbitrage behaviour in each period and does not require resource owners to have any knowledge about the physical amounts available to them. Thus, the price dynamics under the Modified Hotelling Rule are not affected by the criticism of scarcity indices expressed in Norgaard (1990).

10.6 THE HOTELLING PARADOX

The Modified Hotelling Rule requires that the price of the renewable resource increases over time if the interest rate r exceeds the 'natural productivity rate' g_j of the sustainable extraction policy. This section compares the Modified Hotelling Rule with the original Hotelling Rule for exhaustible resources and identifies a crucial difference between the two cases.

The price dynamics of the renewable resource under the Modified Hotelling Rule are formally very similar to the price dynamics of an exhaustible resource under the Hotelling Rule. In both cases, the price of the resource has to rise in order to compensate the resource owner for the losses in earnings that are due to the delay in extraction. However, the formal analogy between the two cases hides a fundamental economic difference. The key difference lies in the fact that the Modified Hotelling Rule applies to a resource that needs to be *maintained* for an indefinite future, while the Hotelling Rule merely applies to a *transition path* from a world where the available stocks of the exhaustible resource are still positive to a world where all resource stocks have been depleted. This difference has important implications for the long-term dynamics of the economy.

Contrast the case of oil with the case of water. Consider oil first. The rising price of oil has two functions. On the one hand, the rising price of oil gives an incentive to the resource owner to allow for a smooth depletetion path and to keep some of his oil stocks in the ground rather than to extract all stocks at once. On the other hand, the rising price of oil makes it possible that alternative energy sources become more competitive as oil stocks decline. On an equilibrium path, all oil stocks will have been depleted when the price of oil has risen up to the point where alternative energy sources become cheaper. After that point, oil ceases to be an economically relevant good. The price rise under Hotelling reflects the *transition path* between two different types of energy sources. No such transition takes place in the case of water. Water is an essential commodity that cannot be fully replaced by other commodities; we may assume that households need a certain minimum amount of fresh water for personal consumption and that the use of water as a productive input exhibits strong complementarities that prohibit a complete substitution by other inputs. Thus, demand for water by households and firms will become highly price-inelastic as water supplies are being reduced. Due to the rigidity in demand, the continual increase in the price of the water resource will *not* generate the transition to an alternative commodity; water remains an economically relevant good for the indefinite future.

This is what may be called the Hotelling Paradox. The Modified Hotelling Rule requires that the price of the water resource rises over time. After an initial adjustment period these continual price rises will no longer induce any further substitution processes. Instead, demand becomes inelastic and producers who use water as an input will have to increase their output prices to recover the continually rising input costs. Similarly, households faced with ever increasing output and water prices will increase their wage demands to defend their real income. In this way, the economy becomes trapped in an inevitable process of continual price inflation. The 'paradox' lies in the fact that the inflationary price dynamics do not reflect any real changes in the economy. In the case of oil, the rise in oil prices was required to guide the economy on the *real* transition path from a world with oil to a world without oil. In the case of water, no such transition takes place. Even if demand and production are completely stable and do not change over time, prices have to rise to prevent resource owners from adopting unsustainable extraction policies.

This inflationary process is not due to any market imperfections or monopolistic behaviour. Rather, it is a consequence of the fact that under unregulated private ownership, resource owners have to be given a reward for abstaining from overexploitation. If the economy is well endowed with water resources, profit-maximizing resource owners may choose initially to allow for a cerain degree of overextraction and quality degradation. However, after an initial adjustment period, demand for water becomes inelastic and resource owners have to resort to sustainable extraction policies. While the option of overexploitation and quality degradation is not actually being used, the mere possibility of this option serves as an effective threat to enforce the continual rise in the price of water resources. The price dynamics of the economy are governed by a threat of resource destruction that never actually materializes.

10.7 POLICY IMPLICATIONS

Under the 'Hotelling Paradox', the continual rise in resource prices does not reflect any ongoing real adjustment processes in the economy but merely acts as a financial incentive for resource owners not to engage in resource destruction. This section shows how the Hotelling Paradox can be avoided by appropriately specified government regulation.

The main point about the Hotelling Paradox is that on unregulated resource markets prices have to control the operation of extraction policies that are never actually used by resource owners; resource destruction acts merely as a threat. This is the point where government regulation comes into play. By simply *prohibiting* resource uses that are unsustainable, the government eliminates the threat that is at the source of the inflationary process. If technological norms make the threat of resource destruction ineffective, resource owners will no longer receive a reward for abstaining from environmental degradation. In the presence of technological norms, competitive prices will not increase to ever higher levels but will converge to their long-run stationary values; the Hotelling Paradox vanishes. Resource owners will still receive a rental income, but this income merely reflects the given scarcity of water and the costs of maintenance, not the potential threat of resource destruction.

More specifically, if a given sustainable extraction policy j is to become competitive without introducing inflationary pressure, technological norms have to rule out any extraction policy i for which the productivity rate g_{ji} is smaller than the interest rate. In the extreme case, only policy j itself is permitted. In that case, resource owners no longer have any choice of the extraction policy they wish to pursue; they merely act as resource managers who collect rental payments and maintenance charges from water users. From the point of view of the user, the supply of water f_j is fixed in the same way in which 'space' is fixed; competition for the given supply of water will then lead to a differential rent that reflects the relative scarcity of water under the given extraction policy.

ACKNOWLEDGEMENTS

I am grateful to colleagues Mike Devereux and Gauthier Lanot and to an anomynous referee for their useful comments. I also wish to express my gratitude to the Daimler–Benz Foundation (Ladenburg) for financial support at an earlier stage. Finally, my thanks go to Publications Manager Sarah Dwyer from C3ED for her assistance.

REFERENCES

Buller, H. (1996), 'Privatization and Europeanization: The changing context of water supply in Britain and France', *Journal of Environmental Planning and Management*, 39.

Conrad, J.M. and C.W. Clark (1987), *Natural Resource Economics*, Cambridge: Cambridge University Press.

Dasgupta, P.S. and G.M. Heal (1979), *Economic Theory and Exhaustible Resources*, Cambridge: Cambridge University Press.

Diedrich, M.E. (1995), 'Environmental resources and the interest rate', *Economie Appliquée*, 48.

Erreygers, G. (1996), 'Sustainability and Stability in a Classical Model of Production', in S. Faucheux, D.W. Pearce and J.L.R. Proops (eds), *Models of Sustainable Development*, Cheltenham: Edward Elgar.

Goudie, A. (1990), *The Human Impact on the Natural Environment*, Oxford and Cambridge (USA): Blackwell.

Hotelling, H. (1931), 'The economics of Exhaustible Resources', *Journal of Political Economy*, 39.

Kluge, T. and E. Schramm (1988), *Wassernöte: Zur Geschichte des Trinkwassers*, Köln: Kölner Volksblatt Verlag.

Leopold, L.L. (1974), *Water: A Primer*. San Francisco: Freeman.

Norgaard, R. (1990), 'Economic Indicators of Resource Scarcity: A Critical Essay', *Journal of Environmental Economics and Management*, 19.

NRA (National Rivers Authority) (1994), *Water: Nature's Precious Resource. An environmentally sustainable water resources strategy for England and Wales*, London: HMSO.

Water Law (1995), *Water Law*, 6 (5-6)

WRI (World Resources Institute) (1986), *World Resources 1986*, New York: Basic Books.

WRI (World Resources Institute) (1992), *World Resources 1992–93*, New York and Oxford: Oxford University Press.

11. Financial Transfers to Sustain Cooperative International Optimality in Stock Pollutant Abatement

Marc Germain, Philippe Toint and Henry Tulkens

INTRODUCTION

It is well known that the transnational character of many environmental problems (for example, greenhouse gas emissions, acid rain, pollution of international waters) requires cooperation among the countries involved if a social optimum is to be achieved. The issues raised thereby have often been addressed, in the economic literature, using concepts borrowed from cooperative game theory (see, for example, Mäler 1989).

However, most of these contributions have dealt only with static (one-shot) games, which are appropriate only for flow pollution models. When the environmental damage arises from the presence of stock pollutants that accumulate (and possibly decay), the problem acquires a dynamic and intertemporal dimension. In this case, differential game theory is a more appropriate tool for the analysis of cooperation, as is done in, for example, van der Ploeg and de Zeeuw (1992), Kaitala, Pohjola and Tahvonen (1992), Hoel (1992) and Tahvonen (1993). Such analysis proceeds by evaluating the gain to be obtained from cooperation, at an international optimum, in comparison with the non-cooperative state of affairs modelled as a Nash non-cooperative equilibrium (open-loop or closed-loop).

Most often, these contributions leave aside the issue of the voluntary implementation of the international optimum. This is an important drawback because in this context no supranational authority can be called upon to impose the optimum. In view of ensuring such implementation, it has often been suggested that financial transfers between the countries involved might reinforce incentives towards cooperation. This property, understood in the sense of the theory of the core of a cooperative game, has in effect been demonstrated by Chander and Tulkens (1995, 1996), who propose a particular transfer scheme based on parameters reflecting the relative intensities of the countries' environmental preferences. The result is obtained, however, for flow pollutants only, that is, in a static game model.

The present contribution establishes that the same property can be obtained for stock pollutants, within the wider context of differential games. It also shows that the transfer scheme implies a sharing rule of the aggregate emission abatement cost between the countries. Moreover, with this cost-sharing interpretation, the transfers appear to be a strategically stable form of joint implementation of the international optimum.

The paper is structured as follows. Section 11.1 presents the stock pollutant model; Section 11.2 characterizes emissions that correspond to an international optimum without transfers, and raises the sustainability issue addressed in the sequel. In Section 11.3, emissions corresponding to a non-cooperative (open-loop) equilibrium are similarly characterized and contrasted with the optimal ones. In Section 11.4, financial transfers are formulated that are shown to induce voluntary cooperation of each country individually, whereas in Section 11.5 these transfers are further specified to achieve cooperation in the core theoretic sense, that is, for all subsets of countries. Section 11.6 considers some issues that arise when the time profile of the transfers, and not only their aggregate present value, is examined. The concluding section emphasizes the political significance of our results.

11.1 THE MODEL

The model we use is a dynamic extension of the well-known one originally presented in Mäler (1989). It is formulated in discrete time. There are n regions or countries, indexed $i \in N = \{1,...,n\}$. Human activity in each country entails pollutant emissions: let $E_t = (E_{1t},..., E_{nt})$ with $E_{iit} \geq 0 \ \forall i, t$, be the vector of these emissions at date t. They spread across the various countries and contribute to the formation of a pollutant stock $S \ (\geq 0)$ which is determined by the equation

$$S_t = [1 - \delta]S_{t-1} + E_t \qquad (11.1)$$

where by definition $E_t = \sum_{i=1}^{n} E_{it}$ is the sum of the emissions and δ is the rate of natural decay of the stock $(0 < \delta < 1)$. Equation (11.1) – often called a 'transfer function' – summarizes the ecological component of the model.

In this formulation, pollution is assumed to be global, in the sense that it spreads out uniformly across countries. Atmospheric CO_2 is the best example of this form of transfrontier pollution. Some pollutions, such as acid rain or river water pollution, do not obey that equation: they are called 'directional'. The results presented below could be extended to directional pollutions, by introducing other forms of transfer functions between emissions and depositions of pollutant (for example Germain, Toint and Tulkens 1995), where we use another function in the framework of a model without pollutant accumulation).

As to the economic component of the model, it comprises two elements. On the one hand, the pollutant stock implies damages for each country i : at period t, and in monetary terms, these amount to $D_i(S_t)$, where D_i is supposed to be a positive, increasing and convex function $\left(D_i > 0 \text{ if } S > 0, D_i \geq 0 \text{ if } S = 0, D_i^{'} > 0, D_i^{''} \geq 0 \right)$. On the other hand, the only means the countries have to keep the stock of pollutant under control is at its source, that is, by reducing their emissions. More precisely, associated with country i is an abatement cost function $C_i(E_i)$, positive, decreasing and strictly convex $\left(C_i \geq 0, C_i^{'} < 0, C_i^{''} > 0 \right)$, that expresses the total costs incurred by the industries of country i due to the fact that total emissions in that country are restricted to E_{it} . The decreasing character of the function reflects the obvious phenomenon of increasing aggregate costs when emissions are abated.

These assumptions, identical to those of Mäler's, are justified in part by realism and in part by analytical convenience: realism in assuming that the damage cost functions $D_i(S_t)$ and the abatement cost functions $C_i(E_{it})$ be increasing and decreasing, respectively; convenience because without convexity the optimization approach we want to use below would require a much heavier mathematical apparatus without much gain in the understanding of the economics at stake.

11.2   INTERNATIONALY OPTIMAL POLLUTANT EMISSIONS AND STOCK

11.2.1 Determining the Optimum

For the economic–ecological system thus described, an international optimum is defined as the joint emission policy, and the ensuing stock, that minimize the sum, over all countries, of the total of both their damage and abatement costs. Formally, this corresponds to the solution of the problem:

$$\min_{\{E_t\}_{t\in T}} \sum_{t=1}^{T} \sum_{i=1}^{n} \beta^t \left[C_i (E_{it}) + D_i (S_t) \right]$$

$$\text{s.t.} \begin{cases} S_t = [1 - \delta] S_{t-1} + E_t; \ S_0 \text{ given} \\ E_{it} \geq 0, \forall t \in T, \forall i \in N \end{cases} \tag{11.2}$$

where β is the discount factor $(0 < \beta \leq 1)$, $T = \{1, ..., T\}$, T being the time horizon of the problem (T positive, integer and possibly infinite).

The necessary conditions for an interior minimum of problem (11.2) yield optimal trajectories for the emissions $\{E_t^*\}_{t \in T}$ and for the pollutant stock $\{S_t^*\}_{t \in T}$ which satisfy the following equations:

$$C_i'\left(E_{it}^*\right) + \sum_{\tau=t}^{T} \beta^{\tau-t} [1-\delta]^{\tau-t} \sum_{j=1}^{n} D_j'\left(S_\tau^*\right) = 0, \forall i \in N, \forall t \in T. \tag{11.3}$$

This expression means that at every moment of time, the marginal abatement cost of country i must be equal to the sum over all countries of their respective marginal damage costs over the entire horizon remaining. In this setting, the higher the damages (either intrinsically *via* the marginal damages D_i' and the stock S, or *via* the weight attributed to these in the future, that is, *via* β), the more important it is to abate and the lower are the optimal emissions; similarly, the slower the pollutant stock depreciates (the smaller δ is).

In the particular case where the damage functions are linear, that is, when

$$D_i(S_t) = \pi_i S_t, i \in N \tag{11.4}$$

we can be more explicit on the time profile of the optimal emissions. In this case they do indeed obey the following equation:

$$C_i'\left(E_{it}^*\right) + \pi_N \frac{1 - \beta^{T+1-t} [1-\delta]^{T+1-t}}{1 - \beta[1-\delta]} = 0, i \in N, t \in T \tag{11.5}$$

where by definition $\pi_N = \sum_{i=1}^{n} \pi_i$. Thus, we get the usual result that, with linear damages, optimal emissions do not depend upon the initial stock (Tahvonen 1993).

We also have that, because the functions $C_i(E_i)$ are decreasing and convex over their domain of definition, optimal emissions are increasing with time if T is finite, whereas they are constant when T is infinite.

Indeed, when T is finite, (11.3) suggests that the incentive to abate (as measured by the discounted sum of future damages) decreases as one gets closer to the horizon; but this does not apply when T is infinite: the second term of (11.5) is then a constant.

11.2.2 The Sustainability Issue

In a Coasian spirit, one may interpret the international optimum as the outcome of a treaty voluntarily signed among the countries involved. However, defining an optimum does not imply that it is an enforceable agreement, not even, if it happened to be reached, that it can be sustained. One of the main reasons for non-sustainability lies indeed in the fact that some countries might consider that the total cost they incur with the optimal joint policy $\{E^*_{it}\}$ is higher than the one they would incur by acting on their own. Of course, this cannot be the case for *all* countries because if it were, the total costs represented by the value of the objective function (11.2) at the solution would not be a minimum.

To evaluate the strength of this argument, the cost of 'acting on her own' should be specified explicitly for each country, and compared with that of the optimal joint policy. This is examined in the next two sections.

11.3 THE OPEN-LOOP NON-COOPERATIVE NASH EQUILIBRIUM

Suppose that, at time 0, each country chooses once and for all its emissions for all future periods, given the pollutant stock S_0 existing at that time, and the emissions chosen by the other countries. Formally, each country i $(i \in \{1,...,n\})$ then solves the following problem:

$$\min_{\{E_{it}\}_{t \in T}} \sum_{t=1}^{T} \beta^t [C_i(E_{it}) + D_i(S_t)]$$

$$\text{s.t.} \begin{cases} S_t = [1-\delta]S_{t-1} + E_t; \ S_0 \text{ given} \\ E_{it} \geq 0, \forall t \in T; E_{jt} \ (j \neq i) \text{given} \end{cases}$$

$$(11.6)$$

The simultaneous solution of the n problems (11.6) consists of emissions and stock trajectories $\{E_t^N\}_{t \in T}$ and $\{s_t^N\}_{t \in T}$, respectively, that are also the solution of the first-order conditions:

$$C_i'(E_{it}^N) + \sum_{T=t}^{T} \beta^{\tau-t} [1-\delta]^{\tau-t} D_i'(s_T^N) = 0, \forall i \in N, \forall t \in T \qquad (11.7)$$

Contrary to what is the case at an international optimum, country i here only takes account of the impact of its decisions *on its own* environment (hence the presence of $D_i'\left(S_t^N\right)$ in lieu of $\sum_{j=1}^n D_j'\left(S_t^*\right)$ in (11.7)).

The emissions and stock trajectories thus defined are of the nature of a Nash equilibrium in non-cooperative games. More specifically, they constitute an 'open-loop' Nash equilibrium, characterized by the fact that each country's strategy is expressed as a function of calendar time alone. See Fudenberg and Tirole 1993, pp. 130 ff. Exogenous changes in the transfer function, or possible deviations from the equilibrium strategies by other countries are not considered.

In the particular case of linear damage costs, the countries' emissions obey the following equations:

$$C_i'\left(E_{it}^N\right)+ \pi_i \frac{1-\beta^{T+1-t}\left[1-\delta\right]^{T+1-t}}{1-\beta\left[1-\delta\right]} = 0, \ i \in \mathsf{N}, t \in \mathsf{T} \tag{11.8}$$

As it was the case at the international optimum, and for reasons that are quite similar (see previous section), emissions are increasing if T is finite and constant if T is infinite.

In view of the fact that $\forall i, \pi_i < \pi_N$, we notice, by comparing (11.5) to (11.8), that when the D_is are linear, the Nash equilibrium emissions of country i are always higher than the internationally optimal ones. This is only natural since at a Nash equilibrium, the abatement decisions of each country are based on their impact on their own environment only.

11.4 TRANSFERS INDUCING AN INDIVIDUALLY RATIONAL INTERNATIONAL OPTIMUM

Let us recall that $E_1^*,..., E_T^*$ and $S_0, S_1,..., S_t^*$ are internationally optimal emissions and stock trajectories. Then:

$$W(S_0)= \sum_{t=1}^T \beta^t \sum_{i=1}^n \left[C_i\left(E_{it}^*\right)+ D_i\left(S_t^*\right)\right] \tag{11.9}$$

is the optimal aggregate total cost of all countries, and

$$W_i(S_0)= \sum_{t=1}^T \beta^t \left[C_i\left(E_{it}^*\right)+ D_i\left(S_t^*\right)\right] \tag{11.10}$$

is the share of $W(S_0)$ borne by country i $(i \in N)$. Of course

$$W(S_0) = \sum_{i=1}^{n} W_i(S_0) \qquad (11.11)$$

Let us keep in mind also that $E_1^N, ..., E_T^N$ and $S_0, S_1^N, ..., S_T^N$ are the emissions and stock trajectories at the Nash non-cooperative equilibrium. Then :

$$V_i(S_0) = \sum_{t=1}^{T} \beta^t \left[c_i \left(E_{it}^N \right) + D_i \left(S_t^N \right) \right] \qquad (11.12)$$

is the discounted total cost of country i at the Nash equilibrium and

$$V(S_0) = \sum_{i=1}^{n} V_i(S_0) \qquad (11.13)$$

is the sum of these total costs over the set of all countries. Clearly, by definition of the optimum, $V(S_0) \geq W(S_0)$.

The above reasoning on sustainability of the optimum can now be formalized as follows. If $\forall i \in \{1, ..., T\}$ $W_i(S_0) \leq V_i(S_0)$, then the optimal trajectories are such that all countries save costs by adopting them; cooperation to achieve the optimum is sustainable in the sense of what is called 'individual rationality' in game theory.

By contrast, a country i, for which $W_i(S_0) > V_i(S_0)$, has no such interest in cooperating. Cooperation, although globally favourable for all countries taken as a whole, is not sustainable in the above sense. In order to gain the cooperation of such a country, some form of compensation must be designed, for example, in the form of financial transfers.

Borrowing from Chander and Tulkens (1992), who dealt with this issue in a static context (as opposed to the intertemporal framework considered here), we propose financial transfers between the countries that are of the following form:

$$\tau_i(S_0) = -[W_i(S_0) - V_i(S_0)] + \mu_i[W(S_0) - V(S_0)], \ i \in N \qquad (11.14)$$

where the parameters μ_i are arbitrary fixed values chosen between 0 and 1 and satisfy

$$\sum_{i=1}^{n} \mu_i = 1 \qquad (11.15)$$

This last condition guarantees that the financial transfers defined by (11.13) be balanced, in the sense that

$$\sum_{i=1}^{n} \tau_i (S_0) = 0. \tag{11.16}$$

If, with international cooperation, country i receives a financial transfer equal to $\tau_i(S_0)$, then its discounted total cost along the optimal trajectory becomes

$$\tilde{W}_i(S_0) = W_i(S_0) + \tau_i(S_0). \tag{11.17}$$

It is easy to verify that this optimal cost *with transfers* borne by i is smaller than or equal to the cost it would bear at the Nash equilibrium. Indeed, it follows from (11.13) and (11.16) that

$$\tilde{W}_i(S_0) = V_i(S_0) + \mu_i[W(S_0) - V(S_0)] \leq V_i(S_0), \forall i \in \{1,...,n\} \tag{11.18}$$

because μ_i is non-negative and $W(S_0) - V(S_0) \leq 0$ by definition of an optimum. Thus with the transfers defined by (11.13), international cooperation becomes individually rational.

11.5 TRANSFERS INDUCING RATIONALITY IN THE SENSE OF COALITIONS

Another dimension of the sustainability of the international optimum is suggested by the notion of 'rationality in the sense of coalitions' offered by the 'core' concept in cooperative game theory. Here, costs savings are considered not only at the level of each individual country but also for groups – called 'coalitions' – of countries. An international optimum is not sustainable for a coalition if its members can achieve lower costs for themselves than those they incur at the optimum; it is sustainable if there is no coalition for which this is possible. Our claim in this section is that the international optimum can be made sustainable in the sense of coalitions, thanks to further specification of the financial transfers. To do so we will adapt to our present dynamic framework the concepts and methodology also developed in Chander and Tulkens (1995, 1996) in a static framework. We first recall the methodology and then state our present result.

11.5.1 The Methodology

A cooperative game in characteristic function form (with transferable utility) is defined by the pair $[N, w(.; S_0)]$, where $N = \{1, ..., n\}$ is the set of players (that is, the n countries) and w is the characteristic function. The space of the players' strategies on which this function is defined is specified as follows: for each country i, this space is the interval of all possible emission levels, that is, $[0, \infty]$. For any coalition $U \subseteq N$, it is the set product of these intervals over the members of U.

The characteristic function of the game may then be defined by using the concept of *partial Nash equilibrium with respect to a coalition*, proposed by Chander and Tulkens (1995, 1996), subject to some adaptation to the present framework. Specifically, the function specifies as follows the vectors $E_t (t \in T)$ of the strategies adopted by all players when a coalition $U \subseteq N$ forms:

(i) For the members of U, the trajectories are described by $\{E_{it}^U : i \in U; t \in T\}$ which is the solution of

$$\min_{\{E_{it}\}_{\substack{i \in U \\ t \in T}}} \sum_{t=1}^{T} \sum_{i \in U} \beta^t [C_i (E_{it}) + D_i (S_t)] \text{ s.t. (1)}, \qquad (11.19)$$

where $\forall j \in N \backslash U$, $\forall t \in T$, $E_{jt} = E_{jt}^U$ as defined by *(ii)*;

(ii) For the players out of the coalition U, the trajectories $\{E_{jt}^U : t \in T\} j \in N \backslash U$, are solutions of the simultaneous resolution of the problems

$$\min_{\{Ejt\}_{j \notin U \in T}} \sum_{t=1}^{T} \beta^t [C_j (E_{jt}) + D_j (S_t)] \text{ s.t.(1)}, j \in N \backslash U \qquad (11.20)$$

where $\forall i \in U, \forall t \in T$, $E_{it} = E_{it}^U$, as defined by *(i)*.

Thus one supposes that if a coalition forms, its members minimize *together* the sum of their total discounted costs, while each country outside of it reacts by minimizing its own total discounted cost. The hypothesis about this last behaviour justifies the expression 'partial Nash equilibrium' used above.

On this basis, the characteristic function may be written

$$w(U; S_0) = \sum_{t=1}^{T} \sum_{i \in U} \beta^t \left[C_i \left(E_{it}^U \right) + D_i \left(S_t^U \right) \right], U \subseteq N \qquad (11.21)$$

where $S_t^U = [1 - \delta] S_{t-1}^U + E_t^U$, $\forall t \in T$ (with $S_0^U \equiv S_0$ given). Because of (11.18), one notes that $w(N; S_0)$ is equal to $W(S_0)$ defined by (11.9), in other words to the optimal total cost of all countries.

For the game $[N, w(.; S_0)]$, any n-dimensional and non-negative vector whose components sum up to $w([N; S_0])$ is called an *imputation* of the game. Thus an imputation may be seen as a way of sharing the optimal total cost between the different players.

The vector $(W_1, (S_0), ..., W_n(S_0))$, where $W_i(S_0)$ is defined by (11.10), constitutes such an imputation, where each country bears itself the abatement and damage costs induced by the optimal strategy $\{E_t^* : t = 1, ..., T\}$. But the possibility of financial transfers between countries implies that there exists (an infinity of) other imputations associated with the same strategy. Indeed, any vector $(\tilde{W}_i(S_0), ..., \tilde{W}_n(S_0))$, defined by (11.16) such that (11.15) is verified, is an imputation.

A *solution* of the game is an imputation that verifies certain properties. Among the imputations we have just defined thanks to the transfers $\tau_i(S_0)$, those who verify the condition

$$\sum_{i \in U} \tilde{W}_i(S_0) \le w(U; S_0), \ \forall U \subseteq N, \forall S_0 > 0 \qquad (11.22)$$

are said *to belong to the core* of the game. The core is thus the set of imputations that attribute to any coalition a share of the aggregate cost $W(S_0)$ less than or equal to the mimimal cost $w(U; S_0)$ this coalition could achieve by itself.

We will call 'rational in the sense of coalitions' any imputation which belongs to the core of the game described above: with such a share, indeed, no coalition has an interest to form because its members, taken as a whole, would bear a total cost greater than what is proposed to them.

11.5.2 The Result

We now show that when *the damage functions are linear* (see 11.4)), such an imputation exists and can be exhibited in terms of specific values of the parameters μ_i appearing in (11.13).

Theorem: Let $\{E_t^* : t = 1, ..., T\}$ be the trajectory of the optimal emissions solution of problem (11.2), and $\{E_t^N : t = 1, ..., T\}$ be the trajectory of emissions at the Nash equilibrium solution of problems (11.6). Let $(W_1, (S_0), ..., W_n(S_0))$ and $(V_1, (S_0), ..., V_n(S_0))$ be the vectors of total discounted costs of each country along these two trajectories (as defined in

Let us define

$$J_t^* = \sum_{i=1}^{n} J_{it}^* = \sum_{i=1}^{n} \left[C_i\left(E_{it}^*\right) + D_i\left(S_t^*\right) \right] \beta^t, \forall t \in T \quad (11.35)$$

$$J_t^N = \sum_{i=1}^{n} J_{it}^N = \sum_{i=1}^{n} \left[C_i\left(E_{it}^N\right) + D_i\left(S_t^N\right) \right] \beta^t, \forall t \in T \quad (11.36)$$

In order to focus the exposition, we will consider here only the three following assumptions.

Assumption 1:

$$J_t^* \le J_t^N, \forall t \in T. \quad (11.37)$$

The international optimum monotonically dominates the Nash equilibrium. In this case, the global surplus generated by cooperation increases every year and the global transfers defined by (11.13) may be decomposed in annual transfers of the form

$$\Theta_{it} = -\left[J_{it}^* - J_{it}^N \right] + \mu_i \left[J_t^* - J_t^N \right] i \in N, t \in T \quad (11.38)$$

One easily verifies from (11.9)–(11.13) and Assumption 1 that $\tau_i(S_0) = \sum_{t=1}^{T} \Theta_{it}$.

Assumption 2:

$$\exists M : 1 \le M < T : \begin{cases} J_t^* < J_t^N & \text{if } 1 \le t \le M, \\ J_t^* > J_t^N & \text{if } M < t \le T. \end{cases} \quad (11.39)$$

The international optimum dominates the Nash equilibrium until a certain year M, starting from which the domination order is reversed. In this case, one verifies that

$$W(S_0) - V(S_0) = \sum_{t=1}^{M} \left[J_t^* - J_t^N \right] + \sum_{t=M+1}^{T} \left[J_t^* - J_t^N \right] > \sum_{t=1}^{M} \left[J_t^* - J_t^N \right] \quad (11.40)$$

The global surplus is inferior *in absolute value* to the surplus obtained during the subperiod $\{1,\dots, M\}$ (both sides of (11.24) indeed represent negative cost differences). If one applies the annual transfer formula (11.23), country i will save $\mu_i \sum_{t=1}^{M} \left[J_t^* - J_t^N \right]$ at the optimum compared to the Nash equilibrium during the first M years, and will lose $\mu_i \sum_{t=M+1}^{T} \left[J_t^* - J_t^N \right]$ during the each of the years $\{M+1,\dots,T\}$. Since the

(11.10) and (11.11)). Then, under the assumptions of convexity of th functions C_i and of linearity of the functions $D_i \, (i \in N)$, the imputatio $(\tilde{W}_i(S_0),... \tilde{W}_n(S_0))$ defined by

$$\tilde{W}_i(S_0) = W_i(S_0) + \tilde{\tau}_i(S_0), i = 1,..., n \qquad (11.23)$$

where

$$\tilde{\tau}_i(S_0) = -[W_i(S_0) - V_i(S_0)] + \frac{\pi_i}{\pi_N} [W(S_0) - V(S_0)] \qquad (11.34)$$

and $W(S_0)$ and $V(S_0)$ are respectively defined by (11.9) and (11.12), belongs to the core of the cooperative game $[N, W(.; S_0)]$.

It is easy to see that the coefficients defined by $\delta_i = \pi_i / \pi_N$ (where the π_i are the coefficients of the damage cost functions (11.4)) have values between 0 and 1 and verify (11.14), and that the financial transfers $\tau_i(S_0), i \in N$ are balanced in the sense of (11.15). By analogy with individual rationality, we call the optimal trajectory with transfers (11.22) 'strategically stable' or 'rational in the sense of coalitions'.

One may note also that this property is satisfied whatever are the initial stock S_0 and the temporal horizon T (which may be infinite).

11.6 THE TIME DIMENSION OF THE FINANCIAL TRANSFERS

The transfers introduced in Sections 11.4 and 11.5 have been defined on a global basis: they are given as total sums related to the complete period $T = \{1,...,T\}$ where cooperation takes place. As a consequence, the question of their precise allocation in time during this period remains open, in particular when the horizon is infinite (see also Zaccour 1994). Even in the case where it is finite, the countries may benefit from parts of the cooperation dividends before the horizon is attained. The purpose of the present section is to briefly analyse some simple situations that may occur.

The first observation is that, if the international optimum globally dominates the Nash equilibrium (in other words $W(S_0) < V(S_0)$ where W and V are defined by (11.9) and (11.12)), this domination is not *monotonic*, in the sense that it does not imply that, for each elementary period (a year, for instance) $t \in T$, the global cost for this period is inferior at the international optimum to that at the Nash equilibrium.

whole procedure is individually rational, the gain in the first period is necessarily superior (in absolute value) to the loss in the second. In this context, if this country wishes to restore, as far as it is concerned, the domination of the international optimum over the Nash equilibrium, it is enough that it levies the loss of the second period from its gains at the first, and then transfers the resulting sum to the second period. Compared to the Nash equilibrium, it will then obtain, at the international optimum with transfers, a gain of $\mu_i[w(s_0) - v(s_0)]$ during the period $\{1, \ldots, M\}$ and of zero during period $\{M+1, \ldots, T\}$.

Assumption 3:

$$\exists M : 1 \leq M < T : \begin{cases} J_t^* < J_t^N \text{ if } 1 \leq t \leq M, \\ J_t^* > J_t^N \text{ if } M < t \leq T. \end{cases} \tag{11.41}$$

The international optimum is dominated by the Nash equilibrium until year M, after which the order of domination is reversed. This is the most plausible situation, in that the optimum implies abatement costs higher than those of the Nash equilibrium, costs which must financed from the date where they are decided while the gains in damages that they induce are obtained only later. In this context, the countries obviously cannot transfer future gains to cover present losses, in order to ensure the domination of the international optimum over the Nash equilibrium during the early subperiod $\{1, \ldots, M\}$. However, if the countries globally lose until $t=M$, the impact of this loss may be very different from country to country. The most affected countries could then benefit from financial transfers from the less affected ones.

11.7 CONCLUSIONS

Using the theory of non-cooperative games in the framework of a model of intertemporal transboundary pollution, we have constructed by means of appropriate transfers a sharing scheme for the abatement costs between the countries involved, which makes their cooperation sustainable in the sense of 'coalitional rationality', that is, that no coalition of countries can guarantee to its members a lower total cost than that obtained at the international optimum with the proposed financial transfers.

That the result was obtained under two restrictive assumptions (linearity of the damage functions, and the open-loop character of the Nash equilibrium considered as reference) should not undermine its political significance. Indeed, the issue at stake is the one whether worldwide agreements on transboundary pollution problems such as CO_2 emissions are at all achievable, and it is a disputed one, as witnessed by the controversy reported in Tulkens (1997). Burden sharing, in particular, is an important economic component of the debate.

The present paper reinforces the optimistic perspective opened by the results of Chander and Tulkens (1995, 1996), by extending these results to stock pollutants. In addition, the constructive nature of this extension – contained in the burden sharing formula (...) – allows for computations that we intend to provide in forthcoming simulations.

REFERENCES

Chander, P. and H. Tulkens (1992), 'Theoretical Foundations of Negotiations and Cost Sharing in Transfrontier Pollution Problems', *European Economic Review*, 36 (2/3), 288–99 (April).

Chander, P. and H. Tulkens (1995), 'A Core-Theoretic Solution for the Design of Cooperative Agreements on Transfrontier Pollution', *International Tax and Public Finance*, 2, 279–93.

Chander P. and H. Tulkens (1996), 'The Core of an Economy with Multilateral Environmental Externalities', CORE discussion paper no. 9550 (revised: March 1996), to appear in *International Journal of Game Theory*.

Fudenberg, D. and J. Tirole. (1993), *Game Theory*, Cambridge, MA and London, UK: The MIT Press.

Germain, M., P. Toint and H. Tulkens (1995), 'Calcul Economique Itératif pour les Négociations Internationales sur les Pluies Acides entre la Finlande, la Russie et l'Estonie', *Annales d'Economie et de Statistique*, 43, 101–27.

Hoel, M. (1992), 'Emission Taxes in a Dynamic International Game of CO_2 Emissions', in R. Pethig (ed.), *Conflicts and Cooperation in Managing Environmental Resources*, Microeconomic Studies, Berlin: Springer Verlag.

Kaitala, V., M. Pohjola and D. Tahvonen (1992), 'Transboundary Air Pollution and Soil Acidification: a Dynamic Analysis of an Acid Rain Game between Finland and the USSR', *Environmental and Resource Economics*, 2, 161–81.

Mäler K. (1989), 'The Acid Rain Game', in H. Folmer and E. van Ierland (eds), *Valuation Methods and Policy Making in Environmental Economics*, Elsevier Amsterdam.

Tahvonen, O. (1993), 'Carbon Dioxide Abatement as a Differential Game', discussion paper in economics no. 4, University of Oulu.

Tulkens, H. (1997), 'Cooperation versus Free Riding in International Environmental Affairs: Two Approaches', Invited keynote speech at the Sixth Meeting of the European Association of Environmental and Resource Economists, Umeå, Sweden, 22 June 1995; revised version (July 1997): *FEEM Nota di Lavoro* 47.97, *Fondazione Eni Enrico Mattei*, Milan and *CORE Discussion Paper* No. 9752, Université Catholique de Louvain, Louvain-la-Neuve. To appear in N. Hanley and H. Folmer (eds), *Game Theory and the Environmen*, Cheltenham, UK and Northampton, USA: Edward Elgar.

Van der Ploeg, F. and A. de Zeeuw (1992), 'International Aspects of Pollution Control', *Environmental and Resource Economics*, 2, 117–39.

Zaccour, G. (1994), 'Side Payments in a Dynamic Game of Environmental Policy Coordination', in M. Breton and G. Zaccour (eds), preprint volume of the 6th international symposium on dynamic games and applications, St Jovite, Québec, Canada, july 1994.

12. The Implementation of the International Climate Regime: How to Finance the Reduction of CO_2 Emissions

Michel Trommetter and Laurent Viguier

12.1 INTRODUCTION

The realization of the impact of global warming on natural ecosystems and on humanity has led countries all around the world to fight against the growth of greenhouse gas (GHG) concentration in the atmosphere resulting from human activities. This preoccupation of the international community led to the adoption of a Framework Convention on Climate Change (FCCC) during the United Nations Conference on Environment and Development of Rio in 1992 which constitutes the cornerstone of a nascent 'international regime'. Starting with a 'soft norm' for the stabilization of GHG emission, the regime will be gradually strengthened. Two institutional forms are generally envisaged: that of 'tradable permits' or that of an 'international carbon tax'. Nevertheless, the numerous difficulties associated with the application of a global instrument oblige us for the moment to consider a 'transitory' regime, based on the development of international cooperation, orchestrated by an intergovernmental organization, the Global Environment Funds (GEF), which is responsible for financing environmental projects in Southern and Eastern countries.

On what basis can we implement the agreements about global warming? What role do international, national and local actors play in the definition of projects which take into account impacts on the global environment?

In this article we emphasize the fundamental role of incentive systems in the implementation of the emerging environmental agreements in the light of the theory of international regimes. The total cost associated with global environment protection is estimated and the distribution of these costs between local, national and international levels is determined so that the projects can be realized.

12.2 PROTECTION OF THE GLOBAL ENVIRONMENT: A REGIME THEORY APPROACH

The development of international cooperation for the protection of the atmosphere collides with the logic of collective action of groups of countries. According to this logic, an unorganized group of countries having a common interest, aware of this interest and with the means to achieve it, can do nothing to champion it (Olson 1966). Consequently, it is necessary to impose a constraint distinct from the pursuit of the common objective, to avoid the failure. Based on this thesis, the international regime theory analyses how international institutions can constrain individual logic in order to make international cooperation less problematical. Krasner's definition of international regimes as 'implicit or explicit principles, norms, rules, and decision making procedures around which actors' expectations converge in a given area of international relations' is generally retained (1982). It allows the collective utility to increase to a level that can be reached by facilitating the cooperation: regimes generate both norms that are internalized by States being able to change the structure of their gains, and information being able to modify the perception that States have of their interest (Oye 1986). After describing the climate regime as a 'negotiated international regime', we define a more refined typology of regimes. This will bring us to describe a 'collaboration regime' based on a hierarchical relationship.

12.2.1 Climate Regime as a Negotiated Regime

Young's analysis of international regimes is based on three classifications: spontaneous, negotiated and imposed regimes. To which category does the climate regime belong? Considering the typology used, Young concludes that it is a negotiated regime. However, it is very difficult to determine clearly the role of leadership in the emergence of a convention on climate change. This difficulty in determining the role of power in the formation of an international institution prompts us to try to refine the typology.

12.2.1.1 Young's typology of regimes

Imposed regimes are linked to the theory of hegemonic stability (Keohane 1984). In this approach, the creation and stability of a regime depends on the presence of a hegemonic power, a country with economic and military resources which permits it to play a dominant role in the establishment of an international order. This hegemony is considered as an elementary condition for the stability of international order. Consequently, imposed regimes are defined as 'regimes established deliberately by dominant actors who succeed in getting others to conform to the requirements of these arrangements through some combination of coercion, cooptation and manipulation of incentives' (Young 1989).

Spontaneous regimes emerge through some process of converging expectations that does not require conscious efforts on the part of those who become participants in the resultant social practice (Young et al. 1995). It refers therefore to situations where institutional preferences converge independently of all will and where a tacit coordination appears without explicit negotiations between the members of the group. Such an approach is based on the influence of social norms on the rational choice of actors. The regulation of conflicts in a group can thus be achieved through the emergence and stability of social norms without the intervention of a central authority responsible for coordinating behaviour (Axelrod 1986).

Negotiated regimes, on the contrary, are institutional arrangement characterized by a conscious effort to agree on mutually accepted provisions. They imply an explicit consent by actors and a formal expression of the commitments made. The formation of this type of regime depends on 'institutional bargaining'. Leadership is an essential condition for the formation of a negotiated regime. According to Young (1991),

> leadership refers to the actions of individuals who endeavour to solve or circumvent the collective action problems that plague the efforts of the countries seeking to reap joint gain or solve common problems.

Leadership therefore should not be confused with hegemony. A leader possesses three essential instruments to facilitate consensus between different members of the group: the use of its power as a bargaining lever (structural leader), the possession of a special skill in concluding the negotiation process (entrepreneurial leader) and the dissemination of its ideas and values in order to modify preferences of other actors (intellectual leadership) (Young 1994).

12.2.1.2 Can we find leadership?

Young considers the climate change regime to be a case of negotiated regime. A phase of institutional negotiation, orchestrated by the International Negotiating Committee (INC), involving countries, intergovernmental organizations (UNEP, IPCC, and so on) and NGOs, had indeed preceded the definition of an explicit agreement expressed in tiie form of a formal institution (the FCCC). Despite their anability to define precisely the 'payoff' associated with each possible option, actors in the negotiation process assumed the existence of a zone of contract: joint gains could be achieved through international cooperation. Institutional negotiation played a central role in this process by allowing parties to attain minimum consensus. Young (1994) points out the absence of truly dominant actors in the process started by the INC. That is explained partly by the timorous attitude adopted by the United States.[1] Internal dissensions on that question have limited the American negotiators' capacity to play the role of 'structural leader' and to make a consensus emerge on actions to take against global warming. Moreover, no 'entrepreneurial leader' has really been able to facilitate the negotiations, notably because of the separation of the negotiation process between different intergovernmental organizations (UNCED Preparatory Committee, UNEP and WMO). Finally, despite the central role of transnational organizations in the scientific expertise that has preceded negotiations, and more particularly that of leaders of the IPCC in the awareness of the international public opinion and negotiators, the real contribution of the 'intellectual leadership' in the formation of the climate regime remains uncertain.

The distinction made by Young between imposed and negotiated regimes appears insufficient to truly determine the role of *power* in the emergence of international institutional arrangements. It appears indispensable to us to define a typology, inspired by that of Young, that would allow us to envisage an intermediate case between imposed and negotiated regimes – that of regimes formed in situations where the preferences of actors are divergent, but where an actor (or a subgroup) has the capacity to negotiate sufficiently strong incentives to make the other members of the group act according to its will.

12.2.2 Climate Regime as a Collaboration Regime

The typology should show that the existence of institutional bargaining is not limited to situations where actors' interests are convergent and that situations of divergent interests can lead to regimes different from an imposed regime. Presented in the form of a 2 × 2 matrix, this typology permits an easier linkage between contributions of the regime theory and that of economic models used for analysing the problem of international environmental cooperation in order to have a better understanding of the climate regime.

12.2.2.1   Redefining the typology of international regimes
Our typology is based on the two following criteria:

(1) *Convergence of institutional preferences*: Institutions are taken into account because of their capacity to facilitate international cooperation. We will postulate that two countries *A* and *B* (or country groups) converge if and only if, individually, their institutional preferences lead them to adopt cooperative behaviour. For *A* and *B* to be divergent, it suffices that one of them does not have an institutional preference. It is necessary to signal that convergence takes place if one of the actors is willing to make use of the formal institutions for cooperation or, on the contrary, it can be spontaneous and depends solely on informal institutions.

(2) *Institutional bargaining*: The negotiation we discuss here is an explicit process between *A* and *B,* aiming to establish formal institutions. Its function depends largely on preferences of individual actors. In cases of convergent interest and existence of a common good, the main objective of institutional bargaining is to make the countries commit themselves to the cooperation. When actors' interests are contradictory, it consists above all in determining the amount of incentives necessary for cooperation of countries that do not have a preference for international action.

Institutional bargaining

	Yes	No
Yes	Coordination	Spontaneous
No	Collaboration	Imposed

Institutional convergence

Figure 12-1 A typology of regimes

As Figure 12-1 indicates, the 2 × 2 matrix identifies four types of regimes:

(1) A *regime of coordination* is formed when actors with convergent interests succeed in defining an institutional arrangement by negotiation. This situation is similar to the 'prisoner's dilemma' where the unsatisfactory result of the game is not due to the absence of

communication between agents, but rather to the absence of a system of sanctions guaranteeing the execution of possible agreements between them. Institutional bargaining plays an essential role in this process since it allows agents to reach a consensus and to define a system that ensures the implementation of mutual commitments. But leadership is essential in the production of public goods (Kindelberger 1988). *Leadership* can be defined as *the capacity of* A *to persuade* B *to act in the common interest.*[2] We therefore adopt a restrictive definition of the concept of leadership that highlights the fact that leadership applies exclusively to the production of public goods and consists of achieving the consent of 'followers' by means of persuasion. For a coordination regime, it is necessary that the explicit negotiation between agents demonstrate the existence of a common interest and that the leader *A* persuade *B* to cooperate.

(2) A *spontaneous regime* corresponds to a convergence of informal institutions integrated by the agents which takes place without any explicit negotiation between them. As underlined by Young, absence of formal negotiations does not mean an absence of coordination. It is possible that the countries individually subsume social norms and values that converge independently of all conscious action and facilitate international cooperation.

(3) An *imposed regime* emerges when institutional preferences are divergent and there is no form of negotiation to take care of the interest of each party. This type of institutional arrangement depends on the existence of a *dominant power*. Kindelberger (1988), extending the analysis of Perroux, considers that 'one country, firm or person dominates another when the second party had to take into account what the first entity did, but the first could ignore the second'. This form of power corresponds to the traditional definition of 'relational power' used by the realist school of international relations: *the power of* A *to make* B *to do something which it would not have done otherwise.* This is achieved by the utilization of coercive force and manipulation. This type of regime is effectively imposed, in the sense that interests of the countries remain fundamentally divergent and the respect of hegemonic institutions entails a utility loss for *B*.

(4) A *collaboration regime* can be formed through a bargaining process when the interests of the countries are divergent. Even if the preferences of *A* and *B* are inconsistent, *A* seeks to *incite B* to act in its interest instead of trying to impose its will by force. Here the aim of the negotiation process is far more complex than in the creation of a regime of coordination. Here the objective of *A* is to ensure that *B* changes its strategy despite its preferences. A regime of collaboration is, therefore, a regime where *A* incites *B* in such a way that *B* does not sustain a utility loss by doing what *A* wants it to do. This type of power

can be termed as *influence*. According to Perroux (1961), influence consists of '*A*'s action on variables that contribute directly to shape *B*'s decision'. Perroux (1973) explains further, '*A* modifies the behavior of *B* without obliging it to act; it inspires the adoption of its values by others; it makes its own objectives attractive and causes imitation of its attitudes and behavior'. *A* can, for instance, bring additional information to *B*, threaten a sanction or promise a financial incentive. Thus a regime of collaboration depends on the existence of *influence*, defined as the *capacity of* A *to incite* B *to do something which it would not have done otherwise*. Institutional choices are not imposed by force but depend nevertheless on the utilization of a form of power by *A*: the capacity to determine international structures by means other than force. One question, however, can be asked: is influence, limited to the use of financial incentives, still power? Perroux answers with great lucidity: 'as such, it [money] is much more than an instrument of unspecified material satisfaction, of a welfare unceasingly modifiable and transformable, but an arm for the tendential assertment of its holder's liberty'. Without doubt 'money is power'.

In response to the criticism made by Krasner,[3] our typology shows more clearly the role of power in the formation of each type of international regime. We will now try to draw a parallel between this typology of regimes and economic models for international negotiation for global environment protection.

12.2.2.2   Economic models and international environmental cooperation

The application to global problems of environmental protection instruments which are conceived to be used in the framework of national policies is not evident. Whether they are inspired by the works of Pigou or Coase, their utilization encounters the same problem: that of the necessity of political intervention.[4] In fact, different modes of 'internalization' are essentially *political processes* which require public authorities to play an active role. As Henry (1993) holds, economic instruments have definite recourse to the invisible hand to make it do what it knows best how to do: induce efficient behaviour in a framework to fulfil the objectives determined by public interest. Applied to a global environment problem, such instruments require the existence of a super-state or a supranational authority. Nevertheless, in addition to methodological difficulties, such an action clashes directly with the will of the countries to preserve their own sovereignty. This has led economists to develop models that allow the possibility of the emergence of environmental cooperation based solely on the will of the countries, that is, on the basis of their individual interests.

Two types of models can be differentiated: game models and agency models.

(1) Game models seek to determine the strategies of countries relating to the global environment and to predict the consequences of their decisions for themselves as well as for the group formed by them. Some models treat especially the questions relating to the emergence, stability and widening of the cooperation. One finds, on the one hand, one-shot games, generally between n countries, based on the hypothesis of complete information (Barrett 1992; Carraro and Siniscalco 1995). These static approaches attempt to determine the conditions for credible commitments by countries that have a common interest in cooperation, but are nevertheless tempted by free riding. On the other hand, dynamic game models consider situations where countries can converge to an optimum through repeated interaction (Mäler 1994; Chander and Tulkens 1992). In both these models, financial transfers (lateral payments) are essential for widening the coalition of cooperating countries. Other game models, first developed by Hoel (1991), are interested in the influence of unilateral commitments on international negotiations. Using evolutionist games, Rotillon et al. (1995) show that the presence of a sufficiently high proportion of countries with strong ecological consciousness can lead to unilateral commitments by countries that can produce a 'ratchet effect' which may form the basis of an international convention. OECD countries, because of their responsibility in the degradation of the atmosphere, should play the role of a *leader*. This leadership consists of committing themselves to starting a bargaining process, presenting their propositions for an overall reduction of their own emissions and defining the proposed amount of transfer to the developing nations (DN). Based on a dynamic game with complete information, Rotillon et al. (1996) show that the attitude adopted by DN is entirely dependent on the initial commitment of OECD.

(2) International negotiation for the protection of the global environment can also be addressed by agency theory.[5] This model has recently been applied by Bromley and Cochrane (1995). The stabilization of the production of GHG at a sustainable level is considered as a 'policy problem' which occurs in case of an agreement between governments of the 'North' (N) wishing to quit the *status quo* and those of the 'South' (S), satisfied by the *status quo,* and depends on the evolution of the behaviour of the two regions. Knowing that atmospheric protection is a major preoccupation of N, the search for a political solution for common global goods depends on the comprehension of two agency problems. The first problem is national: N has to create national institutions to incite its own citizens to modify their behaviour. The

second problem is international: N should succeed in inciting S to take measures for modifying the behaviour of its citizens. This agency problem is hierarchical in nature since N cannot influence directly the behaviour of the citizens of S. S is simultaneously the agent in its relationship with N and the principal in its relationship with its citizens.

12.2.2.3 Power and interest conflicts in the climate regime

Game theory models give us a vision of the problems of international cooperation very similar to that given by what we have called the regime of coordination. These models attempt to develop international coordination games that allow the avoidance of the prisoner's dilemma on a global scale (Snidal 1985). According to this approach, the climate regime depends partly on the role of leaders. The leaders are considered to have the capacity of proposing financial transfers that ensure credible commitments by other countries.

In our opinion, the nascent climate change regime is not a regime of coordination. Even though we are in the presence of a problem of coordination between industrialized countries, the challenge of international cooperation lies in the relationship between the first group of countries having a precautionary principle and concerned with global environment protection and the other group, comprising mainly Eastern and Southern countries, which have other priorities.[6] In fact, if we refer to the 'international cost efficiency' principle which forms the basis of FCCC (art.3(3)), it is evident that the development of international cooperations ought to take place between the richest countries and those in the Eastern and Southern blocks where the marginal cost of emission reduction is much lower than that in developed countries.

Faced with the necessity of building a regime of collaboration between country groups with divergent interests, we should define the problem as that of a group of countries – the principal – having a preference for global environmental protection and wanting the emergence of international institutional arrangements, which negotiates incentives to obtain the participation of countries – the agents – that have other preferences. Consequently, the power exerted within the climate change regime is not one of leadership that we have defined previously, but is rather an *influence* of industrialized countries.[7] We can therefore reconcile the climate regime of collaboration with the agency model.

To conclude, the effectiveness of the climate regime – which must be evaluated for determining to what extent international institutions are responsible for a move towards the objective of reducing emissions with respect to the international cost efficiency principle – will depend essentially on the capacity of the countries to set up a financial incentive system. Using the agency model, we will now analyse how global risks could be integrated in local, national and international strategies.

12.3 PROJECT COSTS AND REDUCTION OF CO_2 EMISSIONS

The development options available to a decision maker may or may not integrate environmental aspects. In order to consider the global environment as a choice criterion, it is necessary to define the notions of short- and long-term costs and benefits as well as of costs/benefits at the local/global level. Thus, the arbitrage process can be between short-term local costs and benefits and long-term global costs and benefits.

This approach has a double objective: to identify all the necessary costs that have to be financed to implement a project and to show the difficulties of measuring the social interest of the reduction of CO_2 at the global level. We are in a situation where environmental protection corresponds to an approach in terms of risk minimization under uncertainty in general and a precautionary principle in particular. Uncertainty plays a crucial role in the analysis: there are uncertainties about ecological impacts at local and national levels, scientific uncertainties about the global warming and its impacts (social costs); possibilities of adverse selection and/or moral hazard exist that can lead to the over or under estimation of project costs. Our approach will involve three levels: local, national and supranational, as in Tobey (1996).

12.3.1 Local / Private Behaviour

In a development programme, there are at least two options[8] available to the decision maker at the local level: one that does not take into account the environment (decision d_1) and the second including environmental aspects (d_2).

12.3.1.1 Hypotheses
(a) Depending on the development option adopted at the local level, we assume that:
- there exists two states of the nature, one negative for the environment and the other without effect on the environment; and
- the probability that the option has a negative effect on the environment is weaker for d_2 (probability q) than for d_1 (probability p)[9] (endogenous uncertainty – Trommetter 1996a).

(b) We assume that the cost of building in the environment constraint increases the total cost of the project in the first period $C_2 \geq C_1$ (environmental excess costs).

(c) Implementation of the environment protection action entails a cost C_4. This cost can be decomposed as: structural cost, knowledge cost, transaction cost, and so on.

(d) There can be a direct diminution of benefit of the programme due to the impact on the environment. This is represented by the passage of B_1 to B_2 (nothing prevents $B_1 = B_2$).

(e) A homogeneous Pigouvian tax can be imposed at the national level in case of a serious ecological catastrophe. This tax T can be zero if the country does not have a strong ecological consciousness (Rotillon et al. 1995) about the impact on the environment or if an institutional failure prevents the imposition of such a tax at the local level.

The behavioural model of the agent at the local level takes into account the uncertainties and the different levels of flexibility depending on the available development options.

12.3.1.2   Solutions

Figure 12-2 represents the decision tree for the local decision maker between two technological choices (the social aspect will be analysed subsequently).

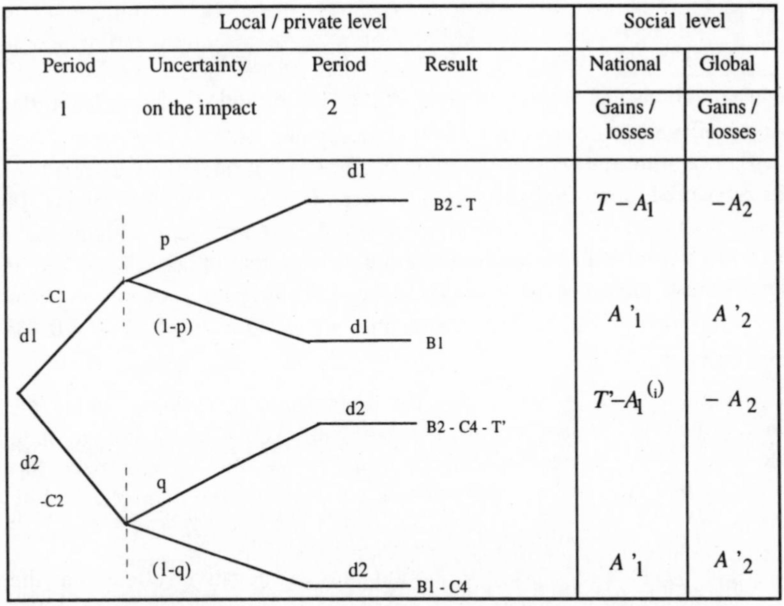

Local / private level				Social level	
Period	Uncertainty	Period	Result	National	Global
1	on the impact	2		Gains / losses	Gains / losses

			Result	National	Global
d1 → p		d1	$B2 - T$	$T - A_1$	$-A_2$
-C1	(1-p)	d1	$B1$	A'_1	A'_2
d2 → q		d2	$B2 - C4 - T'$	$T'-A_1^{(i)}$	$-A_2$
-C2	(1-q)	d2	$B1 - C4$	A'_1	A'_2

Figure 12-2 Model of choice based on the axiom of individual rationality

The decision criterion of the local agent is to choose the option d_2 if and only if:

$$C_1 - C_2 + q(B_2 - C_4 - T) + (1-q)(B_1 - C_4) - p(B_2 - T) - (1-p)(B_1) \geq 0 \quad (12.1)$$

$$(p-q)(B_1 - B_2 + T) \geq C_2 - C_1 + C_4$$

The left-hand side of this expression is positive and represents the gain brought to the local agent by decision as d_2 compared to d_1. This measure of gains is the sum of: direct gains linked to the best probability of the non-negative impact on the environment plus absence of loss as a result of taking into account the environment, which in itself is broken up into losses related directly to the impact on environment, + losses resulting from the installation of a tax system at the national level in case of a negative impact on the environment. The right-hand side is positive and represents the differential of the costs for implementing the new technology.[11]

The tax level for the agent to pass from decision d_1 to d_2 is:

$$T \geq \frac{C_2 - C_1 + C_4}{p - q} + B_2 - B_1 \ (1') \quad (12.2)$$

The difference $(B_1 - B_2)$ represents the loss at the local level of the negative impact of the decision d_1 in the first period. If $B_2 = B_1$, in the economic analysis of externalities we can say that we are in the presence of market equilibrium where the polluting firm is not negatively affected by its own production and there is no internalization of external effects. In such a situation, we cannot approach a Pareto optimum without state intervention through a unitary tax system or a system of subsidies. The tax level that would allow the decision maker to modify his choice is superior to the installation cost of the new technology (even if $q = 0$ or $T' = 0$ for the option d_2).

If equation (12.1) holds, then the project that takes into account the environment will be implemented at the local level without intervention at the national and the international level. In this case, the decision maker has a good perception of local and national environment risks (represented by the tax T). Otherwise, it is necessary to find out whether it is possible to incite the local decision maker sufficiently so that the environment project is implemented, keeping in mind, however, the existence of uncertainties and irreversibilities related to the environmental impact.

We can note already that the implementation of a project with an environmental dimension in a given zone comprises, at least at the beginning, a loss which, in a system of individual choice, has to be compensated (individual rationality axiom). This compensation can be achieved by the direct advantages that the agent derives from this irreversibility (related activities) and/or by incentives justified by (social) externalities that it obtains. Hence, we can visualize the different options and uncertainties that the local decision maker faces, as depicted in the preceding decision tree.

12.3.2 Behaviour at the National and International Level

In the case where incentives are necessary to take into account the environmental option, we must make a distinction between the national and the international level. The problem relates to the financing of projects for environmental protection. In international conventions, each actor is committed to provide, according to its abilities, support and financial advantages to national activities for achieving environmental objectives in accordance with its plans, priorities and national programmes.

12.3.2.1 The national level

If the model of individual rationality (local level) leads to the development of the option d_1, and if the social level (national or international) suffers from the potentially negative externalities of d_1, we have to define an incentive mechanism that can be interpreted by a principal–agent model. Uncertainties and irreversibilities prompt us to use a dynamic approach to represent this relationship, which would allow us to take into account the risks relating to an incorrect evaluation of externalities.

12.3.2.2 Hypotheses

The decision maker at the national level chooses between a set of technologies that take into account the environment in differing degrees. We assume that the environmental characteristics of technologies will be different according to the type of risk (local health risk or global risk).[12] In fact, in many countries, health risks or risks related to national environment are more important than global risks, especially in the case where the country carries out a cost–benefit analysis at the national level. We can use the case of electricity production from a thermal power station as an example. To simplify, two options are available:

(1) the polluting project can be replaced by a technology that minimizes local and national risks, for instance by the introduction of sulphur reduction technologies;
(2) the technology is changed radically by investing in a natural gas power station that reduces both local pollution (SO_2) and global pollution (CO_2) problems.

Decision makers at different levels would choose a technology that corresponds best to their environmental preoccupation. Thus, A_i can include an overall vision of the environmental problem and the possibility for the installation of the gas-based technology is envisaged; alternatively, the possibility of implementing a less expensive alternative technology that takes into account only the local environmental problems can be analysed. Referring back to Figure 12-1, we see that at the national level $(-A_1)$ is the loss related to the relative fragility of its environment: it can, for instance, comprise health expenditures relating to sulphur pollution. It is also necessary to measure the indirect effects of the development programme as an externality for other agents even if it results from other economic activities: benefits at the local and the national level (A'_1). In such a framework, there are two incentive mechanisms that correspond to two different environmental principles: installation of a tax system refers to the polluter pays principle (PPP), or the financial incentive that refers to the potential victim pays principle.

The probability of the expected social value is given by $(p-q)(A_1 + A'_1 - T)$, that is, the absence of loss in social value relating to the action d_2 as compared to d_1 plus the direct social benefit less the loss in terms of tax recovery in case of a negative impact on the environment.

Moreover, we know that $C_1 \le C_2$ and $q \le p$: for the development project d_2 to be retained, the financing requirements at the local level must be inferior to $(C_2 - C_1 + C_4)$, which represents the cost of modification of the development programme (inherent in period $1(C_1 - C_2)$), plus actualized adaptation costs C_4.

12.3.2.3 Solutions

If we add (C_5) that represents the costs of institutional strengthening (credibility of the tax) and/or the costs of building local awareness by the national level which is necessary to ensure long-term sustainability of the system, it implies that financing a programme for environment protection, equal to the amount $(C_2 - C_1 + C_4 + C_5)$, must be accepted at the social level.

The national level can finance only the incremental amount between d_1 and d_2 if

$$(p-q)(A_1 + A'_1 - T) \ge (C_2 - C_1 + C_4 + C_5) - (p-q)T \qquad (12.3)$$

Such a relationship assumes that the tax differential is taken into account at the local level and the differential in benefits is too weak to be taken into account, especially if we assume that there is no impact on the production function at the local level (no integration of the environment). We are in a principal–agent relationship, where the principal has environmental objectives linked to national risk minimization. What type of risk is considered at the national level?

(1) The risks may be same as those analysed at the global level. In this case international regulation will intervene only if the costs of the project are too high at the national level (classical modelling of incremental cost).
(2) The country finances a technology X (taking into account national problems exclusively) in which case international regulation is required to make it adopt a technology Y (beneficial for the global environment) with C'_2 as fixed cost and C'_4 as adaptation cost.

In the standard principal–agent model, the principal maximizes its utility subject to the constraint that the agent is not worse off in case he participates in the contract than in the initial situation. In the case where the principal wants to regulate pollution levels in the presence of scientific uncertainties, it is necessary to define and attain an objective (qualitative or quantitative) at a lower cost, which is represented by the cost-effectiveness analysis. It comprises minimizing risks (or maximizing emission reductions) subject to a budgetary constraint (Trommetter 1996b).

If equation 12.2 holds, it would imply that the country is aware of the ecological consequences of local development. However, this awareness can be of two types: it may be a risk perception uniquely at the national level so that there is no impact at the global level; alternatively, the risk perception may be global, in which case it will finance the entire project if the social value is more than the costs.

This implies the negotiation of a social norm under sustainable development constraints. Otherwise it would be necessary to look at the behaviour at the international level.

12.3.2.4 Model of international behaviour
Hence, it is sometimes necessary to have a regulation at the third level, the international level that one finds in the case of global risks represented by an international financial organization (the GEF), in which developed countries provide new and additional financial resources to allow developing and Eastern countries to meet the excess costs imposed on them for implementing the different measures required to fulfil the obligations of international conventions. The convention encourages developed countries to provide financial resources through bi- or multilateral cooperation.[13] The main function at the international level can then be to finance regional organization costs and/or institutional costs, by comparing them to global benefits of investment projects (A_2 and A'_2).

12.3.2.5 Remarks

(1) The measure of the global benefit is given by $(p - q)(A_2 + A'_2).A_2$ represents the absence of loss related to the installation of less polluting technology and A'_2 the benefits (generally zero except in the case of a transfrontier pollution problem).

(2) It would be necessary to assume that the probabilities for decisions d_1 and d_2, to have a negative effect on the global environment, will be different if the perception of environmental problems varies between the national and the international levels. We will not, however, make this differentiation, with a view of simplification.

(3) The international level will agree to help a country to promote a local development project d_2 only on the following conditions:

Country technology	Decision criterion	Remarks
Gas technology	$(q - p)(-A_2) + (p - q)A'_2 \geq$ $(q - p)(-A_1) + (p - q)A'_1$ $+ (C_1 - C_2 - C_4 - C_5)$ (12.3)	In this case, incremental cost of the project is linked to additional reductions at the national level. Concerning individual projects, we prefer the term 'incremental financing'.
Sulphur abatement technology	$(q - p)(-A_2) + (p - q)A'_2 \geq$ $(C'_2 - C_1 + C'_4 + C'_5)$ $+ (C_1 - C_2 - C_4 - C_5).$ (12.3')	At the international level, the aim is to encourage the installation of gas technology, that is to finance the cost difference between the two techniques (incremental cost).

For an analysis in terms of incremental costs/incremental advantages, if equation 12.3 (resp. 12.3') holds, then the project of CO_2 emission reduction will be implemented. A_2 and A'_2 are measures of avoided losses and global gains related to the project, respectively. We are in a global framework, where scientific uncertainties and anticipations about technological evolutions are very important for the definition of A_i.

Mathematically this presentation remains simplistic. But the analysis of the different costs $(C_2, C_4, C_5, C'_2, C'_4, C'_5)$ are not easy and the evaluation of social benefits (A_1, A'_1, A_2, A'_2) poses problems. The evaluation of social advantages will depend on legal, political, economic and physical conditions, particularly of the countries concerned. The project has to reconcile an approach in terms of sustainable development ('that replies to current generation needs without limiting capacities of future generations to reply to their needs') with an approach in terms of precautionary principles ('in case of serious or irreversible threats to the environment, a lack of scientific certainty does not have to be a pretext for delaying the adoption of efficient measures for providing warning for environmental degradations').

12.3.3 Social Norms and Sustainable Development

The decision makers at each level act under situations of scientific uncertainties about ecological impacts of different technologies and of anticipations about future technological evolution. Because of these uncertainties, the option retained at the international level is not to take a decision using the classical cost–benefit analysis that consists of defining and calculating the A_i and A'_i (for $i = 1,2$) but to define social norms to be achieved in a dynamic cost–benefit analysis framework. The dynamic approach allows the reevaluation of the norm to be achieved depending on the flow of information in the long run at the technological, scientific and social levels. This system of negotiated norms, comprising economic, biological and social requirements (Faucheux and Noël 1995) raises the question of the construction of norms and measures. The right of developing countries to the development process and the underlying social conflicts cannot tolerate a dictatorship by nature which is detrimental to the other two components (conservationist approach) and vice versa. Moreover, in the long run, a gain in information on scientific and technological aspects will entail a renegotiation of the norm in order to attain an equilibrium through public regulations (national and international) at the three levels of analysis (economic, social and ecological) which would guarantee the long run sustainability of projects. These results associated with a cost-effectiveness approach corroborates the works of Ciriacy-Wantrup (1952) on the Safe Minimum Standard for the protection of species which presents an alternative to cost–benefit analysis. This rule amounts to producing a reverse proof: it is necessary to prove that costs are indeed unbearable to renounce the action.[14]

12.4 CONCLUSIONS

The aim of this paper is to show that the climate change regime is a collaboration regime based on an agency relationship between a group of developed countries – the principal – concerned with GHG emissions and seeking to define a system of remuneration that can incite Eastern and Southern countries – the agents – to act in the interest of the Principal. Thus, we focus on the burden-sharing issue, which is crucial for future conferences on climate change, by trying to identify all the costs that need to be financed to guarantee that a programme of global environmental protection can be accepted.

The chances of success of an environment project depend on the level of incentives that are provided at the local and the national levels. We are in a framework where the integration of the global environment in the choice criterion results from risk minimization in a situation of uncertainty subject to an economic effectiveness constraint. As we have seen in the second section, the approach involves three levels of intervention, three representations of risks and two or three available technological options: the national/local dimension in a principal–agent relationship with a twofold incentive: monetary incentive and repressive incentive by taxation; the decision criterion is a social cost–benefit analysis. The relationship between the national and the international level is equally a principal–agent relationship but it is on a cost-effectiveness basis as compared to the objective defined initially (for example, to return to the 1990 level of emissions by the year 2000).

The global risk management in a situation of uncertainty necessitates an approach in several stages, with learning processes, allowing the identification of the totality of factors that influence the decision. This comprises: definition of a norm at the international level (objectives to attain),[15] identification of sustainable development projects in developing and eastern block countries, integration of the precautionary principle in situations of scientific uncertainty and technological anticipations and the non-irreversibility of the situation either by chosen technology or by crossing an ecological threshold.

ENDNOTES

1. Cooper (1992) interprets it as a justified and reflective prudence.
2. According to Kindelberger (1988), 'leadership may be thought of at first blush as persuading others to follow a given course of action which might not be in the follower's short-run interest if it were truly independent'.
3. For Krasner, this literature covers up the role of power in regime formation. According to him, neoliberal speculations 'obscure considerations of relative power capabilities, which draw attention to how the payoff matrix was structured in the first place, how the available options are constrained, who can play the game, and, ultimately, who wins and who loses' (1991).
4. Pigou and Coase are frequently held to be opposite in a fallacious manner, Pigou being considered as 'interventionist'. This opposition relies on an incorrect reference to 'theorem no. 1' of Coase, built on a hypothesis of zero transaction costs, that Coase considers himself as unrealistic (1960).
5. A relationship between two or several economic agents is a agency relationship when one of them, called the agent, acts on the part of, or as representative of, the other, called the principal, in a specific area of decision (Ross 1973).
6. As is underlined by Hurrell and Kingsbury (1992), a fair and acceptable distribution between the industrialized countries will be far from easy. But the principal fissure is between the developed and developing world, and it is the

potential for the global environment to become a major source of confrontation between North and South that renders it such a fundamental international political issue.

7. Hurrell and Kingsbury consider also that the capacity to determine the international agenda is a particularly efficient form of power. According to them, 'industrialized countries have successively focused international attention on those issues which affect them most directly: marine pollution, ozone depletion, global climate change, biodiversity, and deforestation. By contrast, the States and peoples of the South have had less success in securing prominence for environmental problems closely associated with development' (1992).

8. We know that there are options that take into account the environmental factor in different degrees and we shall see that the implementation of a project would depend on the national and international public authorities that finance them.

9. We assume the choice to be between electricity production by coal technology (decision d_1) or by gas technology (decision d_2). The utilization of gas technology reduces CO_2 emissions. Without equipment against CO_2 emissions, a classic coal power station emits, on the average, twice the amount of CO_2 than a natural gas power station (AIE/OECD 1991). Thus, one reduces risks that have a negative impact on the global environment, but without eliminating them completely because: 1) the emission of CO_2 is not null and 2) other negative externalities on the global environment can exist.

10. Unless otherwise indicated, we shall assume in the rest of the essay that $T' = T$ that is, the amount of the tax is not different according to the option taken in first period.

11. To ignore these costs in the arbitration leads to the acceptance of projects that will not take into account transaction costs problems (Viguier 1996) or management of the transition phase.

12. Indeed, developing countries have very different objectives for CO_2 emission reduction policy: insular countries wish an acceleration due to submersion risks, oil-producing countries and China whose natural resources are the main sources of CO_2 have the opposite objective, while the main objective of the Third World countries is to develop to survive (Lédenvic 1996).

13. Bilateral relationships between Norway and Poland are very interesting: for Norway, the aim is to force Poland to set a system that both protects the global environment and limits transfrontier pollutions having an impact on the Norwegian national environment.

14. The economic calculation forms the basis of the negotiation process (Henry 1993).

15. The supranational resources are not unlimited, so it is necessary to define ecological emergency levels by means of criteria and indicators with the definition of norms and the notion of cost-effectiveness.

REFERENCES

AIE/OCDE (1991), *Les émissions de Gaz à l'Effet de Serre. Le rôle de l'énergie*, Paris: OECD.

Axelrod, R. (1986), 'An Evolutionary Approach to Norms', *American Political Science Review*, 80, 1095–111.

Barrett, S. (1992), 'International Environmental Agreements as Games', in R. Pethig (ed.), *Conflicts and Cooperation in Managing Environmental Resources*, Berlin: Springer–Verlag, pp. 11–37.

Bromley, D.W. and J.A. Cochrane (1995), 'A Bargaining Framework for the Global Commons', in D.W. Bromley (ed.), *Handbook of Environmental Economics*, London: Basil Blackwell.

Carraro, C. and D. Siniscalco (1995), 'Policy Coordination for Sustainability: Commitments, Transfers, and Linked Negotiations', in I. Goldin and L.A. Winters (eds), *The Economics of Sustainable Development*, Cambridge: Cambridge University Press, pp. 264–82.

Chander, P. and H. Tulkens (1992), 'Theoretical Foundations of Negotiations and Cost Sharing in Transfrontier Pollution Problems', *European Economic Review*, 36, 388–98.

Ciriacy-Wantrup, S.V. (1952), *Resource Conservation: Economics and Policies*, Berkeley: University of California Press.

Coase, R.H. (1960), 'The Problem of Social Cost', in R.H. Coase (ed.), *The Firm, the Market and the Law*, Chicago: University of Chicago Press.

Cooper, R.N. (1992), 'United States Policy Towards the Global Environment', in A. Hurrell and B. Kingsbury (eds), *The International Politics of the Environment. Actors, Interests, and Institutions*, Oxford: Clarendon Press.

Faucheux, S. and J.F. Noël (1995), *Economie des Ressources Naturelles et de l'Environnement*, Paris: Armand Colin.

Henry, C. (1993), 'Le principe Pollueur–payeur: Vingt Ans Après', *Insee Methodes*, 39–40.

Hoel, M. (1991), 'Global Environmental Problems: the Effects of Unilateral Actions taken by one Country', *Journal of Environmental Economics and Management*, 20, 55–70.

Hurrell, A. and B. Kingsbury (1992), 'The International Politics of the Environment: an Introduction', in A. Hurrell and B. Kingsbury (eds), *The International Politics of the Environment. Actors, Interests, and Institutions*, Oxford: Clarendon Press.

Keohane, R.O. (1984), *After Hegemony. Cooperation and Discord in the World Political Economy*, Princeton: Princeton University Press.

Kindelberger, C.P. (1988), *The International Economic Order. Essays on Financial Crisis and International Public Goods*, New York: Harvester Wheatsheaf.

Krasner, S.D. (1982), 'Structural Causes and Regime Consequences: Regimes as Intervening Variables', *International Organization*, 36 (2), Spring, 185–205.

Krasner, S.D. (1991), 'Global Communications and National Power: Life on the Pareto Frontier', *World Politics*, 43 (3), 336–66.

Lédenvic, P. (1996), 'L'essai de Rio transformé: La conférence de Berlin sur les changements climatiques', Série Responsabilité et Environnement no. 1, *Annales des Mines*, 11–18.

Mäler, K.G. (1994), 'Acid Rain in Europe: a Dynamic Perspective on the Use of Economic Incentives', in E.C. Van Ierland (ed.), *International Environmental Economics. Theories, Models and Applications to Climate Change, International Trade and Acidification*, Amsterdam: Elsevier, pp. 351–72.

Olson, M. (1966), *The Logic of Collective Action*, Harvard: Harvard University Press.

Oye, K.A. (1986), *Cooperation under Anarchy*, Princeton: Princeton University Press.

Perroux, F. (1961), *L'économie du XXème siècle*, Presses Universitaires de France.

Perroux, F. (1973), *Pouvoir et Economie*, Série 'Études Economiques', Paris: Dunod.

Ross, S. (1973), 'The Economic Theory of Agency, the Principal's Problem', *American Economic Review*, 63, 134–9.

Rotillon, G., T. Tazdaït and S. Zeghni (1995), 'Engagement Unilatéral Spontané en Présence de Risques Globaux et Effets d'Entraînements', paper presented at the AFSE, XLIV Congrès Annuel, Paris.

Rotillon, G., T. Tazdaït and S. Zeghni (1996), 'Bilateral or Multilateral Bargaining in the face of Global Environmental Change?', *Ecological Economics*, 18, 177–87.

Snidal, D. (1985), 'Coordination versus Prisoners' Dilemma: Implications for International Cooperation and Regimes', *The American Political Science Review*, 79, 923–42.

Tobey, J. (1996), 'La Biodiversité et les Incitations Economiques', *L'Observateur de l'OCDE*, 198, 25–9.

Trommetter, M. (1996a), 'Les Modèles Séquentiels de Décision en Avenir Incertain: de la Prise en Compte de l'Irréversibilité à l'Arbitrage entre Flexibilité', Colloque 'Tendances nouvelles en modélisation pour l'environnement', CNRS, Paris, January.

Trommetter, M. (1996b). 'Incentive Models and Global Environmental Risks: a Sequential Approach', in International Seminar: 'Do Economists Cope with Environmental Uncertainty and Complexity?', Fondation Universitaire Luxembourgeoise, Arlon, Belgique, October.

Viguier, L. (1996), 'Joint Implementation between Western and Eastern Countries: Institutional Change and Credible Commitment to Reduce Transaction Costs', paper presented at the International Association for Energy Economics Conference, May 1996, Budapest, Hungary.

Young, O.R. (1989), *International Cooperation: Building Regimes for Natural Resources and the Environment*, Ithaca, NY: Cornell University Press.

Young, O.R. (1991), 'Political Leadership and Regime Formation: on the Development of Institutions in International Society', *International Organization*, 45 (3), 281–308.

Young, O.R. (1994), *International Governance. Protecting the Environment in a Stateless Society*, Ithaca, NY: Cornell University Press.

Young, O.R., M.A. Levy, M. Zürn (1995), 'The Study of International Regimes', *European Journal of International Relations*, 1 (3), 267–330.

Index